Communications in Computer and Information Science   **835**

Commenced Publication in 2007
Founding and Former Series Editors:
Phoebe Chen, Alfredo Cuzzocrea, Xiaoyong Du, Orhun Kara, Ting Liu,
Dominik Ślęzak, and Xiaokang Yang

More information about this series at http://www.springer.com/series/7899

Sonajharia Minz · Sushanta Karmakar ·
Latika Kharb (Eds.)

Information, Communication and Computing Technology

Third International Conference, ICICCT 2018
New Delhi, India, May 12, 2018
Revised Selected Papers

 Springer

Editors
Sonajharia Minz
School of Computer and Systems Science
Jawaharlal Nehru University
New Delhi, India

Sushanta Karmakar
Indian Institute of Technology Guwahati
Guwahati, India

Latika Kharb
Jagan Institute of Management Studies
Delhi, India

ISSN 1865-0929   ISSN 1865-0937 (electronic)
Communications in Computer and Information Science
ISBN 978-981-13-5991-0   ISBN 978-981-13-5992-7 (eBook)
https://doi.org/10.1007/978-981-13-5992-7

Library of Congress Control Number: 2018967943

This Springer imprint is published by the registered company Springer Nature Singapore Pte Ltd.
The registered company address is: 152 Beach Road, #21-01/04 Gateway East, Singapore 189721, Singapore

Preface

The International Conference on Information, Communication and Computing Technology (ICICCT 2018) was held on May 12, 2018 in New Delhi, India. ICICCT 2018 was organized by the Department of Information Technology, Jagan Institute of Management Studies (JIMS) Rohini, New Delhi, India. The conference received 295 submissions and after rigorous reviews, 18 papers were selected for this volume. The acceptance rate was around 18.1%. The contributions came from diverse areas of information technology categorized into two tracks, namely: (1) Communication and Network Systems and (2) Emerging Computing Technologies.

The aim of ICICCT 2018 was to provide a global platform for researchers, scientists, and practitioners from both academia as well as industry to present their research and development activities in all the aspects of: communication and network systems, and emerging computing technologies.

We thank all the members of the Organizing Committee and the Program Committee for their hard work. We are very grateful to Professor M. P. Poonia, Vice Chairman, AICTE, New Delhi, as chief guest, Professor Ashraf Elnagar, from the University of Sharjah, UAE, as keynote speaker, Professor Punam Bedi from the Department of Computer Science, University of Delhi, as General Chair, Dr. Sushanta Karmakar, from the Department of CSE, IIT Guwahati as Session Chair for Track 1, and Dr. R. Balasubramanian from the Department of CSE, IIT Roorkee, as Session Chair for Track 2.

We thank all the Technical Program Committee members and referees for their constructive and enlightening reviews on the manuscripts. We thank Springer for publishing the proceedings in the *Communications in Computer and Information Science* series. We would like to congratulate JIMS for organizing such an event and the efforts of the conference secretariat, Dr. Praveen Arora, and the conference conveners, Dr. Latika Kharb and Dr. Deepak Chahal, who really made it happen. Last but not least, we thank all the authors and participants for their great contributions that made this conference possible.

June 2018   Sonajharia Minz

Organization

General Chair

Punam Bedi   University of Delhi, Delhi, India

Program Chair

Sonajharia Minz   Jawaharlal Nehru University, New Delhi, India

Conference Secretariat

Praveen Arora   Jagan Institute of Management Studies (JIMS), Rohini, Sector-05, New Delhi, India

Session Chair for Track 1

Sushanta Karmakar   Indian Institute of Technology (IIT) Guwahati, Assam, India

Session Chair for Track 2

R. Balasubramanian   Indian Institute of Technology (IIT), Uttarakhand, India

Convener

Latika Kharb   Jagan Institute of Management Studies (JIMS), Rohini, Sector-05, New Delhi, India

Deepak Chahal   Jagan Institute of Management Studies (JIMS), Rohini, Sector-05, New Delhi, India

Technical Program Committee

Gerassimos Barlas   American University of Sharjah, United Arab Emirates

Subhash Bhalla   The University of Aizu, Japan

Adeyemi Ikuesan   School of IT, University of Pretoria, South Africa

Marcin Markowski   Wroclaw University of Technology, Poland

Rabindra Bista   Kathmandu University, Nepal

Promila Bahadur   Maharishi University of Management, USA

Renuka Mohanraj   Maharishi University of Management, USA

Muhammad Tanvir Afzal   Capital University of Science and Technology, Islamabad, Pakistan

Prasanta K. Ghosh   Syracuse University, New York, USA

Mee Loong Yang	Auckland University of Technology, New Zealand
Andrew Blyth	University of South Wales, UK
Zoran Bojkovic	University of Belgrade, Serbia
Eduard Babulak	Institute of Technology and Business, Czech Republic
Siti Salwah Binti Salim	University of Malaya, Kuala Lumpur, Malaysia
Busyairah Binti Syd Ali	University of Malaya, Kuala Lumpur, Malaysia
Sophia Rahaman	Manipal University, Dubai
Amlan Chatterjee	California State University, USA
Adrian Fiech	Memorial University, Canada
Jagadeesh Kakarla	IIITDM Kancheepuram, India
Pratyay Kuila	National Institute of Technology, Sikkim, India
S. Prabakaran	SRM University Kanchipuram, India
Zunnun Narmawala	Nirma University, Gujarat, Ahmedabad, India
Parameshachari B. D.	TGSSS Institute of Engineering and Technology for Women, Karnataka, India
C. S. Kumar	Thiagarajar College of Engineering, India
Sunil B. Mane	College of Engineering, Pune, India
Anala Pandit	Veermata Jijabai Technological Institute, Gujarat, India
B. Surendiran	National Institute of Technology Puducherry, India
Vinod Keshaorao Pachghare	College of Engineering, Pune, India
Angelina Geetha	Bsa Crescent University, Chennai, India
Anurag Jain	Guru Gobind Singh Indraprastha University, India
Kathemreddy Ramesh Reddy	Vikrama Simhapuri University, Andhra Pradesh, India
Neetu Sardana	Jaypee Institute of Information Technology, Noida, India
E. Grace Mary Kanaga	Karunya University, Coimbatore, India
Aniruddha Chandra	National Institute of Technology Durgapur, India
Manoj Sahni	Pandit Deendayal Petroleum University, Gandhinagar, India
Subhojit Ghosh	Birla Institute of Technology, Mesra, India
Chandresh Maurya	IBM Research, Bangalore, India
Vladimir Lukin Vasilievich	Kharkov, Aerospace University, Ukraine
Baljit Singh Khehra	Baba Banda Singh Bahadur Engineering College, Fatehgarh Sahib, Punjab, India
Kalman Palagyi	University of Szeged, Hungary
Md Gapar Md Johar	Management Science University, Kuala Lumpur, Malaysia
German Sánchez Torres	Universidad del Magdalena, Colombia
Farzad Kiyani's	Istanbul S. Zaim University, Turkey
Essam Halim Houssein	Minia University, El-Minia Governorate, Egypt
Jonathan Kolo	Federal University of Technology Minna, Nigeria
Farzad Tashtarian	Islamic Azad University of Mashhad, Iran
M. Usman	University of Engineering and Technology Peshawar (Mardan Campus), Pakistan
Gyu Myoung Lee	Liverpool John Moores University, UK

Sachin Gajjar	Nirma University Gujrat, India
Heydari M. Hossain	James Madison University, Harrisonburg, USA
Vicente Hernández Díaz	Universidad Politécnica de Madrid, Spain
Surjeet Dalal	SRM University Delhi - NCR Sonepat, India
Shubhnandan Singh Jamwa	The University of Jammu, Jammu and Kashmir, India
Maushumi Barooah	Assam Engineering College, Guwahati, Assam, India
Ajoy Kumar Khan	Assam Engineering College, Guwahati, Assam, India
Navajit Saikia	Assam Engineering College, Guwahati, Assam, India
Norizan Mohd Yasin	University of Malaya, Kuala Lumpur, Malaysia
K. V. Kale	Dr. Babasaheb Ambedkar Marathwada University, Aurangabad, India
Manoj Patil	North Maharashtra University, Jalgaon, Maharashtra, India
Prem Prakash Jayaraman	Swinburne University of Technology, Australia
Sandeep Dalal	Maharshi Dayanand University, Rohtak, India
Pradeep Tomar	Gautam Buddha University, Noida, India
Arun Solanki	Gautam Buddha University, Noida, India

Contents

Communication and Network Systems

C-Void: Communication Void Avoidance Protocol for Wireless Sensor Networks

Venkatesh[✉] and Y. Nagaraju[✉]

University Visvesvaraya College of Engineering, Bangalore, India
venkateshm.uvce@bub.ernet.in, nagarajuyat22@gmail.com

Abstract. A node on the routing path can not find suitable next-forwarder(s) in its proximity then communication void problem occurs and node is called as *void node*. The presence of void nodes on communication path have implications on network performance. In this paper, we proposed communication avoidance (C-void) protocol based on geographic and opportunistic routing concepts. C-void avoids the void communication nodes by readjusting location of void nodes to restore forwarding path. The proposed protocol consists of three steps. In first step, discovery of one hop and two-hop neighbors through beacon. In second step, the candidate node set from neighbor and forwarding nodes from identified candidate set. In the final step, void node discovery and avoidance of void nodes on communication path. Mathematical expressions are derived to discover void nodes in communication paths. To analyze the performance of the proposed *C-Void* protocol, an extensive simulation have been carried out in NS-2. The simulation results are compared with VBF, DBR and VAPR. The proposed scheme avoids void nodes, improves delivery ratio of packets and energy consumption by 56% and 55% respectively.

Keywords: Communication-void · Candidate node · Two-hop neighbors · Geographic and opportunistic routing

1 Introduction

Wireless sensor networks (WSNs) are collection of sensor nodes and deployed in different applications for gathering a periodic information of event or object. Traditionally, sensor nodes collect neighbor information from the neighbors in the deployed area. The neighbor information is used for the routing data packets. In geographic routing, neighbor node information is used to find potential forwarder or rely nodes to forward the data in the direction of sinks. However, if neighbor node is not available then geographic routing fails to forward data packets. The absent of neighbor nodes for a node create a void region in that node deployed area.

A routing void is also known as a local minimum; this happens due to irregular distribution of sensors. The irregular distribution of sensor nodes leads to the failure of geographic routing. Similarly, any data transmission also fails in such circumstance.

In the literature, bypassing void region, power adjustment, and depth adjustment methods are used to avoid void nodes in the network. In Bypassing void region avoidance method, direct paths are explicitly established to avoid paths which leads to void regions. However, bypassing void avoidance method induces excessively control

S. Minz et al. (Eds.): ICICCT 2018, CCIS 835, pp. 3–16, 2019.
https://doi.org/10.1007/978-981-13-5992-7_1

overheads. To reduce the control overhead, power adjustment or energy change method was proposed. In power adjustment methods, a node's transmission power is adjusted to find next hop forwarder node and data packets are transmitted using greedy method. In depth adjustment, whenever a node encounters void region that node required to be replaced or shifted to new position (depth) to resume the packet forwarding greedily.

Motivation: The main motivation is to design routing scheme that detects and avoid void region (also known as dead node problem) that occurs during data packets transmission from sensor nodes to the control centre or sink node. The proposed protocol is able to select the nearest next level nodes to transfer data packets to the control centre or sink node which is not error prone to the void areas. Update the location of the nodes periodically since. The protocol scheme must improve the data delivery ratio, reduce packet drop to due void region problem and enhance the network lifetime.

2   Literature Survey

To address various constraints such as bandwidth, latency, error prone wireless link reliability and mobility of sensor nodes Xie et al. [1] have designed scheme called Vector Based Forwarding (VBF) protocol, in the proposed scheme the data packets are routed along redundant and inter leaved routing paths. The VBF is geographic routing protocol and self-distributed adaptive algorithm which is resilient to node failure and channel error. However, the VBF is a one simple MAC protocol that is not suitable for mobile network and UWSN.

To improve the performance of VBF, Yan et al. [2] have designed a protocol called Depth Based Routing (DBR) which do not need x, y and z locations of sensor nodes. DBR uses the sensor node's depth information of the sensor to select the forwarding node. However, DBR is Greedy based routing protocol which fails deliver a packet in the presence of void region.

The wireless communication is intrinsically having higher propagation delay and limited bandwidth. It is more prone to loss of packet and results contention and congestion in the network. To overcome these problems Noh et al. [3] proposed a Void Aware Pressure Routing (VAPR) protocol. VAPR includes various parameters such as hop count, sequence number and depth of sensor node. These parameters are encapsulated in the *HELLO* beacons to find next-hop node's direction and directional trail is built based on node's direction.

Data packets forwarding is accomplished through Opportunistic directional on occurrence of void areas with help of directional trail.

Mobile sensor networks have many parameters influence namely interference from other transmission, obstacles in the transmission, mobility of nodes and attenuation of power and signal. Because of these parameters, an evaluation of global algorithm becomes difficult. To solve these problems, Kuhn et al. [4] proposed a new Geometric Ad-hoc routing algorithm (GOAFR) that incorporate concepts of face routing technique and greedy forwarding.

The routing protocols based on Geographic concepts employ greedy data packets forwarding technique to send data packets from source node to destination with help of nearest neighbour closest to destination. However, geographic routing fails to transfer packet whenever it is unable to find a node closest to the destination. To overcome these problems Rodolfo et al. [5] Proposed Depth-Controlled Routing protocol (DCR), where in depth of the nodes are adjusted to forward data when void node encountered.

Rodolfo et al. [6] proposed routing protocol based on greedy geographic concept and topology control based algorithm. In this greedy routing protocol node which is closer to the Sink choosed as a next-hop forwarder. It overcomes the communication void problem by adjusting depth of the sensor nodes. Centralized topology control (CTC) algorithm and Distributed topology control (DTC) algorithm. CTC algorithm finds the nodes that are void nodes and not void nodes on paths to a Sink. In DTC algorithm, where each node computes its new depth when it encounters void region problem. After determining that the node is in void region.

Zuba et al. [7] proposed a Resilient Pressure Routing protocol (RPR), the main objective is to maintain routing in the presence of malicious opponents. RPR uses cryptographic mechanisms, implicit acknowledgement (I-ACKs) and randomization to deliver packet successfully.

It is even more difficult with existing routing protocols to deal with communication voids in UWSN. To overcome these problems Xie et al. [8] proposed (VBVA) a Vector-Based protocol for Void Avoidance. The proposed protocol solves the mobile underwater sensor networks void problems. VBVA approach is based on vector. There are two methods namely back pressure and vector shift to solve the void node problems. The forwarding path in which data packets are transmitted to destination is denoted in the form of a vector. In Vector shift method, VBVA finds a routing path to route the data packets in trajectory of the void nodes. If the void is convex, VBVA delivers packets successfully to the sink node. However, if the void is present at curve of deployed area the vector shift method is unsuccessful in delivering data packets. In that circumstance, VBVA chose back pressure technique to transmit the data packets in reverse order till it reaches suitable nodes to perform vector shift.

To overcome the void region problems in wireless sensor network Aissani et al. [9] proposed an efficient void-avoidance scheme which hinders data packets to reaching void node boundaries. The sender node selects the forwarding region within boundary of determined void nodes based on the sender node locations, the void node position and the destination. Void-discovery algorithm launched by the first stuck node which detects the void. The void centre communicates with all sensor nodes present at void boundary n-hops away.

Wireless sensor network come across many issues like control overhead, delay in transmission and void problem in geographic routing. To address the routing through void nodes in geographic routing. To reduce the transmission delay and control overhead in Wireless Sensor Networks. The node distribution structure for nodes around void nodes are presented and it determine void nodes, an effective directing protocol called bypassing void protocol is proposed based on virtual coordinates [10]. The fundamental thought of the protocol is to transform the irregular structure created from claiming void edge to a virtual circle by mapping edge hubs coordinates. Using these virtual circles the greedy forwarding technique is able to forward data packets because along these lines void nodes are not present. This method reduces control overhead and sourball.

Geographic routing is an efficient routing method because it uses greedy forwarding strategy, but whenever the void regions are encountered due to irregular distribution of nodes. To overcome void problem, long path and high control Dejing et al. [11] has proposed a void routing protocol called as bypassing. It includes virtual coordinate information and geographic. It transforms random structure with void edges into regular one. After transformation of void edges, the void edges which are in virtual circle are assigned with virtual coordinates.

The side-effect of selfish hubs may be horrible, particularly over ongoing transmission. To those creators characterized that a hub need no neighbour on forward, it to drop packets promptly this causes void. Void region problem is a primary variable that harms the execution of ongoing WSNs. In spite of the fact that the childish hubs can spare their energies, they present the vitality utilizations about other nodes, which might in the end abbreviate the existence chance of the system. To overcome this selfish nature of node in UWSN Chi et al. [12] proposed Real Time Fault tolerant protocol (GTRF). GTRF based on Game Theory. It incorporates two procedures: (1) Cluster structure for VA model and (2) Packet Forwarding.

3   Background

In Vector Based Forwarding (VBF) the forward vector is chosen based on the threshold which has been decided earlier. To decide the threshold network requires more energy. Energy consumption is more due to the existence of redundant paths in large networks. Depth Based Routing (DBR) sends the packet using node depth information. It leads to a localization problem because sensor nodes change the location continuously. Resilient Pressure Routing Protocol uses a pair of keys at each node to provide security which requires more energy in each node. VBF, DBR, and RPR protocols fail to recover from communication void area if the packet bound towards the void node then packet is discarded. Void Aware Pressure Routing (VAPR) is not energy efficient because each sensor nodes need to know about the voids in the network, when it identifies the void in the network then it has to broadcast about void node, the broadcasting these requires more energy.

4   Problem Statement

For given set of sensor nodes of sensor network, it is required to design routing protocol that detect and avoid void region in such way that the transmission of a data packets not disturbed. The routing protocol must reduce packet drop ratio and increase the delivery ratio and network life time.

5   Mathematical Model

The sensor nodes $S_n = \{n_1, n_2, \ldots, n_{|N_n|}\}$ are scattered in a geographic area. The Sink nodes $N_n = \{s_1, s_2, \ldots, s_{|N_s|}\}$ are placed at Control unit. Global Positioning System (GPS) and radio transceiver modems are embedded in each sink node.

Network topology represented as an undirected graph $G(t) = (V, E(t))$ at time t, where $V = S$ is group of sensor and sink nodes in the network. Let $E(t) = \{e_{ij}(t)\}$ is communication link between the sensor nodes and sink node. Let u and $v \in V$ are neighbours at time interval t and they are communicated through wireless link, if they can overhear each other at time t. Let $N_u(t)$ represent set of neighbor sensor nodes of u. u is not belongs to $N_u(t)$ and $S_u(t) = \{n_{s1}, n_{s2}, \ldots, n_{sk}\}$ where n_{si} is denoted as the quintuple (seq number, ID, X, Y, Λ) of Sink node ID, present at the (X, Y)-coordinates, it is identified by its $(seq\,number)^{th}$ beacon. The flag $\Lambda = 0$ shows that the node has not disseminated any information to the neighbors.

5.1 Neighbours Candidate Set Selection

A sensor node constructs *HELLO* beacon packets and broadcast beacon packets. These beacon packets are used to determine neighbors that are suitable for directing data packets towards destination node. The progress of packet towards destination is determined as follow; first, find the distance between the source S and the destination D, in second step, find the distance between the neighbor X and D. Subtract distance determined in the first step by distance determined in the second step to obtain the packet advancement. Thus, candidate set of neighbors in C-Void is given as:

$$C_i = \{n_k \in N_i(t) : \exists s_v \in S_i(t) | D(n_i, s_i*) - D(n_k, s_v) > 0\} \tag{1}$$

Let D(a, b) represent the Euclidean distance between a and b nodes and, $s_i \in S_i(t)$ is the closest Sink of n_i as:

$$s_i^* = argmin_\forall \in S_i(t)D(n_i, s_j) \tag{2}$$

5.2 Forwarder Set Construction

The selection of forwarder is based on Eqs. (1) and (2). From neighbor candidate set, the next hop forwarder is chosen. For each neighbor candidate node, the priority is assigned based on maximum packet advancement. However, in wireless communication, higher packet advancement results in signal attenuation due to channel fading. The channel fading results in packet loss. Therefore, the normalized advancement of packet is calculated as:

$$NADV(n_c) = ADV(n_c) \times p(d_c^i, m) \tag{3}$$

Where $ADV(n_k) = d(n_i, s_i^*) - d(n_k, s_k^*)$ is the n_k th packet advancement towards nearest sink s_k^*, d_k^i denotes Euclidian distance from source node to forwarding candidate n_k.

$P(d_k^i, m)$ be the probability of m delivery bits over the distance d_k. Assume F_j subset of C_i obtained from candidate nodes ordered based on the priority. The priority is based on the normalized packet advancement. The expected packet advancement (EPA) of F_j is sum of normalized advancement made by the F_j.

$$EPA(F_j) = \sum_{l=1}^{k} NADV(n_l) \prod_{j=0}^{l-1} \left(1 - p(d_i^j, m)\right) \tag{4}$$

In opportunistic routing, the prioritized node becomes a next-hop forwarder. The low prioritized nodes transmit packets whenever highest priority nodes fail to transmit packets. Lower priority node cancels its transmission on hearing higher priority node transmission.

In C-Void, the ith prioritized node accepts incoming packets; it waits till completion packet propagation and delay propagation time. The delay propagation time includes delay from the 1st prioritized node to the 2nd prioritized node, 2nd priority node to the 3rd prioritized node and include all delay from the $(i-1)^{th}$ to prioritized nodes.

On completion of packet propagation and delay propagation, if the ith sensor node unable to hear a packet transmission from descendent node, then i^{th} node broadcast the packet therefore waiting time of ith node is determined as

$$T_w^i = T_p + \sum_{k=1}^{i} \frac{D(n_k, n_{k+1})}{s} + i \times T_{proc} \tag{5}$$

where T_p represent remaining packet propagation time and T_{proc} represent packet processing time. When sender broadcast a packet, the packets remaining propagation time denotes the delay required for the whole packet propagation. Remaining propagation time is calculated as

$$T_p = \frac{(r_c - D(n_a, n_b))}{s} \tag{6}$$

Let n_a is the node that accept packets, n_b is the node that transmits, and s is the velocity of propagation in wireless medium. In Eq. (5), the total time needed for a node to overhear packet transmission from its descendent prioritized node is the second term.

6 Proposed Algorithm: C-Void Avoidance Algorithm

Algorithm consists of three steps: discovery of neighbor nodes step, Neighbor node's candidate set and Next-Hop Forwarder Set Selection step, Restoration from communication void node step.

Step 1: Discovery of neighbor nodes: Algorithm start with discovery of neighbor nodes and reachable Sinks by broadcasting *HELLO* packets. The nodes that receive *HELLO* beaconing packets respond with *REPLY* with its geographic location and its neighbor node in its transmission range. Each node broadcast *HELLO* packet that contains, *sequence number, nodeID, known Sink locations*, its *x-y-z locations (dept locations)*. Each sensor node identifies its *x-y-z* location through localization services.

Algorithm 1. Neighbour Discovery

1: **procedure** HelloBroadcast(SN)
2: *SN* : sensor node, *hm* : HELLO message, s : Sink, S_i: set of known Sink
3: **while** timer time_out **do**
4:    $hm.locations \leftarrow x\_y\_locations(SN)$
5:    **if** SN $\in$ N(SN)**then**
6:       **for** SN $\in$ N(SN) **do**
7:          **for** s $\in$ S$_i$
8:             **if** flag(s) = 0
9:                hm.(seq_num(s),ID(s),x(s),y(s))   flag(S)=1
10:             **end if**
11:          **end for**
12: **end for** *Broadcast HELLO message*
13: **done** 16: **end procedure**
14: **procedure** recieve_HELLO(SN,hm)
15:    **if** (Sink receives hm) **then**
16:       update entry(S_i(SN),hm)
17:    **else**
18:       update entry(hm.seq_num,hm.id,hm.x_y locations)
19:       **for** (any Sink node belongs to hm) **do**
20:          **if** ((seq_num.Sink, seq_num.hm)>(seq_num.Sink,seq_num.S$_i$)
21:             update entry (S$_i$,Sink)
22:          **end if**
23:       **end for**
24:    **end if**
25: **end procedure**

A Sinks node also determines neighbouring node and other reachable Sinks nodes by broadcasting *HELLO* beaconing packets. Each Sink includes *sequence number*, its *ID* and geographic coordinates values. It is assumed that each Sink is equipped with Global Position System. It is also assumed that Sink has only horizontal movement. The *sequence number* and *ID* is used to determine the current version of *HELLO* beacon packet. Whenever The *HELLO* beacon packet is received from unvisited Sink, a node updates its sink set $S_i(t)$. On receiving recent HELLO beacon packet, a node also updates its sink set $S_i(t)$. For every updates, a node update its *flag* bit to zero, *flag* with zero indicates that information is not yet propagated to its neighbour nodes. Therefore, in next broadcasting, *HELLO* beacon packet includes $S_i(t)$ entry that have zero *flag* and random number between 0 and 1.

Step 2: Neighbor's candidate set selection and Forwarder Set Selection.

Algorithm 2. Forwarder set selection

1: **procedure** forwarders(source sensor node i)
2: **for** each candidate node(CN_i) **do**
3:     Normalized AD $\leftarrow$ Euclidean Distance $\times$ probability of m bits delivery
4: **end for**
5: CN_i are ordered advancement according to Normalized advancement
6: $j \leftarrow 1$
7: $CCN_i \leftarrow CN_i\{CCN_i : Photocopy of CN_i\}$
8: **while** $(|CN_i|>0)$
9:     $FN_j \leftarrow \{SN_i \in CN_i\}$
10:     $CN_i \leftarrow CN_i - \{SN_i\}$
11:     **for** $SN_k \in CN_i$ **do**
12:         **if** $dist(SN_i, SN_k) <$ half of communication radius
13:             $FN_j \leftarrow FN_j \cup SN_k$
14:             $CN_i \leftarrow CN_i - SN_k$
15:         **end if**
16:     **end for**
17:     $j \leftarrow j+1$
18: **done**
19: **for** each F_j **do**
20:     **for** $SN_c \in CCN_i$
21:         **if** $dist(SN_c, SN_t) < r_c \ \forall \ SN_t \leftarrow FN_j$ **then**
22:             $FN_J \leftarrow FN_j \cup SN_c$
23:         **end if**
24:     **end for**
25: **end for** 26: Find EPA based on Equation(4) Highest EPA as forwarder
28: **end procedure**

Algorithm 2 gives a detailed explanation of determining next-hop forwarder set. First, based on the Eq. (3) for each qualified neighbor *NADV* is determined. Secondly, as a result of *NADV*, the neighbor candidates are prioritized. Thirdly, the potential forwarders set F_i are determined from the candidate set C_i. Each potential forwarder set F_j construction begins at highest priority node from C_i and is extended by adding all nodes in C_i which have a distance less than half of communication range r_c. Potential forwarder set F_i is again extended, (copy of nodes) nodes that have distance smaller than the radius of communication r_c for all nodes exist in potential forwarder set added to extended the potential forwarder set F_j. Finally, the potential forwarder set F with the highest Expected Packet Advance (EPA) is selected as the forwarder at next-hop. The potential forwarder set are expanded with condition i.e., a node must over-hear other nodes transmission in particular potential forwarder.

Algorithm 3.1. *DEADEND*

1:          **Procedure DEADEND(N,x,y)**
2:        **for** m = 0 xlength **do**
3:          **for** i = 0 to xlength **do**
4:            $a \leftarrow x[i] - x[m]$
5:            $b \leftarrow y[i] - y[m]$
6:            $if a == 0 \ and \ b == 0$ **then**
7:              continue
8:            $pointradius \leftarrow \sqrt{a^2 + b^2}$
9:            $\Theta \leftarrow atan \ (b/a)$
10:           $\Theta \leftarrow \Theta * (180 \div 3.145926)$
11:           $if a < 0 \ and \ b > 0$ **then**
12:             $\Theta \leftarrow 180 - \Theta$
13:           $if a < 0 \ and \ b < 0$ **then**
14:             $\Theta \leftarrow 180 + \Theta$
15:           $if a > 0 \ and \ b > 0$ **then**
16:             $\Theta \leftarrow 360 - \Theta$
17:           $if pointradius <= r$ **then**
18:             $for k = 0 to 360$ **do**
19:               $if \Theta >= k and \Theta < k + deg$ **then**
20:                 $j \leftarrow ((k + deg) \div deg) - 1$
21:                 $hash[j] + +$
22:               **end if**
23:             **end for**
24:           **end if**
25:         **end for**
27:       **end for**
28: **End Procedure**

Step 3: Restoration from Communication void node: The void nodes in the net- work detected using Algorithm 3.1. Given set of nodes $((x_0, y_0), (x_1, y_1), (x_{n-1}, y_{n-1}))$, the radius r is the transmission region of a source node. The transmission region is divided into several sectors based on predefined angle (i.e., 30). In a sector if there exist at least one node in their transmission region then it ascertained that no void node is present, otherwise in that transmission region there is a void node. To detect the void node, the following steps are followed.

1. Choose source node
2. Mapping the source node to (0,0) and neighbors to (xni - xsi, yni ysi) where ni is neighbor node and s_i is source node.
3. Find the distance between neighbor node and the source node. If the distance is less than radius r then draw the line from source node to neighboring node, find the angle between the source-neighbor line and the x-axis.

4. Now, find quadrant the neighboring node belongs to based on its x, y coordinates.
5. After Finding neighboring node quadrant, determine the angle of neighbor node with reference to x-axis.
6. Steps 3 to 5 are repeated to all the neighboring nodes of source node
7. Ensure that every sector has at least a neighbor node for source node, if so, then that source node is said to be void(dead-end) free, otherwise the source node is dead-end (void).

The restoration from void node region is given in Algorithm 3.2.

Algorithm 3.2. Communication Void Restoration
1: **procedure** Communication_Void_Restoration()
2: **if** (node is void)
3: Change status
4: SN_{vn}: Void node, γ: set of neighbour of SN_{vn}
5: Send (void_node_announcement) to γ
6:
7: $\{\gamma$ set of neighbour of $SN_{vn}.\}$
8: $\{C_D$ candidates to the node $SN_{vn}.\}$
9: **if** $|\gamma| > 0$ **do**
10: **for** $SN_u \in \gamma$ **do**
11: **if** dist(SN_{vn}, SN_u) $\leq r_c$ **then**
16:         $d_u \leftarrow C_D(SN_u, s_u^*)$
17:         $(x_{vn} - x_{s_{vn}^*})^2 + (y_{vn} - y_{s_{vn}^*})^2 + (z_{vn}^* - z_{s_{vn}^*})^2 \geq d_u^2$
18:         $C_D \leftarrow C_D \cup \{z_{vn}^*\}$
19:     **else**
20:         $d \leftarrow \sqrt{(x_{vn} - x_u)^2 + (y_{vn} - y_u)^2}$
21:         **if** $d \leq r_c$ **then**
22:             $(x_{vn} - x_u)^2 + (y_{vn} - y_u)^2 + (z_{vn}^* - z_u)^2 \leq r_c^2$
23:             $C_D \leftarrow C_D \cup \{z_{vn}^*\}$
24:         **end if**
25:     **end if**
26: **end for**
27:     $z = arg\ min_{\forall z_i \in D}\{|z_{vn} - z_i|\}$
28:     SN_{vn} moves to new depth z
31:     Communication_Void_Restoration();
32: **end if**
33: **procedure**

A communication restoration algorithm is used for avoiding void region problem. During communication restoration procedure, void node stops the beaconing, changes its status and sends void node condition to its neighbourhood. The void node calculates new depth or horizontal movement. A neighbor node accepts the *void_node_announcement_message* updates neighbour table by removing the sender from its table and make sure that whether it is a void node or not. communication restoration algorithm is required when the node fails to forward data to next-hop forwarder using greedy forwarding strategy. C-Void not follows the traditional approach which is based on the messages. In existing technique, void nodes are relocated to new position to continue the greedy forwarding. The procedure of communication restoration in C-Void is as follows. When transmission begins, each node examines the neighbourhood locally and finds does it is in a communication void region or not. If the node is located in the region of communication void, then, it has no neighbour node to send packets towards the Sink (C = 0). Therefore, node declares its scenario to its neighbourhood and stop transmission till it obtains any two-hop nodes location information in order to find its new depth location or horizontal movement location. On deciding void nodes depth location or horizontal movement, the void node resumes greedy forwarding.

Whenever node fails to forwarder data packet to sink then void node restoration algorithm is called. In the restoration procedure depth adjustment method is adopted to relocate void nodes to the new location (depth) to continue the forwarding. Void nodes send the beaconing message that contains the e information seq num, x, y, and z location. The neighbour node that receives the beaconing message originated from the void node removes the entry from its routing table. It also ensures that node itself is in the void region or not by sending a void node announcement replay message. Here void node is and it sends void announcement message to neighbours. The node sends the replay to make sure that it is not in void region.

After interval of time void node executes a calculate_new_depth procedure to compute a new location/depth. The calculate_new_depth procedure uses connectivity of hops information received through void_node_announcement_replay message from neighbors that are not void nodes. The new location is determined as follows: the distance from nearest sink to a void node is larger than the distance from nearest Sink to one of the neighbor.

7 Performance Analysis

The simulation parameters used in simulation is summarized in Table 1. An extensive simulation has been carried out using NS-2 simulator and simulation results are compared with the VBF [1], DBR [2], and VAPR [3].

Table 1. Simulation parameter.

Parameter	Value
Number of nodes	50–200
Number of sinks	45
Size of region	750 * 750 * 750
Data packets generation	$\lambda = \{0.01, 0.05\}$pkts – Very Low Traffic $\lambda = \{0.1, 0.15\}$pkts – Low Traffic $\lambda = \{0.2, 0.25\}$pkts – Medium Traffic
Transmission range	250 m
Energy consumption	$Pac_t = 2$ W $Pac_r = 0.1$ W, $Pac_i = 10$ mW $E_{depth} = 750$ mJ/m

Figure 1 illustrates the number of void nodes for entire simulation under various node density. It is observed from Fig. 1 that, as the simulation progress number of neighboring nodes closest to the surface of any sink decrease that leads to more number of void regions. The GUF and GOR have more number of void regions therefore both algorithm fail to route packets. When the number of nodes in the network increased from 150 to 200 and 200 to 250, the number of neighboring nodes closest to the sink increased from 20% to 25% and 25% to 30% respectively. However, the increase in number of neighboring nodes closest to the sink is less in GUF and GOR compared to C-Void. C-Void adopt depth adjustment topology or control mechanism to increase the neighboring nodes closest to the sink and decrease void nodes in the network. C-Void reduces 58% the fraction of void nodes for network of 300 to 350 nodes and approximately 44% in GOR.

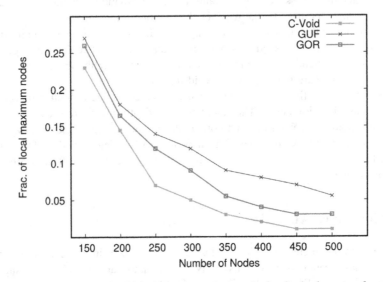

Fig. 1. Presence of void nodes under various node density in the network

Figure 2 illustrate the packet delivery ratio for various network density in C-Void, DBR and GOR. C-Void achieves better packet delivery ratio performance. This is because void node depth adjustment or topology control procedure. When nodes density is low VAPR perform better in comparison to DBR and GOR.

This is because packets generated and forwarded by void nodes are minimum. However, VAPR is not suitable for dense network.

Figure 3 demonstrate that the average number void nodes in C-Void whose depth is reassigned or adjusted. The depth adjustment or topology control increase in the packet delivery. In C-Void, depth adjustment is about 130 m for network of 200 to 300 nodes. The depth adjustment or node movement decrease linearly as the number of nodes are increased. This because the number of neighboring nodes located in communication regions increases.

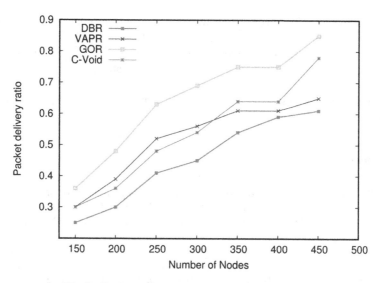

Fig. 2. Packet delivery ratio for various network size

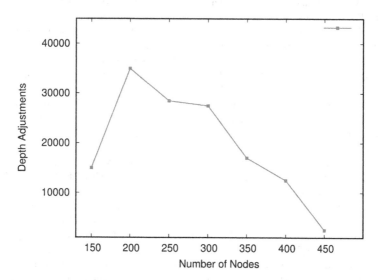

Fig. 3. Average depth adjustment to replace void nodes in the network

8   Conclusions

The proposed C-void protocol based on the geographic and opportunistic routing that reduces number of data transmission, energy cost, and packet collision. The C-Void protocol exploit broadcast nature of wireless communication medium to direct data packets to Sink. The C-Void protocol uses the depth adjustment to avoid communication voids in the transmission path. The performance of the proposed protocol reduces the percentage nodes in the void region about 70%. The simulation result demonstrates that proposed protocol C-Void avoids void region that results in improvement of packet delivery ratio is about 56% in comparison to VBF, DBR, and VAPR. Proposed protocol also reduce packet drop ratio and improves network lifetime. Further, as future work, it is planned to improve propagation latency and energy utilization.

Acknowledgments. Authors' would like to thank all staff members of computer science and engineering.

References

1. Xie, P., Cui, J.-H., Lao, L.: VBF: vector-based forwarding protocol for underwater sensor networks. In: Boavida, F., Plagemann, T., Stiller, B., Westphal, C., Monteiro, E. (eds.) NETWORKING 2006. LNCS, vol. 3976, pp. 1216–1221. Springer, Heidelberg (2006). https://doi.org/10.1007/11753810_111
2. Yan, H., Shi, Z.J., Cui, J.-H.: DBR: depth-based routing for underwater sensor networks. In: Das, A., Pung, H.K., Lee, F.B.S., Wong, L.W.C. (eds.) NETWORKING 2008. LNCS, vol. 4982, pp. 72–86. Springer, Heidelberg (2008). https://doi.org/10.1007/978-3-540-79549-0_7
3. Noh, Y., Lee, U., Wang, P., Choi, B.S.C., Gerla, M.: Vapr: void-aware pressure routing for underwater sensor networks. IEEE Trans. Mob. Comput. **12**(5), 895–908 (2013)
4. Kuhn, F., Wattenhofer, R., Zollinger, A.: Worst-case optimal and average-case efficient geometric ad-hoc routing. In: Proceedings of the 4th ACM International Symposium on Mobile Ad Hoc Networking & Computing, pp. 267–278. ACM (2003)
5. Coutinho, R.W., Vieira, L.F., Loureiro, A.A.: DCR: depth-controlled routing protocol for underwater sensor networks. In: 2013 IEEE Symposium on Computers and Communications (ISCC), pp. 000453–000458. IEEE (2013)
6. Coutinho, R.W., Vieira, L.F., Loureiro, A.A.: Movement assisted-topology control and geographic routing protocol for underwater sensor networks. In: Proceedings of the 16th ACM International Conference on Modeling, Analysis & Simulation of Wireless and Mobile Systems, pp. 189–196. ACM (2013)
7. Zuba, M., Fagan, M., Shi, Z., Cui, J.-H.: A resilient pressure routing scheme for underwater acoustic networks. In: Global Communications Conference (GLOBECOM), 2014 IEEE, pp. 637–642. IEEE (2014)
8. Xie, P., Zhou, Z., Peng, Z., Cui, J.-H., Shi, Z.: Void avoidance in three-dimensional mobile underwater sensor networks. In: Liu, B., Bestavros, A., Du, D.-Z., Wang, J. (eds.) WASA 2009. LNCS, vol. 5682, pp. 305–314. Springer, Heidelberg (2009). https://doi.org/10.1007/978-3-642-03417-6_30
9. Aissani, M., Mellouk, A., Badache, N., Djebbar, M.: A preventive rerouting scheme for avoiding voids in wireless sensor networks. In: Global Telecommunications Conference. GLOBECOM 2009. IEEE, pp. 1–5. IEEE (2009)
10. Ramayajayanthi, R.G.: Improve void routing coordinate fro wireless sensor networks using quality of services. In: International Journal on Engineering Technology and Sciences IJETS, pp. 2349–3976. IEEE (2016)
11. Zhang, D., Dong, E.: A bypassing void routing combining of geographic and virtual coordinate information for WSN. In: 2015 22nd International Conference on Telecommunications (ICT), pp. 118–122. IEEE (2015)
12. Lin, C., Wu, G., Li, M., Chen, X., Liu, Z., Yao, L.: A selfish node preventive real time fault tolerant routing protocol for WSNs. In: 2011 International Conference on and 4th International Conference on Cyber, Physical and Social Computing Internet of Things (iThings/CPSCom), pp. 330–337. IEEE (2011)

Traffic Management and Security in Wired Network

Shivali Dhaka[(⊠)] [ⓘ]

Department of Computer Science, Amity Institute of Technology and Management, Amity University, Gurgaon, India
shivi359@gmail.com

Abstract. Network is nowadays most comprehensible and keen user-friendly requirement of society. All gigantic organizations and institutions can work smartly, competently and proficiently because of this developing network. It has made life simple by doing all trades and transactions whether offline or online on just a click. As network is boon for life, its smooth functioning is necessity of time. Traffic Management and security is essential to deliver the data timely as well as reliably. Inferring filters on different ports, applying ACL's on connecting devices, creating private VLAN's and encapsulating them into secured shell can target both. In this paper, the author has controlled and secured traffic in a Corporate network by simulation of these special secured features. The configuration is done using cisco packet tracer.

Keywords: ACL · VLANs · SSH · Port-Security · Traffic management

1 Introduction

Almost all associations, organizations and institutions comprises of big network connecting them to inside and outside communities, making their task stress-free and easy-going. But this network has to be prevented from traffic to avoid congestion and from intruders to avoid hacking. Some techniques are available today to shelter the network. Here, we are assuming case of corporate network [6] that encompasses four departments- HR, Sales, Marketing and Accounting that are connected with each other for the completion of company targets. For, safe and secure transfer of data and management of traffic, this intranet has to be protected from Intruders who are in rush to enter network and access all the confidential information. In this paper, four approaches have been taken to achieve security target and implemented through cisco packet tracer tool [3]. Firstly, we can craft different private VLAN's in the network area that helps in evading intervention between different departments and Internet and also block access of confidential data by others. Secondly, ACLs are used based on Packet Filtering that can filter unwanted traffic as it passes through a switch and permit or refuse packets from passing specified ports. Packet filtering is a technology used to manage and limit network traffic and hamper network use by intruders and attackers. The data packet coming from outside network is compared by switch or router in the network against applied ACLs. This comparison will help in analyzing the data packet one by one to check if they have the required permission to be forwarded or not. If no such situations

© Springer Nature Singapore Pte Ltd. 2019
S. Minz et al. (Eds.): ICICCT 2018, CCIS 835, pp. 17–30, 2019.
https://doi.org/10.1007/978-981-13-5992-7_2

match, the switch discards the packet. If there are no restrictions, the switch promotes the packet; otherwise, the switch declines the packet [1]. Access Lists are always conFig.d on layer 2 switch to make network secure. Access Lists can be applied both at source and destination. Standard ACL's are applied at source and Extended ACL's are applied at destination to choose which users and outsiders can have access to one's network. Thirdly, traffic management and security can be provided by configuring secure shell [4] on routers and switches of the network to provide encrypted connection to a remote end device. So, it controls safely accessing of data by providing strong encryption when a device is authenticated. Fourthly, security can be implied by blocking the specified ports [5] on the network that can lead to leakage of confidential data to intruders.

2   Practices to Secure a Corporate Network

A Corporate network is gigantic, as it embraces number of sub-departments- HR, Sales, Accounting and Marketing interconnected with each other and working as intranet for their efficient and competent progress. It also deals with outside firms via Internet. But for the smooth running, the essentiality is to keep the network secure. Below are some of the practices proliferating the security and traffic management in the given network (Fig. 1).

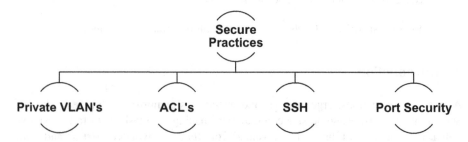

Fig. 1. Secure practices in corporate network

The topology for Corporate exhibiting how different sub-departments are associated with each other via network is shown below in Fig. 2. Here, we have applied different secure practices at various crucial points of network from where data is coming and going out.

2.1   Security via Private VLAN's

One can easily achieve security by creating private VLAN's inside its network. VLANs are used to dispersed subnets and apply security zones [2]. Virtual LANs (VLANs) allow an individual LAN to be divided into numerous apparently separate LANs and are recognized by an identifier. The data packets can travel between VLAN's having same identifier with the effect of regulating the number of hosts that will act as intended recipients for broadcast packet. Due to VLAN's, a network now comprises of multiple networks parted from each other. Private VLAN's helps in attaining security and

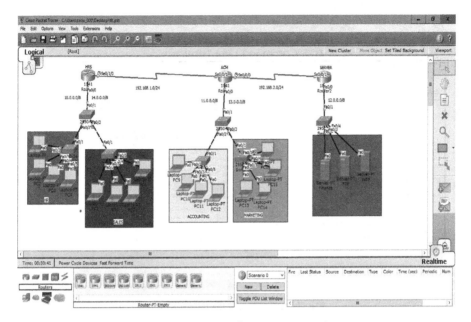

Fig. 2. Topology of corporate network

removing congestion in organizations using wireless Internet. On some of the ports of switch, wireless VLAN's has to be created so that only those ports communicate with Internet and no outside host can access the internal data from servers, as no data traffic will be shared between two logically different networks. Below Figs. 3, 4, 5 and 6 shows VLAN at different departments.

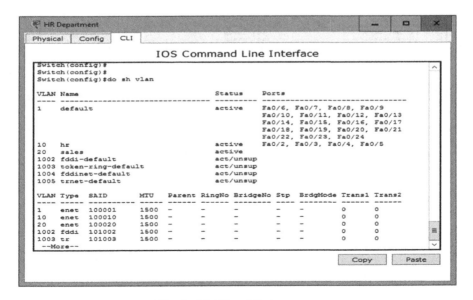

Fig. 3. VLAN on HR department

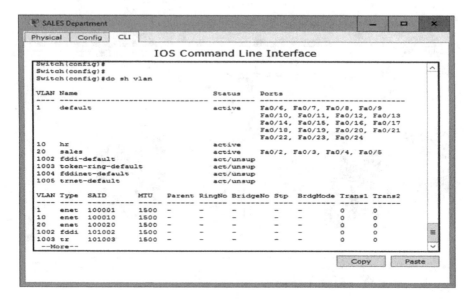

Fig. 4. VLAN on sales department

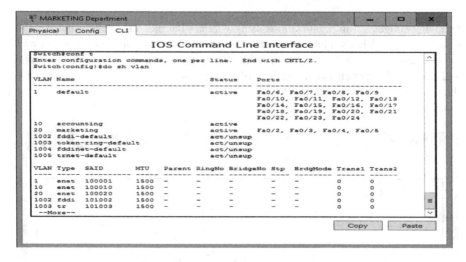

Fig. 5. VLAN on marketing department

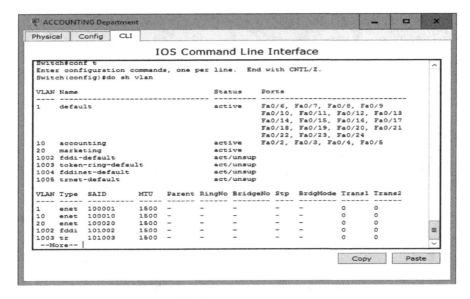

Fig. 6. VLAN on accounting department

2.2 Implementation of ACL's

ACL filters the traffic that arrives and departs the interface by constraining telnet, filtering routing information and ranking WAN traffic with queuing. ACL's can be used to prevent any host to access router connecting the network of Corporate to the Internet. ACL's can be applied in two sequences of numbers. 100 to 199 numbers make use of Standard ACL which is applied on routers near destination in the network and 2000 to 2699 numbers make use of Extended ACL, applied on routers near source in the network. ACL's contain some rules depicting which traffic to allow and which to deny. Routers check every incoming traffic against the rules set in these ACL's to filter unwanted traffic and also to minimize the usage of network by certain hosts to enhance security. Here, we have applied ACL on router connecting HR and sales department named as HRS router and on router connecting Accounts and Marketing named as ACM router. Now, in Accounting department Laptop 9 is having central data that have to be restricted from accessing by others. So, after applying ACL, it can be shown in Fig. 7 below that HR department can access all other PC's except the Laptop 9. Similarly, ACL is applied on ACM router as shown in Fig. 7 restricting PC5 cannot access PC9 (Fig. 8).

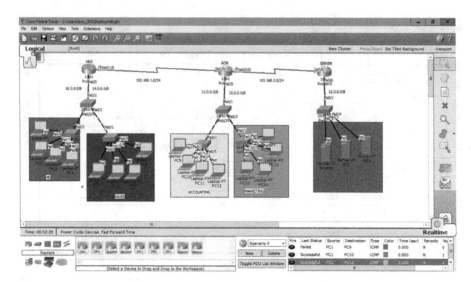

Fig. 7. ACL applied on HRS router (PC1 not communicating with PC9 but communicating with others).

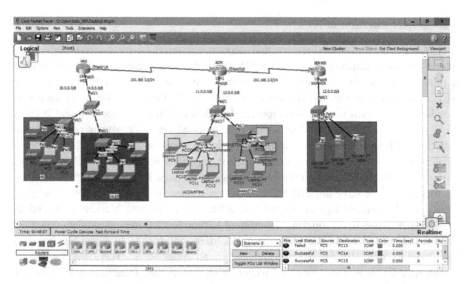

Fig. 8. ACL applied on ACM router (PC5 not communicating with PC13 but communicating with others).

2.3   Secure Shell (SSH) Protection

In big Corporate, remote access of data is very common which usually is the invitation for large number of intruders waiting for the confidential information to hack. Historically, a remote access was possible with TELNET session, rlogin, RSH and RCP that delivers data in plain text readable and snag by anyone. So, the requisite of time give Corporates and institutions a new protocol named Secure Shell (SSH) over insecure network. They provide security by using cryptographic techniques that encrypts the communicated data. SSH Protocol controls Internetworking, all servers on Application layer and network Machines remotely. SSH make use of both public and private keys to identify hosts at client and server sides of network. The client runs SSH key-generate program to generate keys and its identity. The strongest feature of SSH is transforming any insecure TCP/UDP connection into secure SSH connection. SSH is itself applied on the router connecting different sub-networks with each other. Figure 9 is showing the SSH configuration applied on ACM router providing secured and encrypted remote access to every end device connected to it.

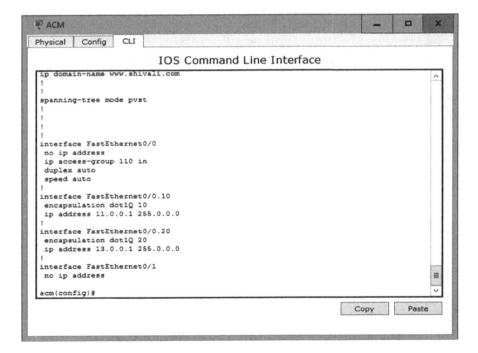

Fig. 9. SSH at ACM router

2.4   Port-Security

By default, when a network is laid down all ports on switches are turned on that can attract a Trespasser to access network through a wall socket causing potential threats for the network. To safe the network in such case required Port Security feature to be applied on particular switches at different interfaces. Port Security applies basically on Layer 2 switches of OSI Model. It helps in controlling traffic in vast network during peak pressure. Port Security as applied on switches near source allows only a specified number of MAC Addresses to enter into the network. This feature smoothen the intranet of Corporate. It blocks data input to all types of Ethernet port when the MAC address of the host struggling to access the port is dissimilar from any of the MAC addresses that are specified for that port. It means only authorized device can access the network and in case any unauthorized device attempt for an entry, the switch will either discard the traffic or shut down that particular port. Port security can be auto configured or enabled manually, defining the maximum number of MAC addresses to be allowed for certain period of specified time. Port-Security feature is applied on switch connecting to each department in which only three end devices are provided access to that particular department. No other third party device can be entered into the network. Figures 10, 11, 12 and 13 is showing Switch-port Security configuration on all departments.

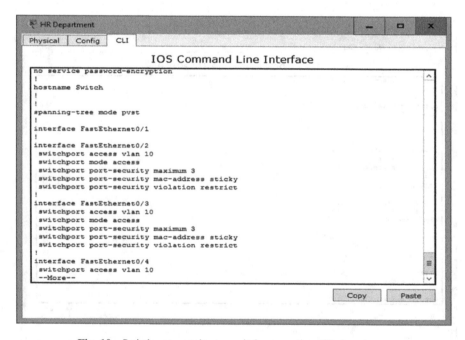

Fig. 10. Switchport security on switch connecting HR department

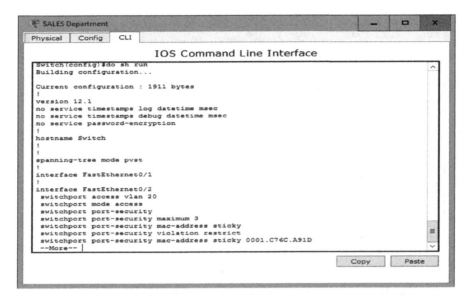

Fig. 11. Switchport security on switch connecting sales department

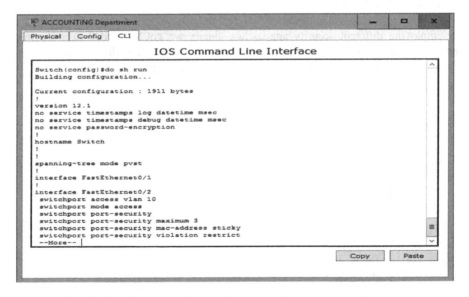

Fig. 12. Switchport security on switch connecting accounting department

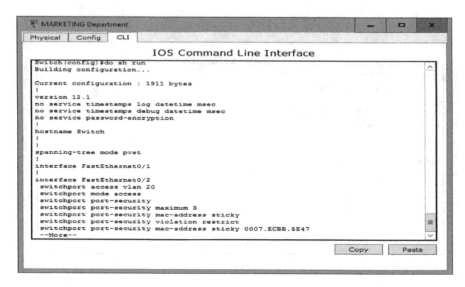

Fig. 13. Switchport security on switch connecting marketing department

3 Result Analysis

By employing different security approaches, finally we got succeeded in achieving secured networks inside corporate. Result analysis is showing the difference before and after applying Access Control Lists, Port-Security and SSH.

(i) **Access Control Lists**
   See Figs. 14(a), 14(b) and 15(a), 15(b).

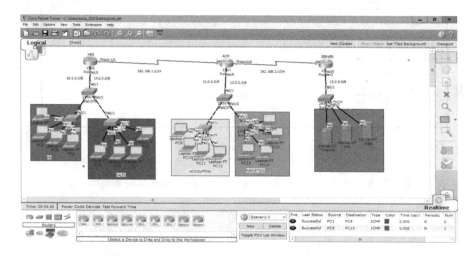

Fig. 14(a). Before ACL is configured at HRS and ACM router.

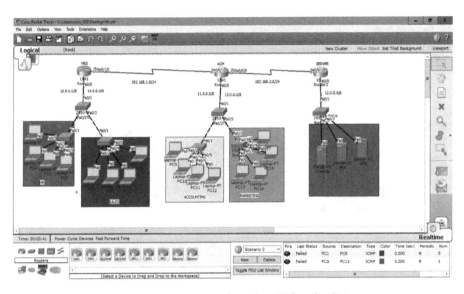

Fig. 14(b). After ACL is configured at HRS and ACM router.

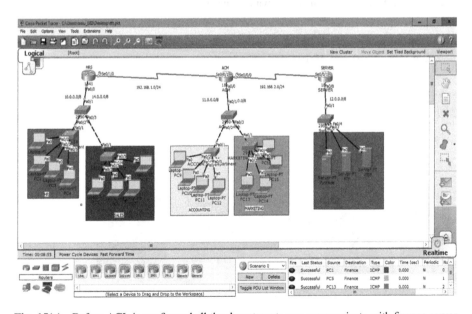

Fig. 15(a). Before ACL is configured all the departments can communicate with finance server.

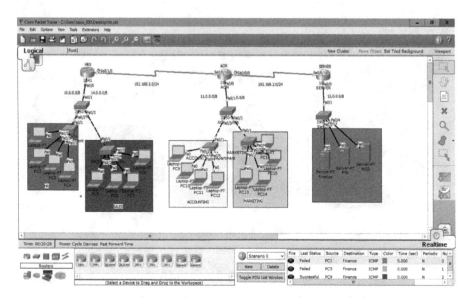

Fig. 15(b). After ACL is configured HR, Sales and Marketing cannot ping finance server only Accounting will be able to communicate with finance server.

(ii) **Port-Security**

See Figs. 16(a) and 16(b).

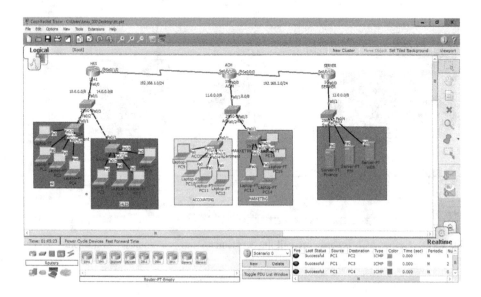

Fig. 16(a). Before applying port-security

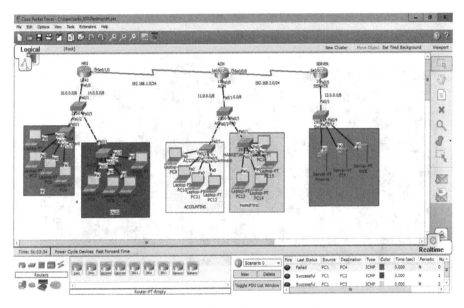

Fig. 16(b). After applying port-security

(iii) **SSH**

See Figs. 17(a) and 17(b).

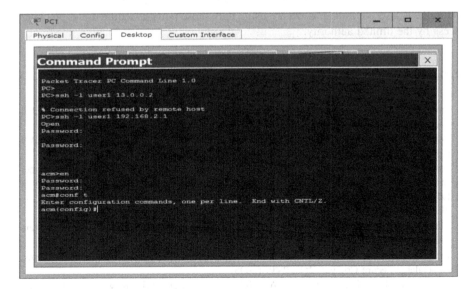

Fig. 17(a). SSH from PC1 to ACM router

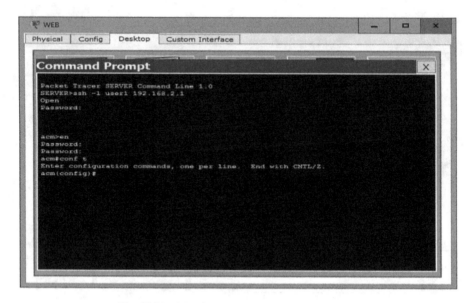

Fig. 17(b). SSH from WEB server to ACM router

4   Conclusion

The result analysis clearly depicted how we can secure the network by just configuring routers and switches wisely by the security approaches, as they are real backbone of the networks. Intruders can not tampered when they try to enter the network. Congestion and traffic is also controlled as we are using only those ports as required and blocking access by the limited authority.

References

1. Suman, S., Agrawal, A.: IP traffic management with access control list using cisco packet tracer. Int. J. Sci. Eng. Technol. Res. (IJSETR) 5(5) (2016)
2. Wang, X., Zhao, H., Guan, M., Guo, C., Wang, J.: Research and implementation of VLAN based on service. IEEE. 0-7803-7974-8/03/$17.00 © 2003
3. Petcu, D., Iancu, B., Peculea, A., Dadarlat, V., Cebuc, E.: Integrating Cisco Packet Tracer with Moodle platform: support for teaching and automatic evaluation. In: Networking in Education and Research, 2013 RoEduNet International Conference 12th Edition, pp. 1–6, 26–28 September 2013
4. Matthews, J.: Computer Networking: Internet Protocols in Action, 1st edn. Wiley, Danvers (2005)
5. Bertino, E., Sanhu, R.: Database security-concept, approaches, and challenges. IEEE Trans. Dependable Secure Comput. 2(1), 2–19 (2005)
6. Nadaf, S.M., Rath, H.K., Simha, A.: A novel approach of enterprise network transformation and optimization. IEEE (2012)

An Improved Driver Assistance System for Detection of Lane Departure Under Urban and Highway Driving Conditions

Anuja Vats[1]([✉]) [iD] and Binoy B. Nair[2]([✉]) [iD]

[1] Department of Electronics and Communications Engineering,
Amrita School of Engineering, Amrita Vishwa Vidyapeetham, Coimbatore, India
anujavats1301@gmail.com
[2] SIERS Research Laboratory,
Department of Electronics and Communications Engineering,
Amrita School of Engineering, Amrita Vishwa Vidyapeetham, Coimbatore, India
b_binoy@cb.amrita.edu

Abstract. One of the major challenges on highways is to avoid an unintended departure from the lane. This paper proposes a lane departure warning system with the help of monocular vision. The efficiency of such a system is subject to clarity of lanes, weather conditions and also method of acquisition. This paper proposes a method of lane detection that is robust to stray edges within the frame. Canny edge detection is utilized on the pre-processed images to obtain maximal intensity edges, followed by lane detection using Hough transform. In this paper we try to utilize selective property of the edges obtained from canny edge detection to reduce noisy edges and improve the false positive rate. The system has been tested to be effective in fully illuminated as well as badly illuminated road conditions with satisfactory results. The average detection rate obtained is 95%.

Keywords: Lane detection · Lane departure · ADAS ·
Edge detection · Hough transform

1 Introduction

The frequency of traffic collisions in India is amongst the highest in the world. A National Crime Records Bureau (NCRB) report revealed that every year, more than 135,000 traffic collision-related deaths occur in India [17]. The "GlobStatus Report on Road Safety" published by the World Health Organization (WHO) identified failure to maintain the lane one of the prime causes of accidents on four lane, non-access controlled National Highways [17]. Improper lane cutting on the Pune-Mumbai Highway in 2016 has contributed to 30% of all road accidents causing fatalities on expressway [18]. Such statistics calls for improvised driver assistance features for increased safety and comfort.

Vision based environment perception is the main enabler for many of these features as it relies on images obtained from front or rear mount low cost cameras as opposed to radar and Lidar based systems. With advancing image processing techniques these

© Springer Nature Singapore Pte Ltd. 2019
S. Minz et al. (Eds.): ICICCT 2018, CCIS 835, pp. 31–43, 2019.
https://doi.org/10.1007/978-981-13-5992-7_3

images can be used in a number of ADAS application like road sign detection, obstacle detection, Lane detection etc. [1–3].

This paper discusses Lane detection and departure warning system for urban traffic based on the feature based approach. Lane detection in urban traffic is subject to a number of challenges, two being:

- Clutter posed by heavy urban traffic, missing lanes, road-side structures including poles, trees buildings etc.
- Significance of achieving reduced computational complexity along with low false positive rate to allow the driver to drive without false departure alarms.

The main contributions of this paper are summarized below:

- Robustness to stray edges: we analysed properties of the edges in the frames obtained from Canny edge detection and chose selective properties to filter out edges contributing strongly to lanes and eliminate edges due to urban clutter.
- Reduced false alarm rate: The lane detection results are segregated into two categories namely abnormal and normal. The normal corresponds to correctly overlaid lanes and is used for a departure estimation and alarm generation, to bring down false positives. The segregation of frames in this way, also brings down computational complexity as the incorrect predictions are excluded from further processing.

We have tested the proposed lane detection on experimental CALTECH data (1225 frames) [16] and Roadmarking data (1439 frames) [15].

The paper is organized as follows: Sect. 2 reviews related works in this domain, Sect. 3 explains the proposed method of lane detection and departure, Sect. 4 shows the experimental results, Sect. 5 concludes the paper along with suggestions of future work.

2   Related Work

Detecting lanes from vision sensors has become increasingly important in recent years for various ADAS applications. A feature based approach for vision applications like Lane detection offers a large range of techniques to optimize time and complexity for better real time performance.

Feature based approach which use visible features in an image such as edges [1, 3, 4] colors, variation in intensities are commonly used. Feature based edge detection comprises of edge detection, lane identification and departure estimation. The most common edge detection techniques are Canny [2, 4], Sobel [5], Prewitt [6] Canny edge detection has proved to be better for robust, single pixel wide edge detection [3]. In order to correctly identify lanes with different colors, an additional intensity based improvement can be done using a stretching function. [4] uses a 5-PLSF function for contrast improvement of the image followed by a lane width model to estimate the missing lanes, this reduces the false warning rate of the system. Dai et al. [5] have used a separate day and night time detection, and used a variant gamma-correction to improve detection in poorly illuminated conditions. [1] have obtained the inverse perspective map of an image and used a score based tracking mechanism for lane detection. For Lane identification from obtained edges Hough transform [2, 4] and RANSAC can be implemented. To reduce the time per frame a Hough transform inspired from RANSAC [1] can also be used for lane identification.

Traditional approach of lane detection are not very effective in the presence of stray edges that appear in urban environment [2]. This paper explains an edge selection technique along with Canny edge detection to filter out stray edges contributed by urban surroundings. This selection significantly improves the output of Hough transform increasing overall accuracy of detection. Another approaches to this application are learning based as in [7] or smartphone based coordination [8]. Learning based approaches have been successfully used for other applications, as in [9–11]. This approach is feature independent but such a method requires a huge labelled dataset to train a convolutional neural network. Efficiency of this system depends hugely on the labelled training samples, which is time consuming.

3   Proposed Method

To overcome the problems mentioned in Sect. 2, we propose an improved lane detection and departure warning system with the following steps. Figure 1 shows the flowchart for proposed technique.

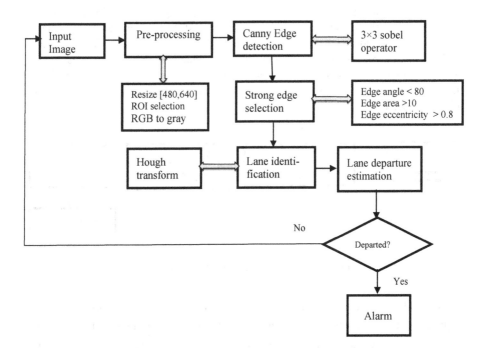

Fig. 1. Flowchart of the lane detection and departure warning system.

3.1 Image Pre-processing

This is a very crucial step in optimizing the overall response time and accuracy of the Lane detection system. The front mounted camera in a vehicle with field of view of 120° captures the road alone with a lot of urban clutter including the roadside structures, trees and view well above the horizon which in turn contribute to a large number of stray edges in the frame. These stray edges are a computational overload for the subsequent step of Hough Transform. Also the presence of strong stray edges reduce the accuracy of the system contributing to a higher false alarm rate.

First step of Image pre-processing is to select an optimal Region of Interest (ROI). Selection of such an ROI reduces the memory requirement per frame along with improving time response of the algorithm. After resizing all the incoming images to a resolution of 480 × 640, we estimated the ROI by dividing the image vertically into four equal regions, and extracting the middle region. This region has proved to be optimal in capturing the road information for varying road widths and front facing camera position.

Second step of image pre-processing is conversion of RGB image into grayscale for further processing, primarily due to the significant reduction in computational complexity offered by this process, as in [12].

3.2 Edge Detection

The purpose of implementing an edge detection at this stage is to significantly reduce the amount of irrelevant information in the image. Edges are completely capable of extracting lane boundaries that can further be used for lane edge selection. The lanes markings on the road surface appear as intensity changes and can be obtained by calculating gradients of the image in x and y direction. Canny edge detection performs better than sobel edge operator [13] with edges that are single pixel wide. The steps in a canny edge detection are shown in Fig. 2.

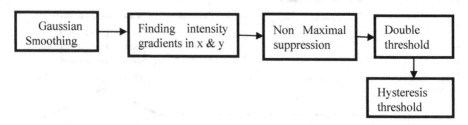

Fig. 2. Flowchart of canny edge detection.

The gradient operators used are 3×3 central difference operators, with more weightage to central pixel. $\frac{\partial f}{\partial x}$ and $\frac{df}{dy}$ are gradients of the mage in x and y directions respectively. The x and y gradients are obtained by convolving the image with the gradient operators Gx and Gy. The resulting gradients in x and y are fx and fy respectively. The magnitude Gmag and phase Gph of the image gradient is given by (4) and (5) respectively.

$$\nabla f = \begin{bmatrix} Gx \\ Gy \end{bmatrix} = \begin{bmatrix} \frac{\partial f}{\partial x} \\ \frac{\partial f}{\partial y} \end{bmatrix} \qquad (1)$$

$$G_x = \begin{bmatrix} -1 & 0 & 1 \\ -2 & 0 & 2 \\ -1 & 0 & 1 \end{bmatrix} \qquad (2)$$

$$G_y = \begin{bmatrix} -1 & -2 & -1 \\ 0 & 0 & 0 \\ 1 & 2 & 1 \end{bmatrix} \qquad (3)$$

$$G_{mag} = \sqrt[2]{(fx^2 + fy^2)} \qquad (4)$$

$$G_{ph} = \tan^{-1}\left(\frac{fy}{fx}\right) \qquad (5)$$

This is followed by non-maximum suppression which suppresses all gradient values to zero, except the local maxima, corresponding to the brightest edge pixel, thereby thinning the edge. The next step in Canny edge detection is to choose a lower and higher threshold to identify strong and weak edges in the resulting edge image. All edges below the lower threshold are attributed by noise and suppressed. The last step that is hysteresis thresholding which checks the neighborhood of a strong edge pixel, if a weak edge pixel is found in the neighborhood it is enhanced and counted as a strong edge based on its connectedness to a strong edge pixel. Figure 3 shows the result of Canny edge detection.

Fig. 3. Result of Canny edge detection on CALTECH lanes [16].

3.3   Strong Edges Selection

The output image of Canny edge selection is a binarized image with strong edges, but it still contains a lot of spurious edges contributed by the urban surroundings like trees, poles, buildings which may be stronger than lane edges especially when the lanes are discontinuous. To combat this, the edges are filtered based on three properties 1. Orientation 2. Eccentricity 3. Area. By applying constraints on these three parameters, the edge corresponding to lanes can be very selectively filtered.

Algorithm : Strong Edge selection
      Input : connected components of Binary Image matrix cc with stray edges
      Output : Binary Image L with lane edges

Idx = 0
Begin
For idx in cc
  cc_2 = find(orientation[cc] < T1 & area[cc] > T2 & eccentricity[cc] > T3)
end
L = cc_2
End Algorithm

Where T1, T2, T3 are threshold values for angle of the connected component, area enclosed by the connected component and the eccentricity of the component respectively.

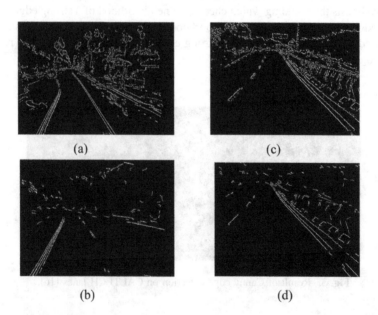

(a)   (c)

(b)   (d)

Fig. 4. (a) and (c) Edges before the use of edge selection. (b), (d) reduction in stray edges after using edge selection.

The values T1 is 80°, T2 as 10 and T3 as 0.8 work reasonably well across different road geometries. Figure 4 shows the result after edge selection.

3.4 Hough Transform

Hough transform is one of the most robust technique for detection of straight lines in an image [14]. It takes a binary edge image as input and transforms every edge pixel into a straight line in the parameter space. Figure 5 shows the geometric representation of Hough transform. The straight lines are described by its angle θ and its distance from the origin ρ. The transformation for each edge point (x, y) is obtained using the Eq. (6).

$$\rho = x \cos \theta + y \sin \theta \qquad (6)$$

Hough transform requires us to describe the ranges for ρ and θ in the parameter space over which the straight lines are likely to span. For each edge coordinate (x, y) the transform finds the number of straight lines passing through is and stores the result in an accumulator array corresponding to that (ρ, θ) value. The strongest edge corresponds to the maxima in this matrix. For Lane identification, with the camera field of view of about 120°, a similar θ will be effective. To ease of computational complexity and reduce processing time the image is split into a left and a right section, with Hough transform applied independently to each.

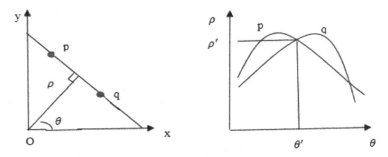

Fig. 5. Geometric representation of Hough transform.

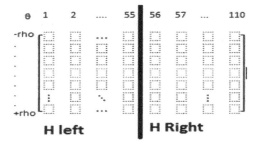

Fig. 6. Right and left Hough Matrix

As shown in Fig. 6 the left Hough matrix ranges $1 < \theta < 55$ and the Right Hough matrix ranges $56 < \theta < 110$. Figure 7 shows the result of Lane detection after Hough transform.

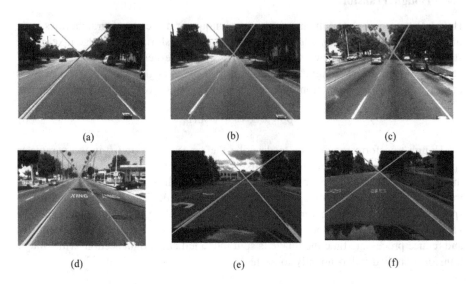

(a)   (b)   (c)

(d)   (e)   (f)

Fig. 7. Result of Lane detection on CALTECH [16]. (a) Cordova sequence 1 (b) Cordova sequence 2 (c) Washington sequence 1 (d) Washington sequence 2 (e) and (f) Road Marking sequence [15].

3.5   Lane Departure Warning System (LDWS)

The lane departure warning system tracks the position of the vehicle with respect to both right and left lanes identified by the Hough transform and indicates a warning to the driver in case of a departure on either side.

In order to make our lane departure warning system more reliable, we separate the result of lane detection into two categories of normal frames and abnormal frames.

This decision is based on the point of intersection of the lanes. The point of intersection will always lie within a rectangle in the mid-section of the image for a frontal mount camera as shown in Fig. 8. An intersection point lying outside this rectangle indicates a false positive or incorrect detection hence categorized as 'abnormal frame'. Such frames are excluded from further processing which helps in reducing computational complexity and increases the reliability of the system.

A Euclidean distance measure id used to estimate departure as shown in Fig. 9. λ_1 is the Euclidean distance between Hough origin (H_o) and the mid-point of the right lane (Mp_r), λ_2 is the distance between Hough origin and the mid-point of the left lane (Mp_l).

$$\lambda_1 = \sqrt{\left(H_{ox} - Mp_{rx}\right)^2 + \left(H_{oy} - Mp_{ry}\right)^2} \tag{7}$$

$$\lambda_2 = \sqrt{\left(H_{ox} - Mp_{lx}\right)^2 + \left(H_{oy} - Mp_{ly}\right)^2} \tag{8}$$

$$\lambda = \lambda_1 - \lambda_2 \tag{9}$$

Algorithm to indicate Departure

Output : Text Warning display , Input : lambda

Begin
    If $\lambda > t1$
        Display('Left Departure')
    Elseif $\lambda < -t1$
        Display('Right Departure')
    Else
        Display('Safe Zone')
    End
    End Algorithm

Where t1 is the departure metric, which depends on Road geometry.

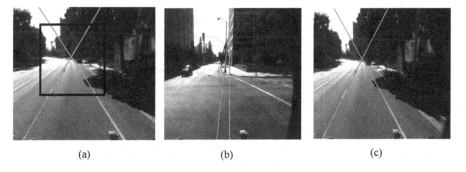

(a)	(b)	(c)

Fig. 8. (a) Region of intersection for normal frames. (b) abnormal frame (c) normal frame on CALTECH lanes [16].

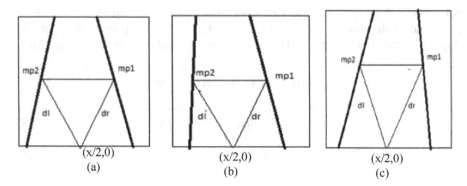

Fig. 9. (a) dl = dr indicating safe zone. (b) dr > dl indicating left departure (c) dl > dr indicating right departure.

4   Experimental Results

The performance of the proposed lane detection system is calculated on standard dataset CALTECH [16] by manual verification of detected lanes with the total number of lanes. The algorithm identifies one lane in each half of the image, hence the lane can be misidentified, but not missed. The algorithm has also been tested on the publically available road-mark data [15] (Table 1 and Fig. 10).

Table 1. Details of dataset used for testing

Dataset name	Number of frames	Road conditions
Caltech	1225	**Daylight/Urban**
Cordova 1	250	Day/Urban
Cordova 2	406	Brightly lit with trees and buildings
Washington 1	337	Shady conditions
Washington 2	232	Brightly lit with trees
Road Marking	1439	**Bad Illumination**
Road Marking Scene	1439	Uneven Light/sunset
Total	2664	

The accuracy has been calculated on the CALTECH [16] and Roadmark [16] dataset based on the total number of lanes in each video segment vs the number of lanes correctly identified.

$$\% \ detection \ Rate = \left(\frac{number \ of \ lanes \ correctly \ detected}{total \ number \ of \ lanes \ to \ be \ identified \ in \ the \ segment} \right) \times 100 \quad (10)$$

Table 2 shows the detection rate achieved before (denoted using B) and after (denoted using A) edge selection.

Fig. 10. (a), (b) departure warning on CALTECH dataset [16] (c) departure warning on Roadmarking dataset [16].

Table 2. Detection rate before Edge selection

Dataset	Total lanes		Detected lanes		False positive/Wrong detection		Lane detection rate (%)		Missing detection	
	B	A	B	A	B	A	B	A	B	A
Cordova 1	476	476	447	465	29	11	93.9	97.6	0	0
Cordova 2	682	682	598	644	84	38	87.6	94	0	0
Washington 1	662	662	552	635	110	27	83.38	95.9	0	0
Washington 2	464	464	399	448	65	16	86.4	96.5	0	0
Road Marking	2798	2798	2483	2593	315	205	88.7	92.6	0	0

The parameter λ obtained from lane departure for roadmarking [15] sequence can be seen for departures in Fig. 11. The thresholds for the safe zone depend on road geometry.

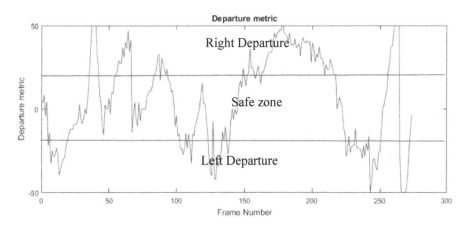

Fig. 11. Graph of departure metric λ vs frame number for the Roadmarking sequence [15].

5 Conclusion

In this paper we presented a lane detection and departure warning system, which performs well for different road geometries in an urban scenario. We focused on improving the robustness of lane detection system in an urban environment with clutter by selecting edges based on their properties. We also reduced the computational complexity of lane detection through Hough transform by selecting the frames with incorrect detections and discarding them from further processing. This significantly brings down false alarms. In addition to that we have also proposed a method to estimate drivers driving pattern based on drive trajectory.

The average accuracy on public dataset CALTECH is 96% and average accuracy on all datasets is 95.3%. This system shows good performance for different environments and levels of illumination. Since an image processing based approach uses handpicked features, which are application dependent, in the future work we will try to address this problem using feature independent learning based approach.

References

1. Lotfy, O.G., et al.: Lane departure warning tracking system based on score mechanism. In: Midwest Symposium Circuits Systems, October, pp. 16–19 (2017)
2. Kortli, Y., Marzougui, M., Atri, M.: Efficient implementation of a real-time lane departure warning system. In: 2016 International Image Processing, Application System, pp. 1–6 (2016)
3. Son, J., Yoo, H., Kim, S., Sohn, K.: Real-time illumination invariant lane detection for lane departure warning system. Expert Syst. Appl. **42**(4), 1816–1824 (2015)
4. Gaikwad, V., Lokhande, S.: Lane departure identification for advanced driver assistance. IEEE Trans. Intell. Transp. Syst. **16**(2), 910–918 (2015)
5. Dai, J., Wu, L., Lin, H., Tai, W.: A driving assistance system with vision based vehicle detection techniques
6. Li, Q., Chen, L., Li, M., Shaw, S.L., Nüchter, A.: A sensor-fusion drivable-region and lane-detection system for autonomous vehicle navigation in challenging road scenarios. IEEE Trans. Veh. Technol. **63**(2), 540–555 (2014)
7. Gurghian, A., Koduri, T., Bailur, S.V., Carey, K.J., Murali, V.N.: DeepLanes: end-to-end lane position estimation using deep neural networks. In: 2016 IEEE Conference on Computer Vision and Pattern Recognition Workshops, pp. 38–45 (2016)
8. Murugesh, R., Ramanadhan, U., Vasudevan, N., Devassy, A., Krishnaswamy, D., Ramachandran, A.: Smartphone based driver assistance system for coordinated lane change. In: 2015 International Conference on Connected Vehicles and Expo, ICCVE 2015 - Proceedings, pp. 385–386 (2016)
9. Jayanth Balaji, A., Harish Ram, D.S., Nair, B.B.: Machine learning approaches to electricity consumption forecasting in automated metering infrastructure (AMI) systems: an empirical study. In: Silhavy, R., Senkerik, R., Kominkova Oplatkova, Z., Prokopova, Z., Silhavy, P. (eds.) CSOC 2017. AISC, vol. 574, pp. 254–263. Springer, Cham (2017). https://doi.org/10.1007/978-3-319-57264-2_26
10. Nair, B.B., Kumar, P.K.S., Sakthivel, N.R., Vipin, U.: Clustering stock price time series data to generate stock trading recommendations: an empirical study. Expert Syst. Appl. **70**, 20–36 (2017)

11. Singh, A.K., John, B.P., Subramanian, S.V., Kumar, A.S., Nair, B.B.: A low-cost wearable Indian sign language interpretation system. In: International Conference on Robotics & Automation for Humanitarian Applications (2016)
12. John, A.A., Nair, B.B., Kumar, P.N.: Application of clustering techniques for video summarization – an empirical study. In: Silhavy, R., Senkerik, R., Kominkova Oplatkova, Z., Prokopova, Z., Silhavy, P. (eds.) CSOC 2017. AISC, vol. 573, pp. 494–506. Springer, Cham (2017). https://doi.org/10.1007/978-3-319-57261-1_49
13. Wang, J.G., Lin, C.J., Chen, S.M.: Applying fuzzy method to vision-based lane detection and departure warning system. Expert Syst. Appl. **37**(1), 113–126 (2010)
14. Duda, R.O., Hart, P.E.: Use of the Hough transform to detect lines and cures in pictures. Commun. Assoc. Comput. Mach. **15**(1), 11–15 (1972)
15. Wu, T., Ranganathan, A.: A practical system for road marking detection and recognition. In: IEEE Intelligent Vehicles Symposium Proceedings, pp. 25–30 (2012)
16. Aly, M.: Real time detection of lane markers in urban streets. In: IEEE Intelligent Vehicles Symposium, pp. 7–12 (2008)
17. Wikipedia Contributors: Traffic Collisions in India. Wikipedia, The Free Encyclopedia, 25 July 2017. Accessed 26 Dec 2017
18. Times of India. Lane Cutting Speeding Big Killers on Stretch in 2016. In timesofindia. indiatimes.com, 17 December 2017

Quality of Service in Dynamic Resource Provisioning: Literature Review

Monika$^{(\boxtimes)}$ (iD) and Om Prakash Sangwan

Department of CSE, Guru Jambheshwar University of Science & Technology,
Hisar, Haryana, India
monikard31@hotmail.com

Abstract. Resource provisioning is major problem in cloud computing because of the rapid growth in demand of resources and these resources are allocated according to dynamic nature of application. Unconstraint use of these resources can lead to two major problems namely under provisioning and over provisioning. Therefore, to implement provisioning is major concern in cloud computing. This paper has discussed and analyzed the methods incorporated in different research papers to understand objectives, performance on various QoS attributes and issues related to current cloud computing environment. This research work also presents details about prior research work, popular factors and future direction in resource provisioning.

Keywords: Cloud computing · Dynamic provisioning · Soft computing · QoS attributes · Literature review

1 Introduction

Cloud computing is a three-layer architecture and used for the delivery of computing resources – computing, storage, software etc. to the customer over the internet. Companies those provide these services are called cloud service provider and user of these services are called cloud customers. These resources are provisioned with minimal effort to users using "pay-for-use-basis" manner. Thus provisioning of resources is the method for distribution and management of resources according to cloud user's requirements. It is a way of executing techniques to enhance the effectiveness and performance of computing resources with satisfaction of QoS parameters. However acceptable QoS can't be delivered to cloud customers until resources provisioning considered as an important task. Therefore, QoS based resource provisioning is a necessary process for efficient utilization of resources [1]. This process can be conducted in several ways i.e. Dynamic provisioning, Static provisioning, User self-provisioning etc. as shown in Fig. 1 and in this paper, we have mainly discussed only dynamic resource provisioning techniques.

Static Provisioning: It is applicable for applications, which have predictable and unchanged resources demand because in this approach resource allocation process is done only once at the beginning of user's application. It is not able to handle unexpected changes in resource demand and leads to insufficient utilization of resources.

© Springer Nature Singapore Pte Ltd. 2019
S. Minz et al. (Eds.): ICICCT 2018, CCIS 835, pp. 44–55, 2019.
https://doi.org/10.1007/978-981-13-5992-7_4

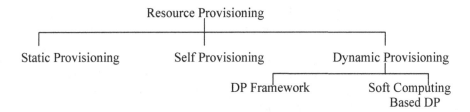

Fig. 1. Classification of resource provisioning

User-Self Provisioning: Self-provisioning is the heart of cloud computing and also called self-service. It allows customer to provision their required resources themselves, and they can use the service without the intervention of service providers or minimal intervention from cloud operator.

Dynamic Resource Provisioning: Dynamic provisioning allows allocation and de-allocation of resources as per user requirements. It is more applicable in cloud computing when application resource's demand more likely to change during application execution time. Due to its dynamic nature, it enables scalability and elasticity of system but incurs resource allocation decision overhead on the system. QoS requirements of users are difficult to satisfy due to high variability of users' needs. To handle this variability, there is need to consider dynamic behaviors in solutions because dynamic behavior can estimate and predict future resources demands which provide better results and improve system performance. Due to the frequent changes in user demands, service providers also need dynamism in provisioning procedures to estimate the total resource requirements of cloud users and to also estimate the number of the resources provided by resource provider in near future [24].

2 Dynamic Provisioning Framework

To handle the dynamic behaviour of user requirements researchers have proposed number of frameworks using varying techniques. Singh and Chana [1] provide QoS based resource provisioning techniques by clustering resources using workload patterns and then again used K-means clustering algorithm to explore the best pairs of resource and workload with reduction in execution time and cost along with other QoS parameters for both homogeneous and heterogeneous cloud environments. The event handling issues related to dynamic resource have been managed by presenting a framework in map reduce computation [3]. Map reduce computation events are dynamic in nature and generated randomly. So to meet the deadlines of map reduce computation and guarantee QoS, it is necessary to identify the task, meet the deadlines of these events and helps in minimize the expenses of virtual machines. A dynamic resource provisioning framework for effective management of workflow ensembles on IaaS clouds was proposed by considering the budget and deadline constraints, uncertainties in task runtime estimators and faults etc. into account [4]. Benfenatki *et al.* [5] proposed a component oriented method for clouds business applications with the aim to moderate the necessity of scientific information and also to decrease the user participation for provisioning of cloud application by using linked USDL to describe cloud services.

A cloud broker resource provisioning technique that solved the task of selection of best service and placement of virtual machines in heterogeneous clouds based on user requirements and constraints with Benders decomposition and integer programming algorithm proposed by Subramanian and Savarimuthu [6]. The approach consists of 3 stages. In first stage, cloud broker collects the service request description and other QoS parameters. The second stage recognizes the set of cloud resources and services filling the service requirement, and the third phase evaluate these cloud providers on SMI. Reddy et al. [9] presented a new two phase provisioning approach which assign low cost resources to users. The first phase approximates the resource requirement for each application and the second phase was used to optimize the cost of Virtual machine wage and cloud providers' service. There was also a need for resource allocation algorithm that serve localized subset of customers by using resource constrained units. Landa et al. [10] presented a mechanism to provide computational capacity in distributed clouds where users compete for resources. It assigns resources based on vickrey auctions that uses the information about locality distribution of clients and produce a high quality probabilistic model that helps customers to estimate the results of such auctions. Clients use the prices information given by system as input to estimate provisioning cost, quality trade-off and better results.

To formulate the problem of dynamic resource provisioning by estimating the currently used resources related to QoS demand during run time, Ran et al. [2] presented an economical provisioning model for satisfying time sensitive demand of computing services by using large deviation principle that does not require any prior information about demand and produce a quick reply in case output does not satisfy QoS demand. Niu et al. [20] presented a model to dynamically adjust fundamental cloud cluster by using job history to develop an online reserved instance provisioning algorithm that reduce cost without effecting the average job wait time. Semi elastic cluster model allows organizations to provision resources within current capacity, user requirement and flexibility. Li and Cai [21] proposed a model by considering factors i.e. interval between tasks, VM loading and data transfer time, workflow deadline and software setup time, and resource utilization using integer programming with the objective of minimizing the expenditure of cloud workflow applications during VM provisioning. It uses 3 rules that matches task with different objectives with time slots: (1) Minimize the rented intervals, (2) total costs minimization, (3) maximize resource utilization. This work was evaluated with workflow, with shorter deadline as well as software setup time i.e. SIPHT etc. An optimized model of VM provisioning by considering various issues i.e. under provisioning, over provisioning, cost, time, delay etc. was presented by Choi and Lim [22] that maximize a provider's revenue while satisfying users QoS requirements and minimizing SLA violations and cost. The prediction of resources was done by using CLT (Control Limit Theorem), AR (Auto Regression) and EWMA (Exponentially weighted Moving Average) for next time interval.

The above discussed resource provisioning techniques are insignificant if scheduling involves computational science or data intensive applications because of requirement of a large amount of computational power by these applications while considering QoS requirement of users. These requirements exceed the amount that is available within the premise of a single organization. In this case a cloud application platform i.e. Aneka is useful because it has capability of provisioning resources obtained from different providers i.e. clouds, clusters, grids etc. Vecchiola et al. [7] presented a provisioning paradigm using aneka, that provides support scientific issues by considering computation time in objective function, besides this Toosi et al. [8] also used aneka platform to handle data intensive application by considering the aspects of data locality, network bandwidth constraints, data transfer time, data associated with each task for resource provisioning in hybrid cloud environment. Wu et al. [18] presented a benefit aware framework that use feedback control theory to solve the problem of SLA violation in multi-tier applications like workload in virtualization based cloud computing. Feedback control theory function is to minimizes the computation cost with satisfying the SLA requirements. Leena Sri and Balaji [24] proposed an automatic resource provisioning based on previous used data so that it can produce estimated resource requirement and can improve the execution time of cloud application to pull more cloud customers. Comparative analysis of various dynamic resource provisioning is shown in Table 1. Factors/attributes taken for the comparison are as follow: sub-category, basic approach, application type, operational environment, objective functions, provisioning criteria, platform used, validating criteria, potential gaps etc. It is concluded form above said comparison that different provisioning algorithms have focused on diverse provisioning criteria and cost and time are the major QoS attributes that majorly effects the overall performance of the dynamic resource provisioning.

3 Soft Computing Based Resource Provisioning

Here, we accomplished a review of soft computing techniques for provisioning of resources in cloud computing because they are used to find a solution to an optimization problem by using some assumption about problem and explores the complete search space. Leslie et al. [11] solved the problem of elastic & reliable provisioning of instances by developing a reliability aware profit maximization resource provisioning framework. Its main aim was to find the instance that maximize the profit while meeting reliability constraints by considering diversity in cloud services.

A bipolar resource management framework was proposed [12] using a ANN based resource predictor and used GA (Genetic Algorithm) for resources management that reduce of job rejection and SLA violation as response time, job rejection rate are important factors of clients' satisfaction. The proposed algorithm consists of two poles. The online pole predict all resources required to client using neural network and the offline pole is responsible for optimization and used genetic algorithm for performance optimization. Islam et al. [13] proposed a prediction based resource measurement and provisioning framework to predict and fulfil the upcoming surge with least drop in performance and availability and results shows that prediction accuracy of neural network demonstrates better effectiveness than other one. An automatic prediction

Table 1. Comparison of dynamic resource provisioning framework

Reference	Sub category	Basic approach	Application type	Operational environment	Objective function	Provisioning criteria	Platform used	Validating criteria	Potential gaps
[1]	QoS-aware	K-means based clustering	Workload	Dynamic & Heterogeneous	Resource without SLA violation	Execution time & cost, delay	CloudSim	Non-QoS based provisioning	–
[2]	QoS based	Large deviation principle	Compute –intensive application	Parallel	To meet time-varying computing workload	Cost, waiting time, utilization ratio	CloudSim	Compared with autoregressive moving average model	Need extra capacity for fluctuation of workload
[3]	QoS based	Solid theoretical analysis based	Map reduce computation	Dynamic	Reduce cost of hiring VM	Cost, deadline, execution time	Event driven RP framework	Static and periodic RP framework	Networking factors not considered
[4]	Cost and deadline constrained based	Workflow-aware admission procedure	Scientific workflow ensembles	Homogeneous	Maximize the completion of user prioritized workflow	Task granularity, uncertainties, delay, failure	Cloud Sim	Experimented with real scientific applications	Exceeds the constraints in less perfect conditions
[5]	Automated provisioning	Matching using SPARQL protocol & RDF query language	Component oriented business applications	Homogeneous	Reduce technical knowledge and human involvement	Cost, response time, availability	Orchestration tool Juju with MADONA web tool	Media Wiki, Word press	Need a preconfigured VM with static compositions
[6]	Architecture based	Mixed integer programming, Benders decomposition algorithm	VM configuration/deployment plan	Heterogeneous	Select the best cloud service with optimal cost	Cost, scalability, response time	AIMMS Language	SMI Cloud, OCRP, Flexi scale etc.	VM migrations effects has not been considered

(continued)

Table 1. (*continued*)

Reference	Sub category	Basic approach	Application type	Operational environment	Objective function	Provisioning criteria	Platform used	Validating criteria	Potential gaps
[8]	Deadline based	By considering available bandwidth and data size	Data intensive applications	Hybrid	Handle size and time of data for allocation of resources	Data transfer time, cost, deadline	Data–aware Aneka	Compared with basic and enhanced Aneka	Not perform well when the deadline is very high
[9]	Cost–effective based	Cloud market broker module with coordinated approach	–	Heterogeneous	Goal of minimizing the user cost	Cost, efficiency, time	Java	Compared with non-coordinated provisioning	Uncertainties in price and demand of resources
[10]	Self-tuning based	Vickrey auction	Decentralized cloud application	Heterogeneous	Effective cost-benefit tradeoff	Monetary cost, QoS cost	–	Different combination of simulation parameters	No equilibrium state due to change in input parameter
[18]	Benefit aware on demand provisioning	Feedback control theory	Multi-tier applications	Heterogeneous	Prevent SLA violation under flash crowd condition	Transition & infrastructure cost, benefit, SLA violation	RUBiS (apache +J2EE Server)	Compared with cost oblivious and cost aware approaches	Accuracy is lower on servers with more cores
[20]	Cost effective	Classic exponential smoothing	HPC applications	Parallel	To deliver a cost effective provisioning	Cost, waiting time	Using SLURM	Using EC2' CCI 8xlarge instances & Google compute engine	Limited self-correcting capacity
[24]	Cost efficient	Central Limit Theorem (CLT), Exponentially Weighted Moving Average (EWMA)	Workload applications	Dynamic	Minimize penalty for SLA violation	SLA violation, profit, cost, response time	CloudSim	Comparison between CLT, EWMA and prediction based technique	Uncertainty not handled accurately

helps to enhance the preciseness of scaling system during the resource provisioning was proposed by the use of the time series prediction algorithm, it uses historical value of performance indicators to forecast future value and reduce the probability of over-fitting problem [17]. ANN and SVM (Support Vector Machine) has been used to evaluate the accuracy of proposed algorithm and also reduce the probability of over-fitting problems.

Fakhfakh et al. [14] used PSO (Particle Swarm Optimization) for resource provisioning by considering the dynamic structural changes of workflow in addition to QoS requirements of user. The algorithm has two stages. The 1st stage i.e. offline stage determine the number of resources required during execution of workflow while 2nd stage i.e. online stage handles the structural changes that raised during runtime. Bi et al. [19] proposed a novel dynamic hybrid metaheuristic algorithm by considering usually ignored factors i.e. SLA, number of rejected requests, amount of finished requests, price of electricity, SLA agreement between service consumer and provider etc. to minimize the energy consumption and increase profit revenue by using simulated annealing and PSO in virtualized cloud data centres. It published a dynamic model to handle work-load of different resource intensive application in virtualized cloud data centres.

Eawna et al. [15] presented a resource provisioning method in layered cloud application using a combination of PSO and SA. They used PSO for identification of Lbest and Gbest, SA for identify Gbest and then made a choice between them. This method compared individually with PSO and SA by considering the factor time and results shows that PSO-SA based resource provisioning takes less amount of time than RP based on PSO and SA algorithm when the number of requests exceed 2500. PSO was also used by Prashanth et al. [23] to handle dynamic workflow, which utilized alternative tasks as additional control over the data flow's cost, resource cost, throughput etc. and satisfy the user defined constraints. The main advantage of PSO is that it can access random population and have large impact on optimization performance.

A dynamic RP using ABC and ACO proposed in multitier cloud computing and results shows that ACO converge faster to optimum solution than ABC or ACO performs better on all combination of parameters [25]. Feller et al. [26] proposed an energy-aware ACO for the placement of resources dynamically according to dynamic load for workload consolidation problem in IaaS cloud computing environment. It used probabilistic decision rule to guide ants toward optimal solutions and the iteration's-best ant was used for pheromone updating. A load balancing algorithm proposed by calculating load index for each node, which is number of the nodes in a particular queue and used firefly algorithm to select the node with least node and to achieve the objective of resource utilization [27]. Fuzzy logic was also used to handle resource allocation in virtualized environment [28, 29]. Budihal et al. [28] used fuzzy approach i.e. fuzzy interface mamdani to handle resource utilization and SLA violation in data centres where as Rao et al. [29] used self-tuning fuzzy control approach which used adaptive output amplification to reduce settling time and flexible selection rule to improve the stability in QoS provisioning. To deal with the problem of appropriate initialization of parameters and convergence speed Amiri et al. [16] used the fuzzy approach that increase the convergence speed of learning and improve the accuracy in resource provisioning. Gurav and Patil et al. [30] proposed heterogeneous-aware

Table 2. Comparison of dynamic resource provisioning using soft computing techniques

Reference	Sub-category	Basic approach	Application type	Operational environment	Objective function	Provisioning criteria	Platform used	Validating criteria	Potentials gaps
[12]	ANN	Online pole to provide resources	Bin packing problems	Homogeneous	Overcome the problem of queuing effect ad delays	Delay, response time, migration time, energy	Testbed	First fit heuristic	Temporal service unavailability affect performance
[14]	PSO	A solution with total execution time closest to deadline	Workflow applications	Homogeneous	Minimizing financial execution cost	Computing time, cost, deadline	Cloud Sim	Real workflow applications	Not considered Heterogeneous workload
[26]	ACO	Probabilistic decision rule	Workload consolidation problem	Homogeneous	Utilize least number of bins	Energy, utilization, time	Java	First fit decreasing	Energy saving at cost of increased computation time
[27]	Firefly	Used load index to find resource with least load weightage	Optimal distribution problem	Homogeneous	Provide a good load balancing	Processing time, stability	Cloud Sim +JAVA	Genetic algorithm	Uncertainty of parameters is not considered
[29]	Fuzzy logic	Extra self-tuning output amplification & flexible rules	Transaction processing council	Homogeneous	CPU allocation under static & dynamic provisioning	Response time, throughput	Testbed	Kalman filter, ARMA	Response time behave nonlinearly in busy state
[31]	GA	Natural selection strategy	Data centres	Dynamic	Load balancing while minimizing makespan	Cost, execution time	Cloud analyst	Compared with FCFS, RR, SHC	Computational complexity is high

dynamic capacity resource provisioning approach using GA that dynamically adjust the number of machines to overcome delay and energy consumption by using information about number of task in the queue during each control period for large scale service applications. Dasgupta *et al.* [31] also used GA for computationally intractable problem to find a global optimum processor for job in a cloud. Table 2 shows details of the above studied soft computing resource provisioning techniques with their objective and operation environment. Most of these metaheuristics approaches performed in homogeneous cloud environments and consider load balancing and resource utilizations as their major resource provisioning attributes.

4 Discussion

A total of 31 research papers have been taken to identify different resource provisioning technique and to provide a brief description of them. Our main focus is to define dynamic provisioning and to identify main searching mechanism, objectives and provisioning criteria used in these provisioning. An orderly technique has been used to find major issues and QoS attributes in dynamic provisioning. This section describes the major finding and QoS attributes of resource provisioning.

Findings: Even after cloud computing has magnificent scope still there are research issues to be solved for flawless understanding.

- The optimal provisioning technique have greater benefit against its cost.
- Initialisation of new VM in cloud is not instantaneous, so service provider takes several minute delay before allocating a new hardware.
- Purchasing of new on demand instances after arrival of new task may backlogged the application because of no reservation for newly arrived task and may also violate SLA.
- It is challenging for a cloud customer to calculate the threshold value for quality attributes i.e. response time, reliability, maintainability etc.
- There is a trade-off always need to be maintained with exactness without delaying time because delay enforced by optimizations techniques produce false results.

QoS Attributes: Major QoS attributes find in above studied literature is shown in Table 3 and Fig. 2 show the number of research papers where these attributes have been considered. Cost (20%) and time (21%) is used in mostly research papers while only 3% research papers used reliability, load balancing and 5% used scalability and availability QoS attributes. Mostly resource utilization (13%), profit (7%), deadline (6%) and SLA violation (8%) used as QoS parameters in studied literature. These QoS attributes perform a very important role in the computation of provisioning objective and overall performance of the system so it is necessary to clearly identify QoS attributes required for particular applications and approaches.

Table 3. QoS attributes affecting dynamic resource provisioning

QoS attributes	References
Cost	[1–6, 8–11, 13, 14, 18–24, 26, 28, 30, 31]
Deadline	[1, 3, 4, 7, 8, 14, 21]
Time	[1, 2, 5–9, 12–15, 17–21, 24–31]
Resource utilization	[1–3, 9, 13, 16, 17, 19, 21, 24, 26–29, 31]
Scalability	[6, 10, 11, 20, 23, 26]
Reliability	[6, 11, 24, 26]
Availability	[1, 5, 11, 13, 23, 27]
SLA violation	[2, 9, 12, 16, 18, 19, 22, 24, 28]
Throughput	[10, 17, 19, 23, 29]
Efficiency	[1, 9, 10, 20, 21, 23]
Load balancing	[6, 27, 31]
Profit	[1, 9, 11, 12, 18, 19, 23, 28]

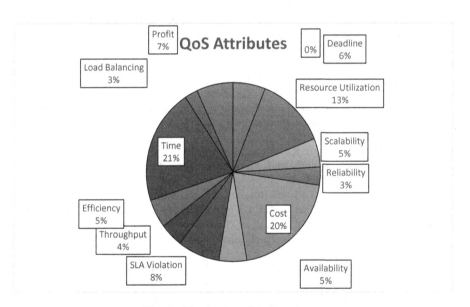

Fig. 2. Distribution of QoS attributes

Conclusion: In this paper, we have largely reviewed the applications of soft computing techniques in the field of resource provisioning to identify major QoS attributes in environment of cloud computing. These soft computing techniques are slower in comparison to deterministic techniques but provide near optimal solution and also improve the quality of solution. Most of the researchers have considered computation time and cost as their objectives whereas others considered makespan, availability, throughput and resource utilization QoS attributes. Comparative analysis of soft computing approach mainly compares the searching mechanism, objectives and provisioning criteria used for improvement and the environment which is used for implementation. Here, various major findings have been described and can be used for further work.

References

1. Singh, S., Chana, I.: Q-aware: quality of service based cloud resource provisioning. Comput. Electr. Eng. **47**, 138–160 (2015)
2. Ran, Y., Yang, J., Zhang, S., Xi, H.: Dynamic IaaS computing resource provisioning strategy with QoS constraint. IEEE Trans. Serv. Comput. **10**, 190–202 (2017)
3. Xu, X., Tang, M., Tian, Y.-C.: QoS-guaranteed resource provisioning for cloud-based MapReduce in dynamical environments. Futur. Gener. Comput. Syst. **78**(Part 1), 18–30 (2018)
4. Malawski, M., Juve, G., Deelman, E., Nabrzyski, J.: Algorithms for cost- and deadline constrained provisioning for scientific workflow ensembles in IaaS clouds. Futur. Gener. Comput. Syst. **483**, 1–18 (2015)
5. Benfenatki, H., Silva, C.F.D., Kemp, G., Benharkat, A.-N., Ghodous, P., Maamar, Z.: MADONA: a method for automated provisioning of cloud-based component-oriented business applications. Serv. Oriented Comput. Appl. **11**, 87–100 (2017)
6. Subramanian, T., Savarimuthu, N.: Application based brokering algorithm for optimal resource provisioning in multiple heterogeneous clouds. Vietnam J. Comput. Sci. **3**, 57–70 (2016)
7. Vecchiola, C., Calheiros, R.N., Karunamoorthy, D., Buyya, R.: Deadline-driven provisioning of resources for scientific applications in hybrid clouds with Aneka. Futur. Gener. Comput. Syst. **28**, 58–65 (2012)
8. Toosi, A., Sinnott, R., Buyya, R.: Resource provisioning for data-intensive applications with deadline constraints on hybrid clouds using Aneka. Futur. Gener. Comput. Syst. **79**, 765–775 (2017)
9. Reddy, K.H.K., Mudali, G., Sinha Roy, D.: A novel coordinated resource provisioning approach for cooperative cloud market. J. Cloud Comput. Adv. Syst. Appl. **6**, 1–17 (2017)
10. Landa, R., Charalambides, M., Clegg, R.G., Griffin, D., Rio, M.: Self-tuning service provisioning for decentralized cloud applications. IEEE Trans. Netw. Serv. Manag. **13**, 197–211 (2016)
11. Leslie, L.M., Lee, Y.C., Zomaya, A.Y.: RAMP: reliability-aware elastic instance provisioning for profit maximization. J. Supercomput. **71**, 4529–4554 (2015)
12. Bahrpeyma, F., Haghighi, H., Zakerolhosseini, A.: A bipolar resource management framework for resource provisioning in Cloud's virtualized environment. Appl. Soft Comput. **46**, 487–500 (2016)
13. Islam, S., Keung, J., Lee, K., Liu, A.: Empirical prediction models for adaptive resource provisioning in the cloud. Futur. Gener. Comput. Syst. **28**(1), 155–162 (2012)
14. Fakhfakh, F., Kacem, H.H., Kacem, A.H.: Dealing with structural changes on provisioning resources for deadline-constrained workflow. J. Super Comput. **73**(7), 2896–2918 (2017)
15. Eawna, M.H., Mohammed, S.H., El-Horbaty, E.-S.M.: Hybrid algorithm for resource provisioning of multi-tier cloud computing. Procedia Comput. Sci. **65**(8), 682–690 (2015)
16. Amiri, M., Derakhshi, M.-R.F., Khanli, L.M.: IDS fitted Q improvement using fuzzy approach for resource provisioning in cloud. J. Intell. Fuzzy Syst. **32**(1), 229–240 (2017)
17. Nikravesh, A.Y., Ajila, S.A., Lung, C.-H.: An autonomic prediction suite for cloud resource provisioning. J. Cloud Comput. Adv. **6**(3), 1–20 (2017)

18. Wu, H., Zhang, W., Zhang, J., Wei, J., Huang, T.: A benefit-aware on-demand provisioning approach for multi-tier applications in cloud computing. Front. Comput. Sci. **7**(4), 459–474 (2013)
19. Bi, J., et al.: Application-aware dynamic fine-grained resource provisioning in a virtualized cloud data center. IEEE Trans. Autom. Sci. Eng. **14**(2), 1172–1184 (2017)
20. Niu, S., Zhai, J., Ma, X., Tang, X., Chen, W., Zheng, W.: Building semi-elastic virtual clusters for cost-effective HPC cloud resource provisioning. IEEE Trans. Parallel Distrib. Syst. **27**(7), 1915–1928 (2016)
21. Li, X., Cai, Z.: Elastic resource provisioning for cloud workflow applications. IEEE Trans. Autom. Sci. Eng. **14**(2), 1195–1210 (2017)
22. Choi, Y., Lim, Y.: A cost-efficient mechanism for dynamic VM provisioning in cloud computing. In: Conference on Research in Adaptive and Convergent Systems, USA, pp. 344–349 (2014)
23. Prashanth, R.H., Pushpalatha, S.: Optimized resource provisioning for dynamic flow on cloud infrastructure using meta heuristic technique. In: Conference on Intelligent Systems and Control, pp. 1–8 (2016)
24. Leena Sri, R., Balaji, N.: Speculation based decision support system for efficient resource provisioning in cloud data center. Int. J. Comput. Intell. Syst. **10**, 363–374 (2017)
25. Eawna, M.H., Hamdy, S., El-Horbaty, E.S.M.: New trends of resource provisioning in multi-tier Cloud computing. In: Conference on Intelligent Computing and Information Systems, pp. 224–230 (2015)
26. Feller, E., Rilling, L., Morin, C.: Energy-aware ant colony based workload placement in clouds. In: IEEE/ACM International Conference on Grid Computing, pp. 26–33 (2011)
27. Florence, A.P., Shanthi, V., Florence, A.P., Shanthi, V.: A load balancing model using firefly algorithm in cloud computing. J. Comput. Sci. **10**(7), 1156–1165 (2014)
28. Budihal, S.V., Mallapur, J., Hiremath, T.C.: QoS based resource provision in cloud network: fuzzy approach. In: International Conference on Advances in Computer Science and Application, pp. 33–40 (2015)
29. Rao, J., Wei, Y., Gong, J., Xu, C.Z.: DynaQoS: model-free self-tuning fuzzy control of virtualized resources for QoS provisioning. In: IEEE International Workshop on Quality of Service, pp. 1–9 (2011)
30. Gurav, R., Patil, D.: Heterogeneity-aware resource provisioning using genetic algorithm. Int. J. Manag. Appl. Sci. **4**(9), 39–44 (2016)
31. Dasgupta, K., Mandal, B., Dutta, P., Mandal, J.K., Dam, S.: A genetic algorithm (GA) based load balancing strategy for cloud Computing. In: International Conference on Computational Intelligence: Modelling Techniques and Applications, pp. 340–347 (2013)

Using a Concept Map Network Based Constructivist Learning Environment to Design a Learning System

Minakshi Sharma[(⊠)] and Sonal Chawla

Department of Computer Science and Applications,
Panjab University, Chandigarh, India
bminakshi@gmail.com, sonal_chawla@yahoo.com

Abstract. Meaningful learning is the desired outcome of every learning system and many theories and learning paradigms aim at achieving this goal. Meaningful learning is best achieved if the approach is student centric. Constructivist theory of learning is one such theory that promotes student centric learning and advocates active participation of learner in the learning process rather than passive assimilation of knowledge. This paper discusses the design of one such tool that enables the educator to create a constructivist learning environment for teaching as well assessing the acquired knowledge. The tool uses concept maps as building blocks for creating the learning component as well as assessment component. The paper further discusses the design considerations for developing both of these components. A prototype of the tool was developed for teaching 'C' programming for the beginners and was tested with undergraduate students who were learning any programming language for the first time. Results indicate that there was a considerable difference in the scores obtained by the learners who were taught the subject using the tool as compared to the learners who were taught the same subject using traditional classroom method and the students taught using the tool performed much better as compared to the other group both in concept based assessments and skill assessments.

Keywords: Constructivist Learning Environment · Concept maps ·
Concept map network

1 Introduction

Learning can be defined as the process of knowledge construction in an individual. Meaningful learning is different from rote learning as in case of meaningful learning, the knowledge presented to learner is fully understood by him and he is able to relate the newly acquired knowledge with what is already known to him [1]. As each learner has a different learning approach, a student-centric approach has become a necessity while designing a learning system. [11, 17] provide some core concepts that a student-centric learning system should have. According to them, a student centric system should create multiple experiences for knowledge construction for the learner and he should be able to choose his learning path from the multiple options provided to him.

© Springer Nature Singapore Pte Ltd. 2019
S. Minz et al. (Eds.): ICICCT 2018, CCIS 835, pp. 56–69, 2019.
https://doi.org/10.1007/978-981-13-5992-7_5

Also, student centric system should provide an environment for collaborative learning by interacting with other learners or teachers.

Theory of constructivism given by Piaget in 1975 provides the guidelines for designing a learning system which is student centric, and which can impart meaningful learning [22].

Student-centric learning and instruction strategies can be provided using various learning techniques like inquiry-based learning, situated learning, project based learning and problem based learning. This research work uses problem based learning method to create a learning environment which provides a learner with learning objective in the form of a solution to specific problem and learning can be carried out either individually or in a group. Problem based learning has been described briefly as below:

1.1 Problem-Based Learning (PBL)

Problem-based learning (PBL) takes a student-centric approach and the teacher acts as a facilitator. The required knowledge and skills are achieved in the process of solving authentic problems [2]. Main objectives of PBL as given by [9] are:

1. It should help the learners in developing cognitive flexibility;
2. Problem-solving skills should be developed as generic skills;
3. Learning should be self-directed;
4. There should be enough motivation from the teachers or peer group to find the solution of given problem.

Although students might learn slightly fewer facts and less content knowledge in a PBL environment, the knowledge they acquire is much more elaborate; thus, students in PBL might perform better in retention and transfer of the knowledge in larger contexts [21].

1.2 Constructivist Learning Environments

Constructivist Learning Environments (CLE) are the learning spaces designed using the principles of constructivism. Peck Jonassen and Wilson [12] define constructivist learning environments as technology based spaces in which students explore, experiment, construct, converse and reflect on what they are doing so that they learn from their experiences. In order to be effective, CLEs should be designed in such a manner that learners can explore the knowledge repositories independently and decide about the concepts to be learnt and in what depth. So, these environments should provide multiple representations of the reality to the learners which they are able to explore.

In constructivist learning environment, the responsibility of learning is on the learners themselves hence encouraging learner-centered approach.

1.3 Concept Maps

A concept map presents relationship between concepts where concepts are linked together using labelled links. Concepts in a concept map are represented using labeled boxes and relationships between two concepts, the propositions, are represented using labelled directed arrows. Hence, a concept-map is a visual representation which represents relationships between different concepts under some context. The context under which these concepts are interconnected in a concept map is given in the form of a focus question. Figure 1 represents an example concept map that provides a context in terms of "Understanding a C Program".

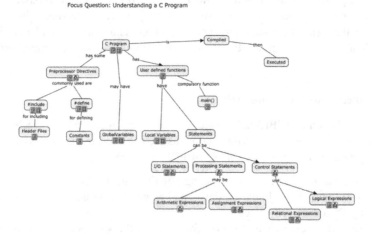

Fig. 1. Example of a concept map

Concept maps have been used in innumerous situations as scaffolds by teachers to make the concepts easy to understand. These can be used as a component for designing a CLE as design of concept maps is fundamentally based in the theory of constructivism.

2   Designing a Concept Map Based CLE

As already discussed, an effective learning environment should be learner centric and by following the principles of constructivism and student centered approach we can aim to create such a learning environment. This paper discusses the design of a learning system which is based on principles of constructivism and uses concept maps as main building blocks. Various design considerations for creating such a CLE were developed and used while designing the learning system. These design considerations are:

2.1   Pedagogical Considerations

Pedagogical considerations focus on what should be learnt and how. Hence, the pedagogical design must focus on the methods in which a learner is able to construct his own knowledge in the process of achieving learning objectives [12, 19]. Also, there should be a strong link between conceptual knowledge and skills for putting this knowledge into practice [15].

While designing the CLE, following pedagogical design considerations should be made:

(i) It should support and satisfy learners' needs and learning objectives;
(ii) System should be flexible enough to let the learner choose the learning content and objectives;
(iii) It should involve learning resources and activities that support active learning [5, 16].

2.2 Social Considerations

Learning can take place individually or socially where learners collaboratively construct knowledge through interactive processes of information sharing, negotiation and modification [7]. Social considerations for designing the CLE should be:

(i) A learning environment must provide tools for sharing knowledge, interaction, reusability of learning objects and interoperability with other learning environments.
(ii) Teachers as well as peers should act as facilitators of knowledge. These interactions may include setting up grounds norms, encouraging participation, monitoring progress and providing information as suggested in [11, 17].

2.3 Principles of Constructivism

In order to put above discussed considerations into practice, following principles of constructivism were identified. The principles were originally given by [14] and have been used by various researchers.

1. CLE model should be learner centric. Learners should discover things themselves rather than being instructed to do so as there should be active construction of knowledge rather than its passive assimilation.
2. Construction of knowledge means that learner should be able to search for similarities between the knowledge he already possesses and the new knowledge presented. Thus, learner should be presented with multiple representations of reality where he can choose any path he desires to.
3. Learners should be able to use their knowledge for solving real-world problems. Hence, a CLE should include activities for learners to test their knowledge.
4. Teachers should serve only as facilitators of learning and not as transmitters of knowledge.
5. Learners should be evaluated constructively using methods that are part of the learning process and take into consideration the learners' individual orientations.
6. There should be collaborative construction of knowledge where learning is also supported through interaction of learners with other people, e.g., instructors, fellow learners.

3 The Tool

Based upon above discussed considerations, a tool was developed which uses concept maps as basic building blocks to create a CLE. This tool provides a framework that can be used to create a learning environment to teach any subject content of which can be arranged in some hierarchical order. Major components of the tool are the learning component as well as the assessment component. Design considerations for both these components are discussed below:

3.1 Designing Learning Component

Learning component of the tool provides a platform where learners can acquire knowledge about the concepts they choose. Effective designing of this component is important as knowledge construction in the learner is facilitated through this component. A poorly designed learning component not only fails to construct the correct and complete knowledge in the learner, it also fails to correct the misconceptions he previously had. An effective learning component will cater to the individual learning needs of the learners and will be able to provide multiple paths of learning to choose from. Learning paths in this component are provided in the form of interconnected concept maps forming concept map network where each concept map provides a context for learning and this context is represented by a focus question. The concepts in a concept map may provide links to the learning stimulus for further learning about the concept or to some other concept map in order to learn about the concept in some other context or to learn about further details of the concept. Hence, the main sub-components of the learning component are concept maps and learning stimulus.

Creating Topics

First step in designing the learning component is the creation of topics to be learnt in a subject curriculum. The topics are derived from the learning objectives to be achieved once the study is over. If the subject to be learnt is part of some curriculum, these topics can be derived from the curriculum provided, otherwise, the subject designer may design the curriculum first in order to identify the learning objectives. Once the topics are created, the designer should identify or create problems that a learner should be able to answer once he learns the topic. Learner's learning objective may be the same as provided by the subject designer in which case, the learner needs to learn all the topics, or, he may also has a different learning objective and select some of the topics to learn. The tool provides facility for the teachers to create these topics.

Designing Concept Maps

Concept maps are the main building blocks of the learning component. In order to design an effective concept map network, the individual concept maps should be meaningful and should answer a focus question. First step is to create a focus question that presents a problem pertaining to the topic selected. Creation of a good focus question is important as it defines the learning context for the student. In the next step, the teacher identifies concepts that will be used to answer the focus question. These concepts are then interlinked using propositions in the form of labelled edges representing the relationship between concepts. Hence, concept map as a whole will provide answer to the problem presented as focus question. Example of a problem based concept map is shown in Fig. 2.

Focus Question: Writing a simple C Program

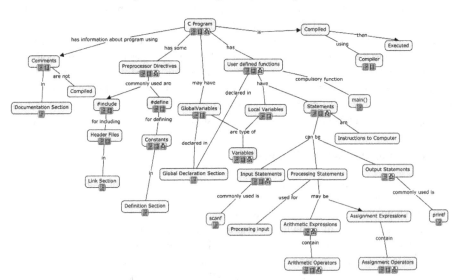

Fig. 2. An example problem based concept map

In addition to the problem based concept maps, there should be other concept maps as well. These maps are linked to the specific concept and explain a concept used in problem based concept maps in more detail. Moreover, these concept maps can also represent the same concept in different context, hence enabling the learner to understand use of a concept under different contexts. All the concept maps are interconnected through concepts forming a concept map network and the learner is free to move from one concept map to another choosing his own learning path.

Learning Stimulus

In order to enable a learner to decide whether and when he wants to learn about the concept, the concepts in a concept map should be linked to learning stimulus. Learning stimulus is a set of learning material that may be in multiple forms like presentations, text, videos etc. and helps the learner in understanding the concepts. This learning stimulus should be stored separately so that same material can be reused in different concept maps wherever the concept appears. This separation of learning stimulus from concept maps helps the designer in providing the links in all the concept maps where the concept appears and learner in deciding when to learn about the concept in detail. Wherever possible, different types of learning stimulus should be presented so that the learner may go with the best possible learning method for him.

The tools uses CMap Tools, an open source software to create the concept map network and stores these on the CMap Server. These concept maps are then linked with the topics through topic management component.

Designing Activities

Activities constitute the problems posed for the learner solving which he can assess the acquired knowledge himself. Importance of activities should not be underestimated as these help the learner in identifying the misconceptions and remove these. Hence, the activities should be such that these are able to help the learner to assess both the theoretical understanding as well as application of the concepts. Ample number of activities should be included in each concept map so that the learner can apply the acquired knowledge and decide which path to follow. The activities are also part of learning stimulus and just like learning material, should be linked to individual concepts.

3.2   Designing Assessment Component

Assessment is an important component of learning as it helps the teacher in under-standing the level of knowledge acquired by the learner. Correct assessment of the acquired knowledge is necessary because it helps the teacher as well as the learner in understanding the kind of knowledge acquired, inconsistencies in the knowledge and misconceptions that should be removed. An ideal assessment task "is objective and reliable, minimizes the influence of context on responses, and captures something of the structural nature of the subjects' knowledge" [18]. As the acquired knowledge is a complex structure that cannot be directly seen, assessment tasks are given to the learner so that he can externalize the knowledge possessed.

Selecting assessment tasks is important as evaluation of these tasks results in evaluation of the knowledge of the learner. The assessment tasks should be easy to understand and perform and should be able to differentiate meaningful learning from rote learning. Traditional pen and paper tests used for assessment of knowledge are not much effective as these cannot effectively externalize the knowledge of learner and promote rote learning. The proposed tool supports two types of assessments: Concept Based assessment, for assessing the conceptual knowledge and the skill assessment, taken to assess whether the learner is able to apply the learnt concepts in solving real life practical problems.

Conceptual Assessments

There are many methods to design conceptual assessments like pen and paper test, multiple choice questions etc., the proposed tool uses two types of conceptual assessment tasks, concept map based assessments and multiple choice questions.

Concept map based assessments pose a focus question to the learner who has to draw a concept map in response to the focus question. Concept maps as assessment tasks have been used in numerous studies and have been found to be more effective as compared to other methods. Concept maps drawn by the learners can give more insight into their knowledge structures as compared to the other methods as structure of concept maps is similar to the mental model in which information is stored inside the brain. Moreover, the concept maps drawn by the learners can provide multiple infor-mation about the knowledge of the learner which is not possible using other methods. Assessment of learner concept maps can tell the teacher whether it is a rote learning or meaningful learning (concept maps from rote learning tend to be linear whereas meaningful learning produces interconnected networked concept map [20]. Also, there is a visible difference between the maps drawn by the beginners and that of a novice. Maps drawn by the experts are more densely connected with elaborate labels on the links whereas maps of novices will contain more number of submaps indicating poorly connected knowledge and basic labels on the links. In addition to such qualitative assessment concept maps can also be assigned scores which can help in quantitative assessment of the maps.

Designing Concept Map Assessments

The tool provides a platform for teachers to create concept map based assignments. First, the teacher selects a topic and then creates a focus question. Focus question created should be precise and clearly indicate what is required from the learner. The teacher also provides solution to the focus question in the form of a concept map which will be treated as expert concept map while assigning scores to the learner's solution to the same focus question. There are many ways in which concept map based assessment tasks may be created right from the filling concept or links in partially designed concept map to creating concept map from the scratch. Although concept map from scratch is treated as the "gold standard" of concept map assessments [25], the students tend to construct better maps if they are provided with the list of concepts [3]. This is because students get a direction about what concepts need to be included in their assessments. This method also helps in assigning the scores automatically by the system. Hence, the tool provides the concepts, that are part of the expert concept map, as list to the learner, along with the focus question.

While drawing the expert concept map for a focus question, the teacher should take care to include all possible links which represent a significant, hierarchical or causal relationship between the concepts as accuracy of scoring by the tool largely depends on the quality of expert map. Figure 3 shows a concept map based assessment as is presented to the learner.

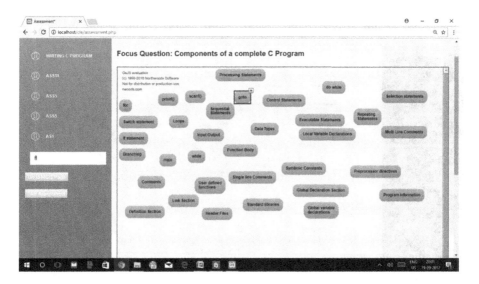

Fig. 3. A sample concept map based assessment task

Designing Multiple Choice Based Assessments

In order to substantiate the results of concept map based assessments, the tool also allows teachers to design multiple choice based assessments. Multiple choice based assessments are most commonly used assessments methods especially in e-learning modules. Although, these tests provide an easy and quick way of assessment, a poorly designed assessment may lead to nothing substantial. Multiple choice assessments have a mixed reputation as they seem less effective as compared to subjective assessments [24], however, carefully designed multiple choice questions can test same high-level cognitive skills as subjective ones if questions are carefully designed [4, 6, 8]. Similar to concept map based assessment tasks, the tool provides a platform to create multiple choice questions. The teacher selects a topic and then designs multiple choice questions (MCQs). Before creating MCQs, the teacher should decide upon the kind of assessment he wants to perform. The questions should not be repetitive, should cover all the concepts under the topic and should also be able to test the understanding of the learner pertaining to that topic. Last but not the least, the MCQ assessment should compliment the concept map based assessment tasks and both together should be able to correctly assess conceptual knowledge acquired by the learner.

Designing Skill Based Assessments

In addition to conceptual assessment, it is important to assess the skills acquired by the learner in order to evaluate his ability to apply the learnt concepts in solving real life practical problems. The proposed tool provides an option to the teacher to create skill based assessments. Again, just like conceptual assessments, skill based assessments are also related to a topic. There can be multiple skill based assessments created for a topic. The learner may select an assignment and provide solution and submit. This submitted assessment is then available to the corresponding teacher who can assess the solution and assign a score as discussed in the next section.

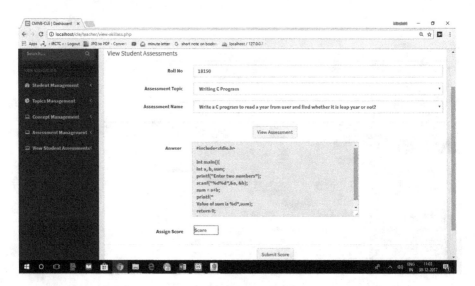

Fig. 4. Teacher's view of the skill based assignment submitted by student

Figure 4 shows the teacher's view of the skill based assessment task submitted by the student.

Assigning Scores to Assessments

In order to quantify the results of assessment evaluation, the assessment tasks submitted by the learner need to be assigned some scores. The tool assigns scores automatically to the concept maps as well as multiple choice based assessments. However, the skill based assessments have to be manually scored by the teacher as there are multiple qualitative aspects related to the skill based assessments. Brief discussion about assessment scores is given below:

Scoring of Concept Maps

Scores assigned to concept maps are based on relation with master map rubric as this method is found to be consistent through many studies [18]. In this method, the concept map submitted by the student is compared with master map drawn by the teacher and is assigned scores. Although, a student is given a liberty to draw new concepts also in addition to the concept list provided, these concept or the links to these concepts are not counted while assigning scores by the tool. However, the teacher while qualitatively assessing the concept map, may consider these concepts and modify scores, if he wants. Qualitative assessment of the maps includes assessment of whether the knowledge acquired by the learner is rote learned or is a meaningful one and how much connectivity is there between the knowledge structure of the learner. The teacher is also provided with the multiple concept maps for the same focus question if the learner has taken the assessment multiple times. This can help the teacher in understanding the change in knowledge structure of the students over a period of learning time. Figures 5 and 6 show the teacher's view of assignments submitted by the student before and after the study.

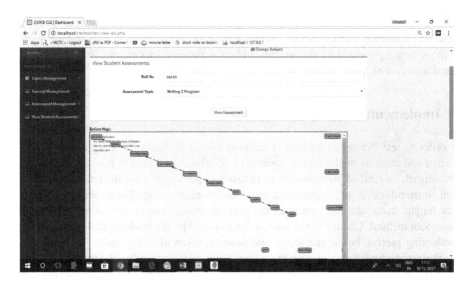

Fig. 5. Concept map based assessment submitted before the test

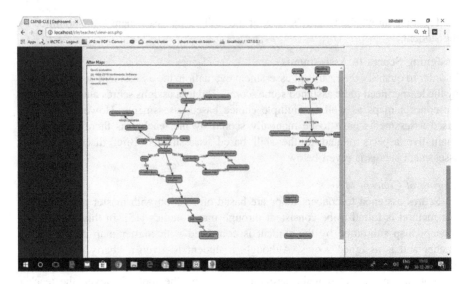

Fig. 6. Concept map based assessment submitted after the test

Scoring of MCQ Assessments

Scoring of multiple choice based assessments is comparatively easier and is fully automated in the tool. Correct choices for the questions is supplied by the teacher and the answers provided by the learner are compared with these stored answers. One mark each is assigned to the correct answers.

Scoring of Skill Based Assessments

As discussed previously, assigning a score to a skill based assessment requires analysis of multiple dimensions. Hence, the tool does not assign any score to these assignments. The teacher can access the assignments submitted by the students, analyse these on parameters like correct use of concepts learnt at the correct place and the level of the solution provided by the student. Figure 4 above shows teacher's view of skill based assessment submitted by the learner.

4 Implementation and Evaluation

In order to test the proposed tool, a learning system to teach 'C' programming was created and implemented with the students of BSc/BCA first year of Panjab University, Chandigarh. A total of 106 students were taken as participants for the study who were then further divided into experiment group and control group. The experiment group was taught using the tool whereas the control group was taught using traditional classroom method. Change in the knowledge acquired by the students was measured by conducting pretest, before the study, and posttest, taken after the study.

Pretests and posttests for both the groups were conducted using the tool in order to bring uniformity in the assessment method. Independent sample test results on post-test scores and difference between post-test and pre-test scores indicate that quality of knowledge acquired by the students taught using the tool was significantly better than the students who were taught using traditional classroom method.

- Comparison of post-test scores between two groups gives M = 70 and SD = 20.31 for experiment group and M = 37.43 and SD = 13.66 for control group denoting highly significant difference between the scores.
- Similarly, for difference score, mean value M for experiment group was 58.39 and standard deviation SD was 23.22 and these values for control group were 23.92 and 14.36 respectively. These values again denote highly significant difference in scores between groups.
- Moreover, here was a significant correlation (Pearson correlation value .496) between scores of students in conceptual assessment and scores obtained in correctness of the practical assignment.
- Similarly, there was a significant correlation (Pearson correlation value .589) between conceptual assessment scores and levels of solution provided by the learner.

5   Limitations

The proposed tool was created as an alternative to traditional classroom teaching where a learner can select his own learning path and decide how to learn. Moreover, the tool provided problem based learning approach providing a learning goal to the students. However, prototype of the tool was developed to teach 'C' programming and all the results obtained are in reference to learning programming languages only. Developing learning system for other subjects may vary especially in case of developing skill based assignments. Other limitations include that the tool was tested only with the students with no prior programming experience. The results obtained may be different when tested with advanced learners.

6   Conclusion

This study proposes a tool for designing a constructivist learning environment that is student centric and uses concept map network as major building block for learning component. While testing the tool for creating learning system for 'C' programming, the tool was found quite effective in implementing the principles of constructivism and designing a student-centric system. However, creation of problem based learning spaces depends upon the approach followed by the teacher while creating the concept maps and linking these with topics and other concept maps. Results obtained from testing the tool for 'C' programming teaching were quite encouraging and the tool can be effectively used to creation of learning system for other programming languages as well.

However, it should be noted that effectiveness of learning system greatly depends upon various factors like quality of concept maps, links to other maps and quality of learning stimulus. Hence, before beginning with designing of the learning system identification of topics should be done along with designing the problems that can provide learning context to the student. After that problem based concept maps should be designed which have focus questions as the problems designed. This should then be followed by creation of learning stimulus and activities and other concept maps.

References

1. Ausubel, D.P., Novak, J.D., Hanesian, H.: Educational Psychology: A Cognitive View, 2nd edn. Holt, Rinehart and Winston, New York (1978)
2. Barrows, H.S., Tamblyn, R.M.: Problem-Based Learning: An Approach to Medical Education. Springer, New York (1980)
3. Cañas, A.J., Novak, J.D.: Freedom vs. restriction of content and structure during concept mapping - possibilities and limitations for construction and assessment. In: Cañas, A.J., Novak, J.D., Vanhear, J. (eds.) Concept Maps: Theory, Methodology, Technology: Proceedings of the Fifth International Conference on Concept Mapping, Valletta, Malta, 17–20 September 2012, vol. 2, pp. 247–257 (2012)
4. Carneson, J., Delpierre, G., Masters, K.: Designing and Managing Multiple Choice Questions. Southrock Corpora, Australia (2003)
5. Chen, T.: Recommendations for creating and maintaining effective networked learning communities: a review of the literature. Int. J. Instr. Media 30(1), 35–44 (2003)
6. Fuhrman, M.: Developing good multiple-choice tests and test questions. J. Geosci. Educ. 44 (4), 379–384 (1996). https://doi.org/10.5408/1089-9995-44.4.379
7. Gunawardena, C.N., Lowe, C.A., Abderson, T.: Analysis of global online debate and the development of an interactive analysis model for examining social construction of knowledge in computer conferencing. J. Educ. Comput. Res. 17(4), 397–431 (1997)
8. Harper, R.: Multiple-choice questions – a reprieve. BEE-j 2, 2–6 (2003)
9. Hmelo-Silver, C.E.: Problem-based learning: what and how do students learn? Educ. Psychol. Rev. 16(3), 235–266 (2004)
10. Hootstein, E.: Wearing four pairs of shoes: the roles of e-learning facilitators (2002). http://www.learningcircuits.org/2002/oct2002/elearn.html
11. Hudson, J.P.: Pathways between Eastern and Western Education. Information Age Publishing Inc., Charlotte (2009)
12. Jonassen, D.E., Peck, K.L., Wilson, B.G.: Learning with Technology: A Constructivist Perspective. Prentice-Hall, Upper Saddle River (1998)
13. Jonassen, D.: Objectivism versus constructivism: Do we need a new philosophical paradigm? Educ. Technol. Res. Dev. 39(3), 5–14 (1991)
14. Jonassen, D.H.: Designing constructivist learning environments. In: Reigeluth, C.M. (ed.) Instructional Design Theories and Models: A New Paradigm of Instructional Theory, pp. 217–239. Lawrence Erlbaum Associates Inc., Mahwah (1999)
15. Kelly, A.E.: Theme issue: the role of design in educational research. Educ. Res. 32(1) (2003)
16. Kirschner, P., Strijbos, J.W., Kreijns, K., Beers, P.J.: Designing electronic collaborative learning environments. Educ. Technol. Res. Dev. 52(3), 47–66 (2004)
17. Land, S., Hannafin, M.J.: Student-centered learning environments. In: Jonassen, D.H., Land, S.M. (eds.) Theoretical Foundations of Learning Environments, pp. 1–23. Erlbaum, Mahwah (2000)
18. McClure, J.R., Sonak, B., Suen, H.K.: Concept map assessment of classroom learning: reliability, validity, and logistical practicality. J. Res. Sci. Teach. 36(4), 475–492 (1999)
19. Merrill, D.: Constructivism and instructional design. Educ. Technol. 31(5), 45–53 (1991)

20. Mühling, A.: Investigating knowledge structures in computer science education. (Doctoral Dissertation, Technische Universität München) (2014). https://mediatum.ub.tum.de/doc/1190967/1190967.pdf
21. Li, N.: Approaches to learning: literature review. IB research paper (2010). https://studylib.net/doc/18404764/approaches-to-learning–literature-review
22. Piaget, J.: The Construction of Reality in the Child. Ballantine Books, New York City (1975)
23. Salmon, G.: E-Moderating: The Key to Online Teaching and Learning, 2nd edn. Taylor & Francis, London (2004)
24. Wood, E.J.: What are extended matching sets questions? BEE-j 1(1), 1–2 (2003)
25. Yin, Y., Vanides, J., Ruiz-Primo, M.A., Ayala, C.C., Shavelson, R.J.: Comparison of two concept-mapping techniques: implications for scoring, interpretation, and use. J. Res. Sci. Teach. 42(2), 166–184 (2005)

Deep Learning in Big Data
and Internet of Things

Dimpal Tomar[1]([⊠]) [iD], Pradeep Tomar[1]([⊠]), and Gurjit Kaur[2]([⊠])

[1] Gautam Buddha University, Greater Noida, Uttar Pradesh, India
dimpaltomar01@gmail.com, parry.tomar@gmail.com
[2] Delhi Technological University, New Delhi, India
gurjeet_kaur@rediffmail.com

Abstract. Due to constant escalation in the pace of information technology, the potential of Big Data and Internet of Things (IoT). Data induce high focus in data science field. As in IoT, large number of smart devices generate or collect enormous amount of data, over the period of time for various domain. However, IoT are basically one of the main source for the generation of big data. This massive volume of data contains valuable information upon which many organizations applying analytics for bang into future technology and favorable for business analysis and decision-making. Deep Learning is the high focus of advanced machine learning and facilitating analytics in various territories of Big Data and IoT by extracting complex feature abstraction or representation from different forms of data through hierarchical process. This review paper putting a focus on the overview of unique and modern technique of machine learning i.e. Deep Learning followed by a detailed consideration on models and algorithms. We also try to cover frameworks, opted for implementing Deep Learning and their use in various Big Data and IoT applications. We also investigate various Deep Learning applications in the realm of Big Data and IoT. Further try to incorporate challenges in several areas of Big Data and IoT. Finally, we conclude this work along with the future work.

Keywords: Big data · Deep learning · IoT

1 Introduction

Every day, unlabeled real-time data in massive amount generating through large number of resources and is being gathered, this immense volume of data are bringing up by the term 'Big Data'. Various issues related to the typical capacity limit and handling ability of conventional data analysis techniques are being posed by Big Data analytics. Thus, innovative and different technologies & architectures are needed for Big Data so it will be easy and make it possible to reveal all the correlations and complex patterns that are hidden.

The impact of IoT on economy by 2025, according to the report of McKinsey [1], it would be assumed that the range from $2.7 to $6.2 trillion may fall to express the annual economy of IoT. The foremost share is occupied by healthcare sector, i.e. around 41%, whereas energy sectors and industry cope up with 7% and 33% of this IoT

S. Minz et al. (Eds.): ICICCT 2018, CCIS 835, pp. 70–81, 2019.
https://doi.org/10.1007/978-981-13-5992-7_6

market, respectively. Other domains such as transportation, agriculture, retail, urban infrastructure and security cover only 15% of the total market of IoT. And that much expectations indicate the tremendous and great evolution in the services of IoT, along with their data generation and successively checking out their associated markets in the upcoming years.

Many applications of IoT and Big Data crop up in various straight up realms in recent years, i.e., banking, health, traffic control system, smart city, agriculture, education, smart home, and many more. Intelligent learning mechanism is the main element of most of these applications for identifying classification, clustering or regression. Machine learning generally focuses on the input data representation and simplification of received patterns that will be further used for concealed data in future. The quality of representation of data has a great influence on machine learner's recital along with the data whereas, an advanced, complex machine learner may suffer in their performance due to the poor representation of data, though relatively high performance of novice machine learner can be led by good data representation [2].

Numerous of IoT applications efficiently make use of Deep Learning among various machine learning approaches, in recent years and has been a great asset in dealing with Big Data because it excerpts high level and intricate abstractions through its intelligence. Representation complex data can be availed from extensive datasets particularly data which is unlabeled and gathered affluently in Big Data. Discriminative tasks, data indexing or tagging, from enormous dimensions of data extracting concealed patterns, fast retrieval of information and streamlining have summarized as Big Data analytics issues. But these complexities can be split down with the help of Deep Learning.

1.1   Related Studies

Various interrelated reviews has been done so far that emphasis on Deep Learning practices in IoT and Big Data realm by providing an outline that rely on various factors i.e. area of interest, existing challenges, methods, and tools. Gheisari [3] discuss upon a broad introduction of Big Data and Deep learning along with the comparative study of various frameworks in addition to that author put a focus on the Deep learning application and its difficulties in Big Data, with its future perspective. Fadlullah [4] addressed how network traffic control systems efficiently utilize Deep Learning approaches and primarily focuses on the infrastructure of network. Tsai [5] presented data mining approaches and other mining algorithms used in IoT used for the purpose of clustering, classification and pattern recognition. Mohammadi [6] focus on the backgrounds on different Deep Learning architectures and algorithms, implementation approaches with the aim to aid learning and analytics in the realm of IoT, by deploying on the fog and cloud centers. Chen [7] put a focus on a brief outline on deep learning, give highlight on the recent research efforts along with its challenges towards big data. Fan [8] emphasis on the present situation and future prediction while mining the big data that covers broad overview of Big Data Mining and its present prominence in various domains and shed a light on the focal point in the near future.

The remaining paper is further systematized in the following manner: Sect. 2 presents generic idea of Big Data and IoT and understanding the characteristics and nature of data that belong to Big Data and data generated through IoT. In Sect. 3, we try to cover an overview of Deep Learning followed by the discussion on various and their related algorithms. Along with that, try to wrap up framework that are used for implementing Deep Learning and their applications. Section 4 talk about various application areas of Big Data and IoT that uses Deep Learning. Section 5 put a focus on the challenges and Sect. 6 concludes the survey of this paper by highlighting various future trends.

2 Big Data and Internet of Things (IoT)

Due to widespread popularity of the IoT and its offspring Big Data, it is imperative for the stakeholders to have a comprehension of what exactly they are, what they are composed of, their capabilities and problems encountered. However, IoT and Big data holds bidirectional relationship. On one hand, for a big data, IoT is a chief source and on other side, the central goal of Big Data analytics is to advance the procedures as well as services provided by the IoTs [6]. Additionally, IoT Big Data analytics contributes to the society by bringing the value. For instance, in Miami, this has been reported by the Department of Park Management that they saved a huge amount of money by just detecting damaged pipes and fixing those [9].

There is a difference between general big data and data generated from IoT. The data from IoT can be streamed constantly or aggregated and become the origin of big data generation. However, attributes of data collected from IoT and its difference from general data need to be explored first in order to improve understanding of the necessities for data analytics in IoT. Following characteristics are exhibited by IoT data [9]:

- **Large-Scale Streaming Data:** Streams of data are continuously generated by distributing and deploying a variety of data acquisition devices for IoT applications. Continuous data of large proportion is generated through this.
- **Heterogeneity:** Data heterogeneity is resulted by gathering different information from myriad of data capturing devices.
- **Time-space interrelation:** Each data item can have a location and time stamp by attaching sensor devices to a specific location in IoT applications.
- **Noisy data:** Because of data fragments in various IoT application errors and noise may be created in most of such data during acquisition and transmission.

Big Data symbolizes broad field of research problems and methods utilized for various application spheres which can accumulate and manage large amount of data for analysis of data i.e. specific to a domain [2]. Data measuring in Exabyte proportion or larger is aggregated and maintained by technology established enterprises like Yahoo, Microsoft, Google, and Amazon. Additionally, huge amount of data is continuously generated by billions of users using social networking companies such as Twitter, YouTube, and Facebook.

General features of Big Data can be described according to several studies [10, 8]. However, while describing the IoT Big Data, the general Big Data depend on the following 6 V's definition:

Volume: Every second, the large volume of data is being generated that forces many organizations to take up new specialized storage and processing solution. The potential to process 'petabytes, Zeta bytes' amount of data become the chief reason to turn up towards the "Big Data Analytics". For example, in 30 min, near about 10 TB of data has been generated by a jet engine, hence everyday likewise 20000 or above aircrafts as one of the data source is responsible for generating petabytes of data.

Velocity: Velocity denotes the rate of data flow with respect to data volume that means the pace at which data is being generated, stored and analyzed in order to meet the demand and challenges. For instance, it took few seconds for a single tweet to get viral on social media, Facebook handles billions of photo upload, similarly YouTube manages to handle thousands of hours of video upload etc.

Variety: Another magnitude of Big Data is Variety that leads to the diversity of data types. However, now a days, we majorly deal with the unstructured form of data like audio, video, sensor data etc. and that does not fit into traditional relational databases.

Veracity: Veracity dealt with integrity or credibility of data which ensures quality. As the data is created in anticipated volume at a very high speed in a variety of formats and it's very much obvious that it affects the accuracy of data and leads to uncertainty of data.

Value: Another convincing side of Big Data is value which determines the importance of data i.e. substantial worth of data to any enterprise. However, the data value is directly proportional to the veracity. As the large volume of data hides meaningful insights that is valuable and needs to be analyzed which is the challenging task for the organization.

Variability: Variability, in Big Data environment, specify to the data whose meaning keep on changing which affects the homogenization of data and leads to inconsistency. However, variability is quite a different aspect from variety.

However, Big Data characteristics can better be understood by classifying them into several classes and five aspects needs to be considered upon which classification depends, i.e.: (i) Data sources (ii) Data stores (iii) Data processing (iv) Content format (v) Data Staging [11].

As the requirements for analytic response for the two approaches is not the same, they should be treated differently. Insight from Big Data analytics performed on streaming data should be available within a few hundreds of milliseconds to few seconds although the insight from analytics performed on Big Data may be delivered after generation of data for several days.

3   Deep Learning: Models, Algorithms and Frameworks

One of the biggest difficulty of machine learning techniques i.e. traditional one, is to deal with the process of feature extraction. The principal idea of Deep Learning is to extract abstractions or presentation from the date with full automation. Based on multiple layers of artificial neural network (ANN), Deep Learning composed of unsupervised and supervised learning methods to learn and imitate hierarchical abstractions. Basically, Deep Learning algorithms inspired from the structure of neurons present in human brain for processing signals.

As compared to the traditional machine learning models, Deep Learning models and architectures have increased more consideration as of late. These models and architectures are deliberated as version of shallow learning architectures of Deep Learning.

3.1   Models and Algorithms

Deep Learning algorithms are indeed the consecutive layers of deep architectures. Each and every layer composed of assorted units which are known as neuron that accept various signals as the input. Those signals get multiplied with associated weighing factor of neuron that will be optimized during the process of training. Basically, each and every consecutive layer of deep architecture put nonlinear transformation on its own input node and then generate representation or abstraction as its output. That means the sensual data, for instance pixel in a picture, is provided to the main layer that is first one. Therefore, the yield of each processing layer is fed as the next layer's input. Deep Learning models are broadly categorized into three classes i.e. (i) Discriminative Model, (ii) Generative Model and (iii) Hybrid Model

- *Discriminative models:* Machine learning use the class of model from discriminative model. These models usually support those approaches based on supervised learning and hardly go for unsupervised learning. Discriminative models are also known as conditional models.
- *Generative models:* Generative models, as opposed to discriminative model, practice for unsupervised learning techniques in machine learning with the objective for either directly modelling the data through probability density function or form a conditional probability density function as an intermediate step.
- *Hybrid model:* Hybrid model assimilating the advantages of both the models that is discriminative and generative models.

The above mentioned models of deep machine learning have number of popular algorithms. Table 1 summarizes the popular algorithms of Discriminative Generative and Hybrid Models.

3.2   Frameworks for Developing Deep Learning

In the recent years, the breakneck advancement of concern is to apply various models and algorithms of Deep Learning in different field that has been promoted by offering various frameworks for Deep Learning. Each and every framework has its own stability

Table 1. Popular algorithms of discriminative generative and hybrid models

Model	Algorithms	Description	Reference
Discriminative (Supervised Learning)	Recurrent Neural Networks (RNNs)	• Typically, Input Data: Serial & time-series i.e. sensor data of various length • Operates on sequential data through internal memory • Effective for time-dependent data, in IoT applications	[12, 13]
	Long Short Term Memory (LSTM)	• Serial, long time dependent data, time-series form of data • Extension of RNN • Data with long time lag bring out good performance • Gates are used to protect the accessing of memory	[14]
	Convolutional Neural Networks (CNNs)	• Typically, Input Data: 2D Input (E.g. Speech and Image signal) • Substantial portion of computations is done by Convolution layers • As compared to DNNs require less connections • For visual tasks, a large dataset for training is required	
Generative (Unsupervised Learning)	Autoencoders (AEs)	• Input Data: Various form of data • Appropriate algorithm for reduction in dimension and feature representation (extraction) • Require input and output units in the same number where the output unit is used to regenerates the input data • Unlabeled data is used for working	[15]
	Restricted Boltzmann Machine (RBMs)	• Input Data: Various form of data • Relevant for feature representation, classification and dimensionality reduction purpose • One of the most expensive training process	
	Deep Belief Network (DBNs)	• Input Data: Various form of data • Good enough to discover hierarchical features • Greedy approach used to train the whole network	[16]
	Variational Autoencoders (VAEs)	• Input Data: Various form of data • Belong to the category of Auto-encoders • Handy for scarcity of labelled data	[17]
Hybrid (Semi-Supervised)	Generative Adversarial Networks (GANs)	• Input Data: Various form of data • Good enough to handle corrupt data	[18]
	Ladder Networks	• Input Data: Various form of data • Good enough to handle corrupt data	[19]

depending upon Deep Learning architectures, algorithms for optimization and ease of development and deployment [20].

Various frameworks for efficient training of deep neural network have been broadly used in the domain of research. They are: H2O, Torch, Tensorflow, Theano, Neon and Caffe.

H2O: A machine learning Framework that support a broad spectrum of interfaces for Java, Python, Scala, R, Coffee-script, JSON. Based Feed Forward Neural Network, H2O implement the Deep Learning algorithm which is trained by Stochastic Gradient Decent (GSD) with back propagation. Though, H2O support sufficient number of models.

Torch: An open source Framework that has been developed in LVA programming language and widely supported by light weighted and fast Deep Learning algorithms for machine learning by providing interface for C and C++ programming language [21]. However, it is adopted by various organizations and Research Laboratories such as Twitter, Google and Facebook for training deep neural networks by powerful parallelization packages.

Tensorflow: An open source library of different types of deep neural network models for machine learning algorithms. Originally, implemented for Google Brain Project [22]. Tensorflow is used by various popular products of Google such as YouTube, Google search, Google Translate, Google map and many more.

Table 2. Frameworks used in big data and IoT applications

Frameworks	Big data and IoT applications
H2O	• A pervasive, personalized framework for smart societies focuses on the advancement of teaching-learning process through the use of IoT, advance computing Deep Learning and Big Data, named as UtiLearn
Tensorflow	• Apply Deep Learning in automotive space for the formulation of large datasets i.e. Big Data, enabling automatic extraction of features from dissimilar automobiles
Theano	• Modelling, prediction and analysis of traffic flow by applying advanced Deep Learning techniques on large scale "Taxi" data
Torch	• Apply Deep Learning in automotive space for the formulation of large datasets i.e. Big Data, enabling automatic extraction of features from dissimilar automobiles • To develop an initial understanding of smart device/resource characteristics on performance, requirements and implementation blockages while modelling deep learning in order to identify their different types of behaviour
Caffe	• Development of recognition model for identifying plant disease using leaf image classification and Deep neural networks [25]
Neon	• Development and demonstration of Deep Learning algorithms and framework to handle weather pattern from large climatic datasets

Theano: An open source framework based on Python programming language, developed for powerful machine learning algorithms by employing (i) CUDA library for the Optimization of complex nodes to be run, (ii) Parallelism on CPU and (iii) Support Graph Representation.

Neon: Yet another Framework for Deep Learning, available as an open source, based on Python language come up for modern deep neural networks with high performance such as GoogleNet, AlexNet [23] and reinforces easy switching of back-end platform.

Caffe: An open source C++ based framework, supported by the interfaces for MATLAB and Python, introducing Deep Learning algorithms and a set of reference models [24]. Caffe is helpful for easy changing between back-end platform and good at convolutional networks (Table 2).

4 Applications of Deep Learning in Big Data and Internet of Things (IoT)

The Big Data technologies can provide data stores to the generated data through IoT applications while finding valuable information through the use of Deep Learning which has turn out to be a main interest in this current phase of technologies. In the following subsections, we highlight upon various IoT and Big Data applications that use Deep Learning as their intelligence engine.

Smart Homes: This is the time of smart homes where the household appliances are getting smarter with the help of technology. Appliances are getting connected to the internet creating IoTs that are generating sensor data in large volumes. This data is processed with techniques of Big Data Analytics. Smart homes are making life of people very easy and convenient and improving quality of the lives. The owner of the smart home can control the household appliances from anywhere and anytime. But in order to going a step ahead Deep Learning is applied to this sensor generated big data to get a deeper inside of the data. For example, Microsoft and Liebherr are using Cortana Deep Learning on the information fetched from sensors installed in refrigerator. These analytics proved to be helpful in controlling their home supplies and expenditure and also can be used for the health related predictions by applying the Deep Learning in smart appliances. We can improve the efficiency of the devices and also predict the future needs of energy consumption based on date analytics.

Smart Cities: If we consider smart cities as Deep Learning application territory in big data analytics, we noticed that heterogeneous data is being generated from various domains resulting in big data. A smart city covers up various domains generating voluminous data in various forms like smart transportation system, smart parking systems, smart waste management systems. For example, in transportation system the deep learning can be applied to human mobility data or GPS data collected from metro stations or bus stands in a locality that predicts the rate of increase or decrease in commuters during a particular time period and can be utilized to control the frequency of trains or buses coming to the station. In Smart parking systems, deep learning can be applied to vision based parking lots where deep learning algorithms run on visual data stream coming from a CCTV camera that can help in identifying weather the parking lot is empty or occupied by a vehicle with the help of computer vision techniques [26].

Smart Grids: Smart energy meters installed in homes generate data that can be utilized by smart grids for analysis of power consumption and generating power consumption bills. This data can be provided as input to Deep Learning techniques for big data analytics and aid to forecast the future trends of power consumption or demand in a locality or city that will be a great help in managing energy generation.

Smart Traffic Management System: Let us consider the GPS data being generated by radio taxies in a particular locality by applying Deep Learning based data analytics, systems can be developed that could predict the evolution of traffic jams in a particular area on a particular time and efficient traffic management could be implemented [27].

Healthcare Sector: Deep Learning in classification & images processing is a substantial area in medical sciences. People came up with idea to detect Parkinson's disease at the early stage by handwriting recognition of the patient.

Agriculture & Horticulture Sector: Deep Learning can be used in agriculture and horticulture in various ways. For example, plant diseases can be detected with the help of systems that can capture and analyze the images of plant and their leaves and classify them. Deep Learning can be deployed in autonomous farming equipment and machines, for example in lawn mowers for obstacle avoidance, that mows the lawn without hitting an object say a chair or table lying in the lawn by detecting the presence of the object after analyzing the images captured by mounted camera [25].

Prediction of Natural Calamities: We can harness the potential of IoTs by conjunction of IoTs with Deep Learning in predicting the natural disasters such as cyclones, storms, forest fires, landslides, etc. by monitoring the environment. For prediction of landslides, we can utilize the optical remote sensing images. Image patterns of climate events can be used as data sets for training purpose of the system developed, that could help in detection of hurricanes, cyclones, floods, etc.

Damage Detection and Control in Civil Structures: It could be an amazing use of Deep Learning in damage detection/surveying of civil structures like, roads, bridges, flyovers, buildings, etc. A local person can click a picture with the help of smart phones and send it to the local civic authority server. Although the person is not an expert to detect any damage, but the image submitted to the server can be analyzed with the implementation of Deep Learning algorithms that could process the images for assessing the damage.

5 Deep Learning Challenges in IoT and Big Data Analytics

In this consequent segment, the noticeable difficulties of Deep Learning encountered by big data analytics and internet of things while extracting high level features from large amount of data, has been discussed and taken into consideration.

Identifying the Appropriate Service Node for Analytics: With the adoption of IoTs, the need for accessing the big data more quickly, and locally, arise that results in introduction of "Fog Computing." Fog computing: a distributed framework, where certain services or operations are being performed and managed by smart devices or nodes at the ends of the network. Now in such environment it become tough to identify and locate a suitable node for performing a certain required process of analytics and become an issue that need to be resolved.

Load Distribution Among Available Service Nodes: Another big challenge is efficient distribution of tasks or operations among the available nodes as Deep Learning models need to be partitioned and executed on various nodes for processing of fast streaming data from numerous smart devices. And it's very critical in case of time-sensitive applications such as tsunami, cyclone or landslide prediction and alerts as final results from various nodes need to be aggregated and submitted for the action.

Mobile Edge: As mobile edge computing environment is ubiquitous in nature and offer a great contribution for the analytics of big data generated from IoTs. It results in dynamicity of such environment as mobile nodes are free to join and leave the system. This dynamicity of computing environment the need to be considered as a huge challenge.

Continuous Learning in Fast Streaming Data: Another challenging aspect is dealing with fast streaming data, when we are implementing Deep Learning to data analytics. A need of algorithms will always remain in demand that can deal the fast streaming data deluge. Need of incremental learning for new feature extraction, will always there, that were never introduced before to the learning system. So we have to add up new processing nodes in Deep Learning models [2].

6 Conclusion and Future Work

Big Data and Internet of Things: the most significant shifts in the modern era of IT technology and the growing demand of both the technologies has taken Deep Learning to new heights as the conjoin of these technologies established to create positive impact on our lifestyle, metropolis, and around the globe. However, Big Data is all about data only whereas IoT is about the main source of Big Data along with the significant focus on smart devices and the Deep Learning techniques are used to extract features and generates remarkable abstractions and provide prominent insights of data so that IoT services can be improved and finely tuned up.

In this paper, we focused on the overview of modern machine learning technique i.e. Deep Learning followed by a discussion on three categories of models i.e. Distinctive, Generative and Hybrid models and their related algorithms. We also try to cover frameworks used for the implementation Deep Learning i.e. H2O, Caffe, Torch, Tensorflow, Neaon, Theano and their use in various Big Data and IoT applications. We also investigate various application areas of Big Data and IoT in Deep Learning such as smart cities, agriculture, smart homes, health sectors, smart grids and covers various other sectors. Further try to incorporate challenges in the realm of Big Data and IoT.

However, there is lot of future scope in the extent of "Use of Deep Learning in Big Data and Internet of Things". Researchers, practitioners and scholars can explore the Deep Learning techniques with mobile Big Data for better advancement in the services of various IoT domain, another direction can cover the exploration of Deep Learning approaches for Analytics of Big Data over cloud computing platform and various conjoin of these technologies to delve into other new domains.

References

1. Manyika, J., Chui, M., Bughin, J., Dobbs, R., Bisson, P., Marrs, A.: Disruptive technologies: advances that will transform life, business, and the global economy. McKinsey Global Institute San Francisco (2013)
2. Najafabadi, M.M., Villanustre, F., Khoshgoftaar, M.T., Seliya, N., Wald, R., Muharemagic, E.: Deep learning applications and challenges in big data analytics. J. Big Data **2**(1), 1 (2015)
3. Gheisari, M., Wang, G., Bhuiyan, M.Z.A.: A survey on deep learning in big data. In: Proceedings of IEEE International Conference on Computational Science and Engineering and Embedded and Ubiquitous Computing (2017)
4. Fadlullah, Z., et al.: State-of-the-art deep learning: evolving machine intelligence toward tomorrow's intelligent network traffic control systems. IEEE Commun. Surv. Tutorials **19** (4), 2432–2455 (2017)
5. Tsai, C.W., Lai, C.F., Chiang, M.C., Yang, L.T.: Data mining for internet of things: a survey. IEEE Commun. Surv. Tutorials **16**(1), 77–97 (2014)
6. Mohammadi, M., Al-F, A.: Enabling cognitive smart cities using big data and machine learning: approaches and challenges. IEEE Commun. Mag. **56**(2), 1–8 (2017)
7. Chen, X., Lin, X.: Big data deep learning: challenges and perspectives. IEEE Access **2**, 514–525 (2014)
8. Fan, W., Bifet, A.: Mining big data: current status, and forecast to the future. ACM SIGKDD Explor. Newslett. **14**(2), 1–5 (2013)
9. Chen, M., Mao, S., Zhang, Y., Leung, V.C.: Big Data: Related Technologies, Challenges and Future Prospects. Springer, Heidelberg (2014). https://doi.org/10.1007/978-3-319-06245-7
10. Hilbert, M.: Big data for development: a review of promises and challenges. Dev. Policy Rev. **34**(1), 135–174 (2016)
11. Hashem, I.A.T., Yaqoob, I., Anuar, N.B., Mokhtar, S., Gani, A., Khan, S.U.: The rise of "big data" on cloud computing: review and open research issues. Inf. Syst. **47**, 98–115 (2015)
12. Pascanu, R., Gulcehre, C., Cho, K., Bengio, Y.: How to construct deep recurrent neural networks (2013)
13. Hermans, M., Schrauwen, B.: Training and analysing deep recurrent neural network. In: Advances in Neural Information Processing System, pp. 190–198 (2013)
14. Hochreiter, S., Schmidhuber, J.: Long short-term memory. Neural Comput. **9**(8), 1735–1780 (1997)
15. Baldi, P.: Autoencoders, unsupervised learning, and deep architectures. In: ICML Unsupervised and Transfer Learning, pp. 37–50 (2012)
16. Bengio, Y.: Learning deep architectures for AI. Found. Trends R Mach. Learn. **2**(1), 1–127 (2009)
17. Doersch, C.: Tutorial on variational autoencoders (2016)
18. Goodfellow, I., et al.: Generative adversarial nets. In: Advances in Neural Information Processing Systems, pp. 2672–2680 (2014)

19. Rasmus, A., Berglund, M., Honkala, M., Valpola, H., Raiko, T.: Semi-supervised learning with ladder networks. In: Advances in Neural Information Processing Systems, pp. 3546–3554 (2015)
20. Bahrampour, S., Ramakrishnan, N., Schott, L., Shah, M.: Comparative study of deep learning software frameworks (2016)
21. Collobert, R., Kavukcuoglu, K., Farabet, C.: Torch7: a matlab-like environment for machine learning. In: BigLearn, NIPS Workshop (2011)
22. Abadi, M., et al.: Tensorflow: large-scale machine learning on heterogeneous distributed system (2016)
23. Krizhevsky, A., Sutskever, I., Hinton G.E.: Image net classification with deep convolutional neural networks. In: Advances in Neural Information Processing Systems, pp. 1097–1105 (2012)
24. Jia, Y., et al.: Caffe: convolutional architecture for fast feature embedding. In: Proceedings of the 22nd ACM International Conference on Multimedia, pp. 675–678. ACM (2014)
25. Sladojevic, S., Arsenovic, M., Anderla, A., Culibrk, D., Stefanovic, D.: Deep neural networks based recognition of plant diseases by leaf image classification. Comput. Intell. Neurosci. **6**, 1–11 (2016)
26. Song, X., Kanasugi, H., Shibasaki, R.: Deep transport: prediction and simulation of human mobility and transportation mode at a citywide level. In: IJCAI (2016)
27. Tian, Y., Pan, L.: Predicting short-term traffic flow by long short-term memory recurrent neural network. In: Proceedings of IEEE International Conference, pp. 153–158 (2015)

Quantitative Service Reliability Assessment on Single and Multi Layer Networks

Harshit Pandey[1]([✉]) [iD] and Cher Ming Tan[2,3,4,5,6]

[1] Department of Electrical and Electronics Engineering,
Amity School of Engineering and Technology, Noida, Uttar Padesh, India
harshitpandey16@gmail.com
[2] Centre for Reliability Sciences and Technologies,
Chang Gung University, Taoyuan, Taiwan
cherming@ieee.org
[3] Department of Electronics Engineering, Chang Gung University,
Taoyuan, Taiwan
[4] Department of Urology, Chang Gung Memorial Hospital, Taoyuan, Taiwan
[5] Department of Mechanical Engineering, Ming Chi University of Technology,
Taoyuan, Taiwan
[6] Institute of Radiation Research, College of Medicine,
Chang Gung University, Taoyuan, Taiwan

Abstract. Congestion that might build up due to bottlenecks in a conventional data transmission network because of constrained capacities poses the main problem. This paper aims to model the two scenarios of data transmission in the network via the single and multi layer network architectures based on the queuing theory analysis for data packets, and various parameters are seen to yield results that substantiate vividly the benefits of multi layer architecture over the single layer by summarizing outputs in terms of service reliability. Analysis in terms of throughput and waiting time, the two modeled architectures deduce conclusions that effectively prove how layered networks are much more capable than single layered networks in terms of service Reliability.

Keywords: Single layer · Multi layer · Congestion · Utilization ·
Public internet · Peer to peer networks · Buffering · Message passing

1 Introduction

The meaning of communication today has absolutely no room for data disruptions and essentially aims for instant, uninterrupted and timely reception of information. Conveying data digitally entangles information to be sent as packets [1] through the intertwined network and is thus subsequently received at the destination. Internet as a humongous collection of nodes [2] serves as an abstract medium for information interchange. Modern day communication requires being reliable especially in applications tending severe serious arenas like military deployments [3] medical emergencies, space missions and many more. According to [4] a reliable network is one which is capable enough to carry out communication without compromising in the quality,

S. Minz et al. (Eds.): ICICCT 2018, CCIS 835, pp. 82–92, 2019.
https://doi.org/10.1007/978-981-13-5992-7_7

whereas [5] describes reliability as probability of a network being functional even after encountering congestion or failure and [6] elucidates reliability of network as timely delivery of packets with lesser waiting time for each packet in the queue. Thus, it is inferred that a more reliable service aims at significantly reducing the waiting time of entities in a queue and diminishing the rate of packet loss during transmission.

Kelly and Jain in their work [1, 7] have discussed about information being lost midway which is seen as losing/dropping a packet amidst transmission due to overload in the system. Accessing high quality videos and graphics, gaming and enormous data transmission pose an overload to internet services today. The flow of data through networks can be modeled with a substantial base of queuing theory wherein the data packets are en queued and treated as Poisson arrivals en route source to destination [8]. En route, these packets have to wait [8] in the line and waiting time depends on the congestion faced by the network and the type of routing paths the network offers. If due to heavy congestion a packet is timed out then it is dropped and information is lost [1]. Layered networks prove to be an effective and efficient alternative to this issue with multiple layers employing various node interconnections to effectively transmit data.

Chu et al. in [10] described a framework for assessment of network reliability by minimizing probable failures for a digital subscriber line (DSL) network. The work of Tsilipanos et al. [11] proposed a system of systems model analyzing hazards and probabilities of network failures. Reliability of complex networks is seen in [12] where assessment of service oriented architecture is considered. Layered networks often face link failures which have been discussed in [13] and simulations have been performed that lead to analysis of layered network reliability. To the best knowledge of the authors of this work, the quantitative analysis of service reliability in single and multi layer networks is lacking. Thus, in this work, we simulate the packets while being transmitted and model two architectures of packet flow viz. single layer transmission of information and transmission through a combination of multiple layers, each working independently and individually following the service of first come first serve for packets of information.

Comparing both the models, questions like "what is the difference between the time delay or latency of packets of information", "what inferences can one deduce by the rate of packets being lost" and "what is the effect of layering the network" are major service issues that will be approached and underlying simulation results will be used to substantiate the conclusions that follow. The major motivation of this work lies in clearly enumerating as to why employability of a layered network is much more significant than a single layer network in terms of service reliability, the inference of which leads us to meticulously relate reliability into our understanding with proving explicit vulnerability of the latter network during times of congestion and overload. In the upcoming sections we describe queues and their mathematical representation, then the formation of models is discussed which is followed by results, conclusions, future work and finally the references.

2 Queue Formation and Waiting Time

In a network where data is transmitted in the form of packets [1] of information, these packets are analogous to entities forming a queue which wait for their turn to be transmitted. In networks, the standard assumption for arrivals of packets is considered to be Poisson with exponential inter-arrivals distributions [8]. Figure 1 shows how typically the queues of data packets are built up while data is transmitted over a network.

In this paper we look at the waiting time for packets for both type of network architectures considered here namely single and multiple layer. The waiting time in a queue [8] is given as:

$$W = (q - U)/A \tag{1}$$

Where W represents the effective waiting time of the packets, q is the average length of the queue, U is the utilization of the network which implies the interim for which the network is busy routing packets, and if its value reaches unity it implies that the network is overloaded and cannot route data packets robustly and thus subsequently incurs loss of information. A is the arrival rate of packets (packets/second) and is generally Poisson with exponential distribution for inter arrivals. Equation 1 illustrates the relation between the waiting time and the utilization, average queue length and the rate of arrivals.

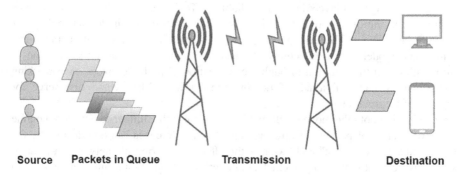

Source   Packets in Queue   Transmission   Destination

Fig. 1. Queuing of packets while transmission

3 Model Formulation

The transmission of data in the network is like a discrete event transmission system as information is contained in discrete packets which are then transmitted from one end to the other and this property motivates to formulate models in the discrete event toolbox of MATLAB. Simevents toolbox is employed in the formulation of the models. The Simevents toolbox allows discrete modeling of events which have attributes that are distinct and effectively models a process that includes queue, server and routing type of problems. Also this toolbox allows the modeling in areas of inventory control and capacity management.

Figures 2 and 3 represent the models, where the former is for single layer transmission in which the network has one single layer of data transmission and the latter is for multi layer transmission in which the network is layered without the loss of generality into three distinct layers with the assumption that each layer works individually. In multilayer routing model, the main layer of transmission is branched into three individual layers without any loss of generality with the assumption that each works independently whereas in the single layer model there exists only one layer for packet transmission. The output switch in Fig. 3 distributes packets prioritizing that layer which gets free from the previous packet routing first so that the packets can be sent simultaneously in all the three layers and the probability of formation of bottlenecks is reduced substantially and information is received at the destinations effectively.

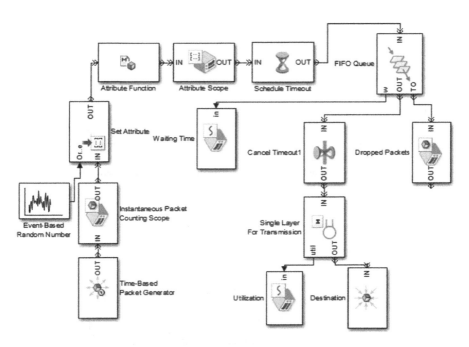

Fig. 2. Representation of single layer network with packet transmission

Considering heaps of packets in the queue, the flow balance is not essentially balanced which poses probable congestion while maintaining homogeneity. Persistence prevails and loop less flow is modeled with the considerations of an open network [8]. Packets that hold information are generated by the inbuilt time based packet generator block and for both the models the packet generation is at the same rate as seen in Fig. 4. All the packets that are generated have features that are completely different from

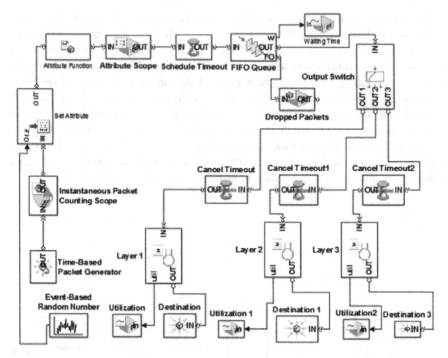

Fig. 3. Representation of multi layer network with packet transmission

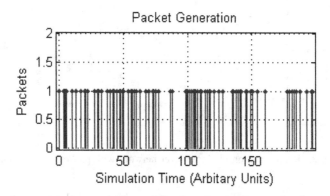

Fig. 4. Packet generation for both models with exponential distribution.

each other and this is done through the attribute function and the event based random number generator as seen in the models. Figures 5 and 6 represent two major characteristics, namely the time taken by the network to route a packet from source to destination, and the time till which a packet exists in the queue during congestion after which it is dropped by the network.

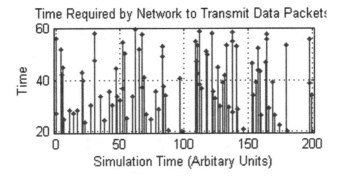

Fig. 5. Time taken by network to route different packets from source to destination.

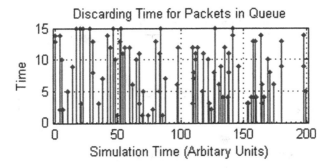

Fig. 6. Time for a packet to exist in the queue after which it is dropped.

Both these have completely random values which depend upon the type of data being transmitted and the duration to reach the destination, after which they are timed out due to traffic encountered in the path.

4   Results and Discussions

The models described in Figs. 2 and 3 were simulated under same assumptions of inputs for both cases. Analysis of four major parameters led to interesting yet substantial results pertaining to the transmission of packets via both architectures.

Figures 7 and 8 represent the variation of waiting time for packets in the queue when they are being transmitted from source to the destination which can be diagrammatically visualized from Fig. 1. It is observed that for the same number of packet arrivals, the average time for packets to wait in the queue for single layer network is much more than for multi layer networks. Ideally, the lower waiting time is preferred as instantaneous data transmission means better Quality of Service.

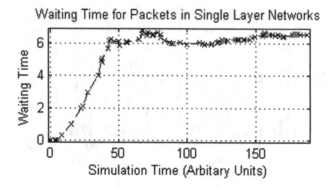

Fig. 7. Variation in waiting time for packets in queue for single layer networks.

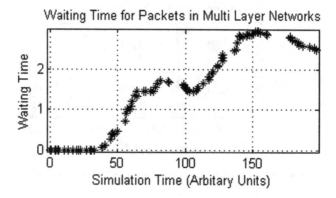

Fig. 8. Variation in waiting time for packets in queue for multi layer networks.

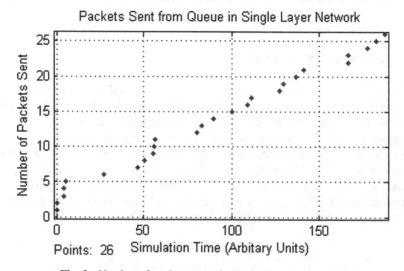

Fig. 9. Number of packets sent via single layer architecture.

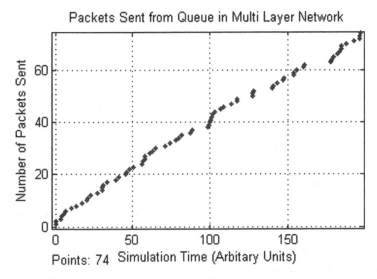

Fig. 10. Number of packets sent via multi layer architecture.

Figures 9 and 10 represent the amount of packets that are transmitted by the two architectures in the same simulation period. It is observed that for the same simulation time period the amount of packets routed from source to destination in multi layered architecture is more than that routed in single layer architecture as is seen. The number of packets routed is 74 for multilayer and 26 for single layer which elucidates that performance is boosted by an approximate of three times which is another aspect for improved Quality of Service.

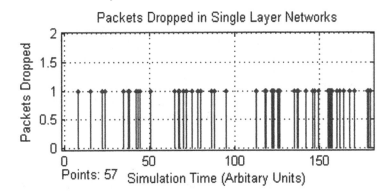

Fig. 11. Number of packets discarded/dropped by single layer architecture due to congestion.

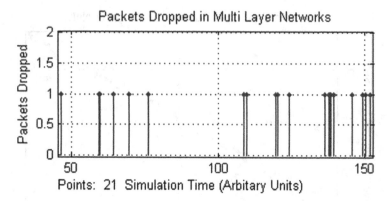

Fig. 12. Number of packets discarded/dropped by multi layer architecture due to congestion.

Figures 11 and 12 represent the number of packets that the network architectures drop due to the fact that the network is heavily occupied and till the time the packet reaches the actual transmission stage, the data is timed out due to prolonged waiting and the network eventually drops these packets. The number of packets dropped in single layer is much more than in multi layer thus inferring that despite same arrivals for both architectures as seen in Fig. 4, the single layer develops more congestion and bottlenecks are more prominent and frequent leading to packet drop. This again is a parameter of Quality of Service.

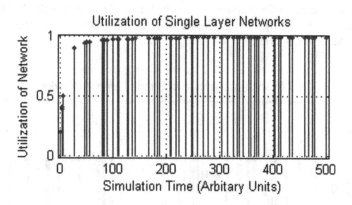

Fig. 13. Utilization of network via single layer architecture.

Utilization of a network is a parameter used to define whether a network is busy routing packets or is idle and can route packets [9]. Figures 13 and 14 represent the utilization of the network via the two architectures. It is observed that in a single layer architecture, the whole network is used to route the packets and thus has a utilization which approaches unity with the increase in simulation time. This parameter analysis indicates that the network is busy for most of the time and thus more bottlenecks are

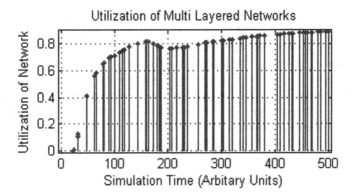

Fig. 14. Utilization of network via multi layer architecture.

formed in the network. On the contrary, the multilayer network has a utilization which is about 0.8 and indicates that the network is comparatively free for routing packets and can support more transmission without posing congestion. Utilization is another parameter that is a part of Quality of Service.

5 Conclusion

Quality of Service in a Network is related to various parameters that combinedly can be analyzed to infer and deduce conclusions that substantiate the overall service reliability behavior of the network considered. The results of simulation as obtained in previous section consider various parameters of interest in the network architectures considered. Lesser waiting time implies more speedy transmission and more throughput means lesser congestion and more output based approach. In any communication system, the losses are expected to be negligible and reduced losses mean better efficiency of the network. Also utilization of the network as a parameter of interest should be lesser and this low value implies that the network is free with lesser traffic and is idle enough to transmit more. All these parameters when compared and analyzed for both cases viz. single and multi layer architectures reveal that multi layer architecture proves to be an architecture which provides better Quality of Service to the users. This parameter when summed up on the whole is found to dictate better terms of service in case of Multi layered architecture over Single layered architecture and thus infers that layering the network makes the transmission system much more reliable.

6 Future Work

In the present network modeling architecture of multi layer network, the assumption that each layer works individually in routing data packets is considered. Also the packet generation is considered to be exponential but in real life scenarios a static continuous packet generation is not necessarily the case as users log in and out of the network almost instantly and the total number of internet users are large, which if considered will lead to more intriguing and substantial results. The most important part that is a milestone still to be reached is the exploration of how many layered the network can be and till what level we can go on layering it. In addition to layering, what will be the major criteria apart from cost that will pose probable constraints in layering the network is an open platform. Explorations can been done further to produce the same comparisons in the two network architectures when the various layers in Multi layer architecture modeling are made to work in a manner that the nodes of one layer can interact with nodes of other layer and completely new paths can be evolved for data transmission.

References

1. Kelly, F.: Mathematical modelling of the internet. In: Engquist, B., Schmid, W. (eds.) Mathematics Unlimited—2001 and Beyond, pp. 685–702. Springer, Berlin (2001). https://doi.org/10.1007/978-3-642-56478-9_35
2. Pandey, H., Ranjan, P., Tripathy, M.R., Pushp, S.: Optimal rate allocation in multi layer networks. In: Proceedings of ICDECT, (2017, to appear)
3. Felemban, E., Lee, C-G., Ekici, E., Boder, R., Vural, S.: Probabilistic QoS guarantee in reliability and timeliness domains in wireless sensor networks. In: Proceedings IEEE 24th Annual Joint Conference of the IEEE Computer and Communications Societies INFOCOM 2005, vol. 4, pp. 2646–2657. IEEE (2005)
4. Richard Harris Network Reliablility. http://seat.massey.ac.nz/143465/Lectures/Network%20Reliability_2_1s.pdf. Accessed 28 Jan 2018
5. Obeidat, I.M., Berkovich, S.Y.: Reliability of network connectivity. In: First International Conference on the Applications of Digital Information and Web Technologies. ICADIWT 2008, pp. 435–441. IEEE (2008)
6. Orhan Ergun: Why is Reliability Important in Networking (2016). https://orhanergun.net/2016/09/reliability-network-design/. Accessed 28 Jan 2018
7. Jain, R.: Congestion control in computer networks: trends and issues. arXiv preprint cs/9809091 (1998)
8. Galant, D.C.: Queuing theory models for computer networks (1989)
9. Standards for Technology in Automotive Retail (2012). http://www.starstandard.org/images/guidelines/DIG2012v1/ch02s02.html. Accessed 28 Jan 2018
10. Chu, C.-H.K., Chu, M.: An integrated framework for the assessment of network operations, reliability, and security. Bell. Labs Tech. J. 8(4), 133–152 (2004)
11. Tsilipanos, K., Neokosmidis, I., Varoutas, D.: A system of systems framework for the reliability assessment of telecommunications networks. IEEE Syst. J. 7(1), 114–124 (2013)
12. Yang, M., Feilong, W., Wang, S., Li, D.: Reliability assessment method of SOA architecture software system based on complex network. In: 2014 IEEE 4th Annual International Conference on Cyber Technology in Automation, Control, and Intelligent Systems (CYBER), pp. 653–657. IEEE (2014)
13. Lee, K., Lee, H.-W., Modiano, E.: Reliability in layered networks with random link failures. IEEE/ACM Trans. Networking (TON) 19(6), 1835–1848 (2011)

Optimized Power Allocation in Selective Decode and Forward Cooperative Wireless Relay Communication with MIMO Nodes

E. Bindu[1(✉)] and B. V. R. Reddy[2]

[1] Department of ECE, Amity School of Engineering and Technology,
GGSIP University, New Delhi, India
bindue25@gmail.com
[2] USICT, GGSIP University, New Delhi, India

Abstract. In wireless communication, Multiple Input Multiple Output (MIMO) technology has proven to improve reliability through spatial diversity. Cooperative relay transmission is an emerging concept, which involves the users to share their resources to improve overall system performance. In this work, Selective Decode and Forward (SDF) cooperative relaying scheme is analyzed. This paper describes power optimization in relay nodes for a dual hop half-duplex SDF based cooperative relay communication system, with nodes using multiple antenna. For the proposed system model, average end-to-end probability of error is derived, leading to evaluation of asymptotically tight upper bound under high signal to noise ratio. Optimal power allocation to minimize the bit error rate (BER) is formulated and a closed form solution for this convex optimization problem is derived and verified through simulation. The BER performance of the system is compared with that of cooperative relay network having single antenna at the participating nodes. Results show sharp decline in error rate with increase in the number of participating antenna. Simulation results reveal that cooperate scheme with optimal power allocation has an improved performance, compared to its direct link counterpart.

Keywords: Cooperative communication ·
Selective decode-and-forward relay · MIMO · Virtual MIMO ·
Convex optimization

1 Introduction

Relay assisted communication is a promising strategy that uses the spatial diversity available among a collection of distributed terminals, for both centralized and decentralized wireless networks [1]. Cooperative relay scheme with nodes having single antenna can emulate MIMO channel since the destination node receives multiple copies of the message from participating relay nodes. This virtual MIMO system helps the single antenna devices to attain some benefits of spatial diversity without the need of actual antenna arrays, which is favorable in scenarios where there are physical limitations to implement multiple antennas on the device due to constraints on cost, size or hardware implementation [2, 3]. Multiple-input multiple-output (MIMO) techniques

© Springer Nature Singapore Pte Ltd. 2019
S. Minz et al. (Eds.): ICICCT 2018, CCIS 835, pp. 93–106, 2019.
https://doi.org/10.1007/978-981-13-5992-7_8

can improve the communication reliability by sending multiple copies of same signal through different paths, hence allowing better reception at the destination. Hence if the participating relay nodes can afford multiple antenna, then this relay system can out-perform its single antenna counterpart. Most widely used relay protocols are amplify-and-forward (AF) and decode-and-forward (DF). DF relay protocol receives informa-tion from source and re-transmits the signal to destination after decoding and re-encoding the message. A sub-variant of DF strategy is selective DF (SDF) in which the relay decides whether or not to forward the message to destination, based on certain threshold criterion on the received signal [4]. Fixed DF transmission does not offer diversity gains for large signal to noise ratio (SNR) since the relay has to fully decode the information received from the source node. SDF perform better under such con-dition. Moreover this strategy reduces the chance of error propagation [5, 6].

Application of SDF in different communication scenarios are given in literature. For a dual hop relay system using SDF, the energy efficiency optimization is proposed in [7]. Performance analysis of SDF based single and multiple hop cooperative MIMO relay under fading scenario is done in [8] and SDF applied to spatial modulation (SM) is carried out in [9]. A new variant of SDF, named dynamic-SDF (D-SDF) is proposed in [10] under slow fading channel conditions. Energy consumption issues in wireless sensor networks (WSN) using SDF protocol is studied in [11].

This paper focus on dual hop SDF based cooperative relay system. Average bit error rate (BER) for the system is formulated and closed form expression for asymp-totically tight upper bound is found. Power optimization to obtain minimal end-to-end BER is carried out by framing and solving the convex objective function. Theoretical results were substantiated through simulations. Numerical results show that using MIMO system at relay and destination nodes can improve error performance consid-erably, compared with that of single antenna relay link.

Rest of the paper is arranged as follows: Sect. 2 explains system model and analysis. System model for source-destination (S-D) direct link, followed by source-relay (S-R) and relay-destination (R-D) are analyzed. Then SNR and probability of error (P_e) for each link is evaluated and symbol error rate (SER) of S-D and S-R-D link is calculated. This is followed by formulation of power optimization problem. Section 3 contains simulation results which validate the proposed solutions. Section 4 concludes the paper.

2 System Model

Wireless relay based cooperative communication network consisting of source (S), a single relay node (R), and destination (D) is modeled in Fig. 1. It is assumed that source node is having single antenna and relay and destination nodes are equipped with multiple antenna, N_r, N_d respectively. The relay system modeled is SDF and operates in half duplex mode. This protocol is divided into two phases.

In the first phase, the information is broadcast by source. The received message at the relay is analyzed. In the second phase, the relay re-encodes and transmits the message to destination, only if the signal received in the first phase is error free and decodable. Frequency-selective, independent and identically distributed (*i.i.d*) Rayleigh

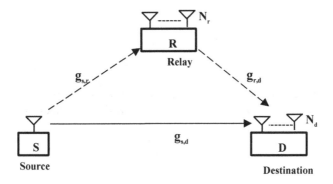

Fig. 1. System model

fading channel is assumed with perfect channel state information (CSI). Perfect CSI means the relay knows channel condition in S-R link and the destination knows channel perfectly for S-D, R-D links so as to perform Maximum Likelihood (ML) detection at the destination [12]. The proposed cooperative relay scheme uses MIMO system [13].

2.1 Selective DF Transmission

For the Rayleigh fading channel between any two nodes A and B, with channel vector $g_{a,b}$, let the fading channel coefficient magnitude be $\omega_{a,b}$ and average channel gain for the kth link be $E\left\{\left|g_{a,b}(k)\right|^2\right\} = \xi_{a,b}^2(k)$. Corresponding probability density function (PDF) can be given as

$$f_{\Omega_{a,b(k)}}\left(\omega_{a,b}(k)\right) = \frac{2\omega_{a,b}(k)}{\xi_{s,r}^2}\exp\left(-\frac{\omega_{a,b}^2(k)}{\xi_{a,b}^2(k)}\right) \tag{1}$$

Message transfer between S-R and S-D happens in two phases.
Phase1: Source broadcasts signal to both destination and relay nodes

$$r_{s,d}(k) = \sqrt{P_S}g_{s,d}(k)s + n_{s,d}, 1 \le k \le N_d \tag{2a}$$

$$r_{s,r}(k) = \sqrt{P_S}g_{s,r}(k)s + n_{s,r}, 1 \le k \le N_r \tag{2b}$$

Where P_s is source power and s is transmit symbol with average power $E\{|s|^2\} = 1$.
Phase2: In selective DF relay transmission, relay forwards decoded symbols to destination if relay decodes the symbol correctly

$$r_{r,d}(k) = \sqrt{P_R}g_{r,d}(k)s + n_{r,d} \tag{3}$$

P_R is power employed at the relay and is given as

$$P_R = \begin{cases} P_R \text{ if decoded correctly} \\ 0 \text{ if decoded incorrectly} \end{cases} \tag{4}$$

Decoding at the relay is done based on SNR threshold criterion. If error at relay, then only one link exists between S and D, and corresponding SNR at destination is

$$SNR_d = P_S \frac{\sum_{k=1}^{N_d} |g_{s,d}(K)|^2}{\sigma^2} \tag{5}$$

If no error, then there do two paths exist between S and D, i.e. S-D and S-R-D, and received signals are

$$\begin{bmatrix} r_{s,d} \\ r_{r,d} \end{bmatrix} = \begin{bmatrix} \sqrt{P_S} g_{s,d} \\ \sqrt{P_R} g_{r,d} \end{bmatrix} S + \begin{bmatrix} n_{s,d} \\ n_{r,d} \end{bmatrix} \tag{6}$$

At the destination, optimal receiver performs MRC with the weighing coefficients calculated as $w = \frac{g}{\|g\|}$

SNR at destination is $SNR_d = \dfrac{P_S \sum_{k=1}^{N_d} |g_{s,d}(K)|^2 + P_R \sum_{k=1}^{N_d} |g_{r,d}(K)|^2}{\sigma^2}$ $\qquad(7)$

2.2   SER Analysis

Assuming BPSK modulation with SNR $\rho = P/\sigma^2$, P_e can be obtained using Craig's formula [14],

$$Pe = Q\left(\sqrt{\frac{P}{\sigma^2}}\right) = \frac{1}{\pi} \int_0^{\frac{\pi}{2}} exp\left(-\frac{\rho}{2 \sin^2 \theta}\right) d\theta \tag{8}$$

Let Ψ denote the event of error at the relay. Then error probability is

$$Pe(\Psi) = Q\left(\sqrt{\frac{P_S \sum_{k=1}^{N_r} |g_{s,r}(K)|^2}{\sigma^2}}\right) = \frac{1}{\pi} \int_0^{\frac{\pi}{2}} \prod_{k=1}^{N_r} exp\left(-\frac{\rho_s \omega_{s,r}^2(k)}{2 \sin^2 \theta}\right) d\theta \tag{9}$$

Therefor the average probability of error $\overline{P_e}(\Psi)$ at the relay is

$$\overline{P_e}(\Psi) = \frac{1}{\pi} \int_0^\infty \int_0^{\frac{\pi}{2}} \prod_{k=1}^{N_r} exp\left(-\frac{\rho_s \omega_{s,r}^2(k)}{2\,sin^2\theta}\right) f_{\Omega_{s,r}(k)}\left(\omega_{s,r}(k)\right) d\theta \, d\omega_{s,r}(k)$$

$$\overline{P_e}(\Psi) = \frac{1}{\pi} \int_0^{\frac{\pi}{2}} \left(\frac{1}{\left(1 + \frac{\rho_s \xi_{s,r}^2}{2\,sin^2\theta}\right)^{N_r}}\right) d\theta \tag{10}$$

The probability of error e at destination, knowing Ψ is

$$P_e(e|\Psi) = Q\left(\sqrt{\frac{P_s \sum_{k=1}^{N_d} |g_{s,d}(k)|^2}{\sigma^2}}\right) = \frac{1}{\pi} \int_0^{\frac{\pi}{2}} exp\left(-\frac{\rho_s \sum_{k=1}^{N_d} \omega_{s,d}^2(k)}{2\,sin^2\theta}\right) d\theta \tag{11}$$

Therefor the average probability of error $\overline{P_e}(e|\Psi)$ at the D is evaluated as

$$\overline{P_e}(e|\Psi) = \int_0^\infty P_e(e|\Psi) f_{\Omega_{s,d}(k)}\left(\omega_{s,d}(k)\right) d\theta \, d\omega_{s,d}(k) = \frac{1}{\pi} \int_0^{\frac{\pi}{2}} \left(\frac{1}{\left(1 + \frac{\rho_s \xi_{s,d}^2}{2\,sin^2\theta}\right)^{N_d}}\right) d\theta \tag{12}$$

Since Ψ is the event of error at the relay, let $\overline{\Psi}$ be the event of correct decoding. Hence in this event, R retransmits the message to D and D employs MRC on signals received from S and R. The SNR at destination, given $\overline{\Psi}$ is

$$SNR_d = \rho_s \sum_{k=1}^{N_d} |g_{s,d}(k)|^2 + \rho_R \sum_{k=1}^{N_d} |g_{r,d}(k)|^2 \tag{13}$$

Probability of error e at destination, knowing $\overline{\Psi}$, i.e. $(P_e(e|\overline{\Psi}))$ and corresponding average probability of error $(\overline{P_e}(e|\overline{\Psi}))$ are

$$P_e(e|\overline{\Psi}) = Q\left(\sqrt{SNR_d}\right) = \frac{1}{\pi} \int_0^{\frac{\pi}{2}} exp\left(-\frac{\rho_s \sum_{k=1}^{N_d} |g_{s,d}(k)|^2 + \rho_R \sum_{k=1}^{N_d} |g_{r,d}(k)|^2}{2\,sin^2\theta}\right) d\theta$$

$$P_e(e|\overline{\Psi}) = \frac{1}{\pi} \int_0^{\frac{\pi}{2}} \prod_k^{N_d} exp\left(\frac{\rho_s \omega_{s,d}^2(k)}{2\,sin^2\theta}\right) \times \prod_k^{N_d} exp\left(\frac{\rho_R \omega_{r,d}^2(k)}{2\,sin^2\theta}\right) d\theta \tag{14}$$

$$\overline{P_e}(e|\overline{\Psi}) = \int_0^\infty P_e(e|\overline{\Psi}) f_{\Omega_{s,d},\Omega_{r,d}(k)}\left(\omega_{s,d}(k), \omega_{r,d}(k)\right) d\omega_{s,d}(k) d\omega_{r,d}(k) \tag{15}$$

Since Rayleigh channel fading coefficients are assumed independent, the joint PDF can be written as product of individual PDF's.

Substituting and solving,

$$\overline{P_e}\left(e|\overline{\Psi}\right) = \frac{1}{\pi}\int_0^{\frac{\pi}{2}} \left(\frac{1}{\left(1+\frac{\rho_S\xi_{s,d}^2}{2\sin^2\theta}\right)^{N_d}} \times \frac{1}{\left(1+\frac{\rho_R\xi_{r,d}^2}{2\sin^2\theta}\right)^{N_d}} \right) d\theta \tag{16}$$

The end-to-end error probability of error **e** at destination is

$$P_e(e) = P_e(e|\Psi) \times P_e(\Psi) + P_e(e|\overline{\Psi}) \times P_e(\overline{\Psi}) \tag{17a}$$

$$E\{P_e(e)\} = \overline{P_e}(e|\Psi) \times \overline{P_e}(\Psi) + \overline{P_e}\left(e|\overline{\Psi}\right) \times \left(1 - \overline{P_e}(\Psi)\right) \leq \overline{P_e}(e|\Psi) \\ \times \overline{P_e}(\Psi) + \overline{P_e}\left(e|\overline{\Psi}\right) \tag{17b}$$

As $\sin^2\theta \leq 1$, we can substitute and simplify (17b) to find tight upper bound for end-to-end SER as

$$P_e(e) \leq \frac{2^{N_d+N_r-2}\sigma^{2(N_d+N_r)}}{\left(2\sigma^2+P_S\xi_{s,d}^2\right)^{N_d}} + \frac{2^{2N_d-1}\sigma^{4N_d}}{\left(2\sigma^2+P_S\xi_{s,d}^2\right)^{N_d}\left(2\sigma^2+P_R\xi_{r,d}^2\right)^{N_d}} \tag{18}$$

At high SNR, asymptotically tight upper bound for end-to-end BER is obtained as

$$P_e(e) \approx \\ ^{2N_d-1}C_{N_d} \times {}^{2N_r-1}C_{N_r} \times \frac{1}{(2^{N_d+N_r})(\xi_{s,r}^{2N_r}\xi_{s,d}^{2N_d})(\rho_S^{N_d+N_r})} + {}^{4N_d-1}C_{2N_d} \times \frac{1}{(2^{2N_d})(\xi_{s,d}^{2N_d}\xi_{r,d}^{2N_d})(\rho_S^{N_d}\rho_R^{N_d})} \tag{19}$$

Let total power be constrained as $P_S + P_R = P_t$ and let $P_S = \gamma P_t$, then $P_R = (1-\gamma) P_t$, where γ is the cost function for fractional power allocation. Modifying (19) we can get expression for asymptotically tight BER

$$P_e(e) \approx \\ ^{2N_d-1}C_{N_d} \times {}^{2N_r-1}C_{N_r} \times \frac{1}{(2^{N_d+N_r})\left(\xi_{s,r}^{2N_r}\xi_{s,d}^{2N_d}\right)} \frac{\sigma^{N_d+N_r}}{\left(\gamma^{N_d+N_r}P_t^{N_d+N_r}\right)} \\ + {}^{4N_d-1}C_{2N_d} \times \frac{1}{(2^{2N_d})\left(\xi_{s,d}^{2N_d}\xi_{r,d}^{2N_d}\right)} \frac{\sigma^{2N_d}}{\left(\gamma^{N_d}(1-\gamma)^{N_d}\right)\left(P_t^{2N_d}\right)} \tag{20}$$

Diversity order of the system is $N_d + min\{N_r, N_d\}$, where as if the terminals are using single antenna, then due to virtual MIMO effect, the diversity order is 2.

2.3   Optimal Power Allocation

We need to find optimal γ which minimizes $Pe(e)$. Assuming high SNR, based on (20) the objective function can be formulated as

$$min\, P_e(e) \quad s.t \qquad P_S + P_R = P_t \qquad (21)$$

This problem can be solved through convex optimization [15]. Applying Karush–Kuhn–Tucker (KKT) conditions, optimal γ can be obtained as root of equation below,

$$
{}^{2N_d-1}C_{N_d} \times {}^{2N_r-1}C_{N_r} \times \frac{1}{(2^{N_d+N_r})\left(\xi_{s,r}^{2N_r}\xi_{s,d}^{2N_d}\right)} \times \frac{(\sigma^{N_d+N_r})N_d+N_r}{\gamma^{1+N_d+N_r}P_t^{N_d+N_r}}
$$
$$
+ {}^{4N_d-1}C_{2N_d} \times \frac{1}{(2^{2N_d})\left(\xi_{s,d}^{2N_d}\xi_{r,d}^{2N_d}\right)} \times \frac{N_d\gamma^{2N_d-1}(1-\gamma)^{N_d-1}(1-2\gamma)\sigma^{2N_d}}{\gamma^{2N_d}(1-\gamma)^{2N_d}P_t^{2N_d}} = 0 \qquad (22)
$$

If $N_r > N_d$, then the optimum of is around $\gamma = 0.5$, that is, equal power to be allocated to source and relay.

3   Results and Discussion

Simulation results are now presented to demonstrate the performance of the proposed source power optimization in wireless SDF relay network. Dual hop, half duplex communication is assumed for the cooperative relay channel. Relay and destination are having multiple antenna, and the system has perfect CSI at the nodes. Number of antenna considered for MIMO system are 2, 3, 4 and 10. Transmitted power is assumed as 0–20 dB in the interval of 5 dB. Channel model is Frequency-selective, *i.i.d* Rayleigh fading channel with channel gains taken as unity. Modulation scheme is BPSK with 10000 symbols per block. Monte-Carlo simulation is executed in Matlab with 1000 iterations.

Figure 2 shows error rate performance of Cooperative communication system against full transmit power, without optimized power allocation. Comparison is done for participating nodes using 2 antennas (MIMO) against nodes using single antenna (Virtual MIMO), which forms reference. In case of single antenna system, the BER curve for cooperative link follow the same slope as that of direct link, for lower transmit powers, but drops faster at high at high SNR. For 20 dB, the BER for direct link is 7.8×10^{-3}, and using cooperative relay communication, the value comes down to 1.745×10^{-4}. Use of dual hop relay system with single antenna at all three nodes, brings in a reduction of BER of the order of 10^{-2} in cooperative link. This is due to the virtual MIMO effect in which the destination receives multiple copies of the same message and hence attaining the diversity gain. But in a worst case scenario in which the relay link breaks, there is a graceful degradation in performance with an approximate roll off from BER of 0.2632 at 0 dB to 2.1×10^{-3} at 25 dB. The error performance see a tremendous improvement when the number of antenna in R and D are doubled and the improvement is clearly visible for higher transmit powers. At transmit power of 10 dB, BER for direct link with single antenna is 0.0653 which drops down to 4.225×10^{-3} for link with dual antenna. For the same transmit power, dual antenna dual hop cooperative link has even better BER of 6.507×10^{-5} against its single antenna counterpart (2.09×10^{-2}). Error performance further improves to 1.3×10^{-7} for the dual antenna system for 15 dB transmit power. The improvement in error performance is due the diversity gain achieved through the use of MIMO system.

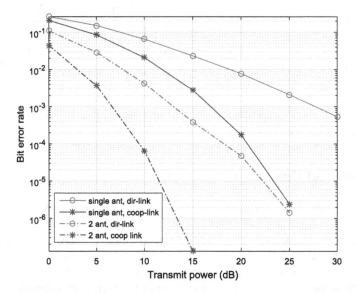

Fig. 2. BER performance comparison of cooperative SDF relay network using single antenna (Virtual MIMO) and 2 antenna at R and D nodes, without power optimization

Our objective is to optimize the average BER performance through optimal power allocation to the source. Solving the objective function as in Eq. (22), it is obtained that, for an optimal power of 60% allotted to the source, the cooperative system is giving minimum BER. Convex optimization technique is used to simulate the optimization problem and to get the optimal value.

Figure 3 is graphical representation of Comparison of direct and cooperative SDF relay link using single antenna and 2 antenna at R and D nodes, for power allocation factor ranging from 1% to 99% with $P_t = \times 1$ w. Here also, the dual antenna cooperative relay network outperforms single antenna counterpart. The optimal BER for single antenna cooperative system is 0.01928 where as that of dual antenna system is 1.1×10^{-3}. Dual antenna system shows a decrease in error rate compared to single antenna direct communication system.

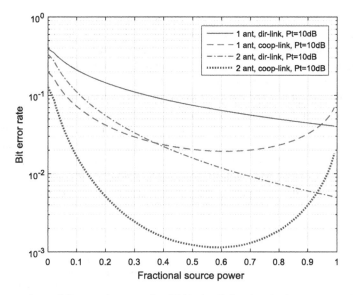

Fig. 3. Comparison of direct and cooperative SDF relay link using single antenna and 2 antenna at R and D nodes, for power allocation factor ranging from 1% to 99% with $P_t = 1$ w.

Figure 4 depicts BER performance comparison of cooperative SDF MIMO relay network, without power optimization. This is an extension to Fig. 2, where we compared single antenna and dual antenna nodes participating in dual hop relaying. Graph

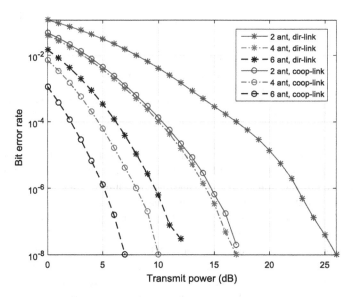

Fig. 4. BER performance comparison of cooperative SDF MIMO relay network, without power optimization

shows that as number of antenna increases, error decreases due to increase in diversity. As the transmit power increases, the rate of decrease in BER for system with higher number of antenna become more steep. To achieve a BER of 10^{-6}, a dual antenna system requires 22 dB of transmit power, where as a six antenna MIMO relay network needs only 5 dB power. It is observed that the rate of decline is more steep as we increase total transmit power from 0 dB to 25 dB. This is because the SNR improves as power increases and BER is nonlinearly related to SNR, as given by Eqs. (9) and (11).

Figure 5 has Comparison of error performance for SDF cooperative communication link (S-R-D) with optimal power allocation for different number of antenna at nodes, for a constant P_t of 5 dB. The optimum value for dual antenna system is 0.01928 where as if MIMO with 10 antenna are used in R and D, the error rate decreases to 1.1×10^{-6}. So power optimization aids to improved error performance.

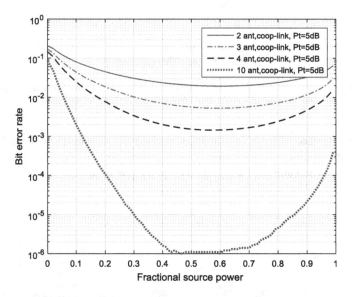

Fig. 5. Comparison of error performance for SDF cooperative communication link (S-R-D) with optimal power allocation for number of antenna at nodes, for a constant $P_t = 5$ dB

Figure 6 is comparison of error performance for direct communication link (S-D) with optimal power allocation for different number of antenna at nodes, for a constant $P_t = 5$ dB. For full transmit power allocated to the source, without optimization, the BER decreases rapidly as the number of antenna increases.

Figures 7 and 8 indicates BER for direct and cooperative communication for dual hop dual antenna nodes for different transmit powers ranging from 0 dB to 20 dB. As total transmit power increases, the BER for direct as well as cooperative links improve, which is very intuitive. But the rate of variation is different for high transmit power. This is due to the nonlinear relation between SNR and average probability of error. For an optimal power allocation, BER of direct and cooperative links are 1.6×10^{-2} and 1.14×10^{-3} for 10 dB transmit power. As total transmit power increase to 20 dB, the

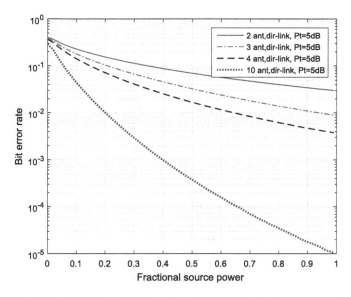

Fig. 6. Comparison of error performance for direct communication link (S-D) with optimal power allocation for different number of antenna at nodes, for a constant $P_t = 5$ dB

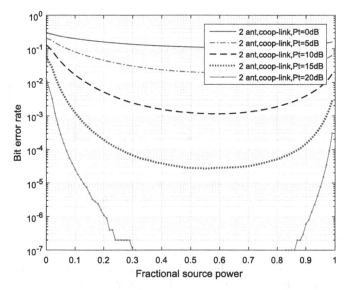

Fig. 7. Comparison of error performance for SDF cooperative communication link (S-R-D) with optimal power allocation for different transmit powers, with nodes using 2 antenna

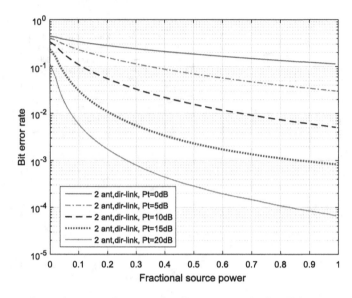

Fig. 8. Comparison of error performance for direct communication link (S-D) with optimal power allocation for different transmit powers, with nodes using 2 antenna

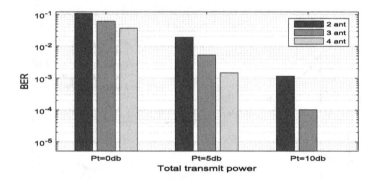

Fig. 9. Comparison of error performance for SDF communication link with optimal power allocation for different transmit powers and MIMO configurations

BER values become 2.7×10^{-4} and approach zero. If Fig. 5 is compared with Fig. 7, rate of decrement in bit error is faster in case of transmit power increase, which has a direct link to SNR improvement. Figure 9 is bar chart comparing error performances for SDF communication link with optimal power allocation for different transmit powers and MIMO configurations.

4   Conclusion

This paper discussed average end-to-end error performance of cooperative relay using selective decode-and-forward scheme with nodes using multiple antenna, under optimized source power allocation. BER performance is compared with cooperative relay network with single antenna per node. System simulations indicate improved system performance in terms of BER, with diversity gain due to MIMO effect. The formulated power allocation optimization problem for the relay system is observed to be convex in nature with a constrained power. Closed form analytical expression is derived for optimal power allocation. Monte-Carlo simulation of the proposed solution is carried out for different source powers and antenna configurations to validate the analytical result. The simulation results are in perfect agreement with the analytical solution and indicates improvement in BER performance with the optimal power allocation.

References

1. Zhang, C., Yin, H., Wang, W., Wei, G.: Selective partial decode-and-forward schemes for distributed space-time coded relaying networks. In: 69th IEEE VTC, Barcelona, Spain, pp. 1–5 (2009). https://doi.org/10.1109/VETECS.2009.5073844
2. Moço, A., Teodoro, S., Silva, A., Gameiro, A.: Performance evaluation of virtual MIMO schemes for the UL OFDMA based systems. In: 4th IEEE WMC, Athens, Greece, pp. 71–76 (2008). https://doi.org/10.1109/ICWMC.2008.61
3. Nahas, M., Saadani, A., Hachem, W.: Outage probability and power optimization for asynchronous cooperative networks. In: 17th IEEE ITC, Doha, Qatar, pp. 153–159 (2010). https://doi.org/10.1109/ICTEL.2010.5478646
4. Atay, F., Fan, Y., Yanikomeroglu, H., Poor, H.V.: Threshold-based relay selection for detect-and-forward relaying in cooperative wireless networks. J. W/L Commun. Netw. (EURASIP), 1–9 (2010). https://doi.org/10.1109/10.1155/2010/721492
5. Li, Y., Wang, W., Kong, J., Peng, M.: Subcarrier pairing for amplify-and-forward and decode-and-forward OFDM relay links. IEEE Commun. Lett. 13(4), 209–211 (2009). https://doi.org/10.1109/LCOMM.2009.080864
6. Kim, S.-I., Kim, S., Kim, J.T., Heo, J.: Opportunistic decode-and-forward relaying with interferences at relays. J. WPC 68(2), 247–264 (2013). https://doi.org/10.1007/s11277-011-0449-6
7. Farhat, J., Brante, G., Souza, R.D., Rebelatto, J.L.: Secure energy efficiency of selective decode and forward with distributed power allocation. In: International Symposium on Wireless Communication Communication Systems, Brussels, Belgium, pp. 701–705. IEEE (2015). https://doi.org/10.1109/ISWCS.2015.7454439
8. Varshney, N., Krishna, A.V., Jagannatham, A.K.: Selective DF protocol for MIMO STBC based single/multiple relay cooperative communication: end-to-end performance and optimal power allocation. IEEE Trans. Commun. 63(7), 2458–2473 (2015). https://doi.org/10.1109/TCOMM.2015.2436912
9. Varshney, N., Goel, A., Jagannatham, A.K.: Cooperative communication in spatially modulated MIMO systems. In: Wireless Conference and Networking Conference, Doha, Qatar, pp. 1–6. IEEE (2016). https://doi.org/10.1109/WCNC.2016.7564938

10. Mohamad, A., Visoz, R., Berthety, A.O.: Dynamic selective decode and forward in wireless relay networks. In: 7th International Congress on Ultra-Modern Telecommunications and Control Systems and Workshops, Brne, Czech Republic, pp. 189–195. IEEE (2015). https://doi.org/10.1109/ICUMT.2015.7382426

11. Grira, L., Bouallegue, R.: Energy consumption analysis of SDF and non-cooperative schemes over Nakagami-m channel and under outage probability constraint. In: 13th IEEE WCMC, Valencia, Spain, pp. 1834–1839 (2017). https://doi.org/10.1109/IWCMC.2017.7986563

12. Yang, W., Yang, W., Cai, Y.: Outage performance of OFDM-based selective decode-and-forward cooperative networks over Nakagami-m fading channels. J. WPC **56**(3), 503–515 (2011). https://doi.org/10.1007/s11277-010-9986-7

13. Zhou, G., Wang, T., Wu, Y., Zheng, G., Yang, G.: Energy-efficient power allocation for decode-and-forward OFDM relay links. Mobile and Wireless Technologies 2016. LNEE, vol. 391, pp. 13–24. Springer, Singapore (2016). https://doi.org/10.1007/978-981-10-1409-3_2

14. Tellambura, C., Annamalai, A.: Derivation of Craig's formula for Gaussian probability function. Electron. Lett. **35**(17), 1424–1425 (1999)

15. Boyd, S., Vandenberghe, L.: Convex Optimization. Cambridge University Press, Cambridge

Emerging Computing Technologies

Exudate Detection in Fundus Images: Multispace Clustering Approach

Sanjeev Dubey$^{(\boxtimes)}$ and Utkarsh Mittal

Cluster Innovation Centre, Rugby Sevens Building, University Stadium,
University of Delhi, GC Narang Marg, New Delhi 110007, Delhi, India
getsanjeevdubey@gmail.com, utkarshmttl@gmail.com

Abstract. Retina is the outer lining of human eye where the image formation takes place. Any threat to retina causes severe eye defects and may lead to complete blindness. During a defect the retina gets distorted. To measure the severity of a disease we need to determine different damage causing elements. Exudates are one such artefact that play a vital role in disease prediction. Diabetic Retinopathy is the leading cause of blindness in the working-age population of the world. Exudates act as a feature to predict this condition. This work aims to automatically segment exudates from fundus images using Image Processing and Machine Learning algorithms.

Keywords: Exudates · Diabetic Retinopathy · Optic disk

1 Introduction

According to a report from WHO on vision impairment and blindness, there is an estimate that 39 million people in the world are blind [10]. The early signs of many of diseases causing blindness can be found by retinal examination. The image of retina is taken through fundus photography. Fundus images are then analyzed by ophthalmologists who look for certain patterns and defects in the image to predict diseases. One such defect is presence of exudates. Exudates are bulges of yellow and white colors appearing in the fundus. Exudates are very crucial indicator of Diabetic Retinopathy. Exudates consist of extracellular lipid which has leaked from abnormal retinal capillaries.

Based on known physical characteristics of exudates we generate three different candidates of a single fundus profile and aggregate them to get final candidate image. We have employed edge detection to generate one profile. Then clustering has been performed in two different spaces - Hue-Saturation space and Deviation from mean space. Results of these clusterings and sharp edge profile have been combined. The results are very effective in providing a good representation of exudates in the images. Further various classifiers have been used to get actual exudates pixels from final candidate profile and segmentation results have been provided. The work has been

---

S. Dubey and U. Mittal contributed equally to this manuscript.

described in different sections. First section puts together the work researchers have been doing in this field. In the next section segmentation of blood vessels has been described. Next section thoroughly explains the entire architecture and detail of procedures involved in the exudate segmentation process. Finally there are results and work has been concluded.

2 Database Description

We would like to extend our sincere gratitude to the maintainers of DIARETDB1 [9] database.

3 Literature Review

Exudate detection for retinal disease prediction is an active research area. People have been working on it for a long time. There have been various methods devised to detect exudates and other bright lesions. Sopharak et al. [1] have used mathematical morphology to detect optic disk and exudates in retinal images. Welfer et al. [2] applied morphological operators on LUV color space of image and obtained good segmentation results. Their work does not involves pre-detection of any other retinal structures and has average sensitivity of 70.48%, and an average specificity of 98.84% on pixel level classification. Jaafar et al. [3] used a splitting algorithm based on dividing image into small regions which are then merged to form larger regions under a homogeneity criterion. They claim to have sensitivity and specificity of 89.8 and 99.3 respectively. They evaluated their method only on images which had signs of exudates in DIA-RETDB1 dataset. Karegowda et al. [4] have used an artificial neural net classifier on some image features. Their claim of best performance with sensitivity of 99.97% and specificity of 100% is based only on 10 fundus images from DIARETDB1. Harangi et al. [11] created a 14-feature space and fed it to an improved naive bayes classifier and obtained good results. Their method has a sensitivity 63, PPV 85 and 0.72 F-Score. Kumar et al. [5] obtained sensitivity of 88.45 on DIARETDB1 by using multi channel histogram analysis. The corresponding specificity obtained is 99.45.

Luangruangrong et al. [6] implemented Frangi's algorithm based on Hessian filtering for blood vessel detection. Later fuzzy clustering was used to detect exudates. The method seems very effective in locating exudate pixels in the image. Ram et al. [7] used multi-space clustering for segmentation of exudates in retinal color photographs. Combining results obtained from different spaces he was able to cover most of exudate pixels. The sensitivity of this method was 71.96% and also the algorithm was time efficient than other clustering based works. Further this work was modified by Araújo et al. [8] in which they replaced k-means clustering by fuzzy c-means clustering. Also elimination of optic disk and further classification have improved the model to a sensitivity of 79.10%. Note that here people have used different metrics to calculate accuracy, sensitivity and specificity. Also choice of different datasets and test-train split between various datasets affects evaluation results.

4   Materials and Methods

4.1   Detection of Blood Vessels

Detection of blood vessels becomes very important as they play a crucial role in segmentation of nearly all other artefacts. Alternate sequential Filtering (ASF) along with other established image processing techniques has been used to extract blood vessels. Green channel of image is extracted for segmentation because it has greater contrast. To further increase contrast Contrast Limited Adaptive Histogram Equalization is applied. Applying ASF on this image gives us another image with average intensity of each region applied over it. Later we subtract this image from output of CLAHE. This gives us an image which contains faint traces of blood vessels with optic disk and other light components removed. We binarize this image with a threshold and get blood vessels segmented. The final image also contains noise and some undesirable elements. Noise is removed by eroding the image once. Undesirable elements are removed further by taking into account that blood vessels are linear in shape (Fig. 1).

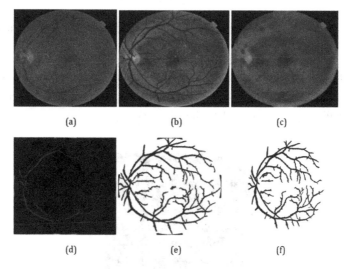

Fig. 1. Various steps in blood vessel segmentation. (a) Input image of fundus (b) Output of CLAHE on green channel (c) Alternate Sequential Filtering of b image (d) Subtraction result of b and c images (e) Thresholded image with noise and extra elements (f) Segmented blood vessels

4.2   Detection of Exudates

To detect exudates following framework has been followed. In this method we have generated three different candidates based on different characteristics of exudates and merged them to get aggregate candidates (Fig. 2).

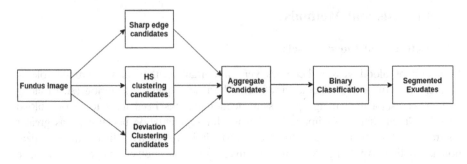

Fig. 2. Framework for exudate detection

Initially the input color image is converted into grayscale. The canny edge detector is applied on grayscale channel. This result creates edges around every dark lesion, bright lesion and blood vessels. Since blood vessel pixels are large in number they add huge no of unwanted pixels in candidate image. So to remove them following steps are taken:

1. The blood vessels are dilated. This enhances the blood vessels so as now it can entirely overlay a non-dilated (previous) version.
2. Using logical operations between edges of blood vessels and dilated version we can get rid of these extra edges, leaving only edges of dark/bright lesions and optic disk.

Next, a dilation operator has been applied to enhance candidate pixels. This serves as one of candidates for exudate detection (Fig. 3).

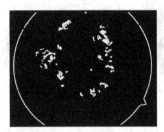

Fig. 3. Sharp edge candidates for exudates

Edge detection alone does not cover all the pixels which represent exudates in the fundus image. Also edges are very hollow as they are only edges of candidates and not the actual pixel cluster. To add those remaining pixels in the candidate set we have applied k-means clustering on images. Ram et al. [7] have shown that applying clustering on multiple spaces and aggregating those results has an impressive result. In our work we have applied clustering on multiple spaces and obtained two candidate regions with certain constraints to get good results. To do so images are converted into Hue-Saturation-Intensity spaces. From observation we know that exudates have effects of yellow, brown and slightly white colors. This is a good factor for distinction between exudates and non exudates pixels. (H_0, S_0) has been taken as a reference pixel point for exudates. Manhattan distance is calculated between centres of clusters and our reference pixel value. The cluster with minimum distance corresponds to exudate cluster. Note that hard exudates clusters contain small no of pixels. So if a cluster contains more than a particular percentage P it is not included in the candidates (Fig. 4).

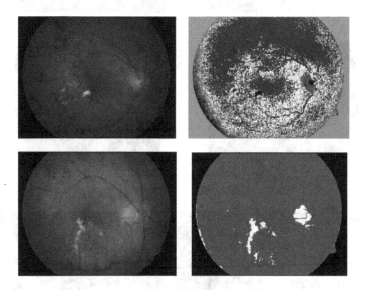

Fig. 4. HS space clustering results

Another filter was applied on hue channel. The cluster whose centre is very close to hue and does not have many counts are also included in the candidates. This covers some more candidates which can possibly represent exudate pixels.

Exudates which are small in shape and have only slightly higher intensity than their neighbourhood are missed in the above approach. In this approach the space has been taken in a way so as it tries to include those pixels as well. To calculate this space a small window is hovered onto image while calculating deviation of pixels from mean intensity of that window. The difference between pixel values and mean intensity of their neighbourhood has been fed to clustering algorithm.

Following are the results (Fig. 5):

While combination of candidates the marks of blood vessels in above clustering results are masked out using technique described in Sect. 4.2. Finally we get candidates with pixels which have intensity higher than its neighbourhood. Now since we have three candidate regions for one profile of fundus. We add them together using arithmetic OR operation. All the candidates have some pixels in common and some new pixels to contribute to final candidate (Fig. 6).

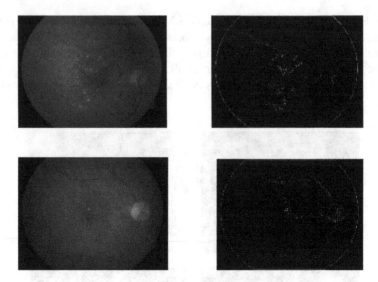

Fig. 5. Deviation space clustering results

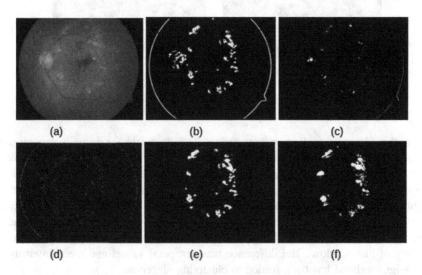

Fig. 6. (a) Input image of fundus (b) edge-detection candidate (c) H-S Space clustering results (d) deviation-space clustering candidate (e) aggregated candidates (f) label image

In the above results final image has been displayed after optic disk removal and a masking which removes white pixels present near the circumference of fundus images. It can be justified as mostly exudates are observed to be present near fovea and mid-fundus region only.

Note: Optic disk has been detected manually.

Final candidate has a lot of positive pixels which should not be treated as exudates which came due to lenient thresholding in each step to avoid loss of positive pixels. To detect actual no of exudates in the images we have to classify these candidate pixels as exudate and non exudate. Features that have been used for classification using Support Vector Machines with linear kernel are:

Hue value, Saturation Value, Intensity value, Red Channel value, Green Channel value, Deviation value from neighbourhood window.

5 Results and Discussions

The algorithm has been trained on 12 images & tested on 36 images of DIARETDB1 which had signs of hard exudates. Actual labels are obtained by thresholding over given polygons of DIARETDB1 labels which is similar to work of Ram et al. [7]. In this case one crucial metric is Positive Predictive Value. The approach has produced very good results on images which have large number of exudates, as their PPV value is high. This method also includes exudate pixels with less intensity and area. Here is a result sample (Fig. 7):

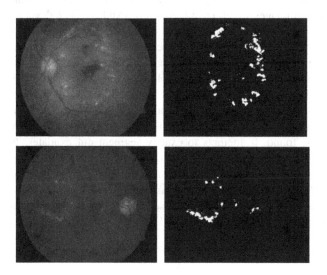

Fig. 7. Results of exudate segmentation

The following bar plots shows images in DIARETDB1 database and their respective PPV value (Fig. 8):

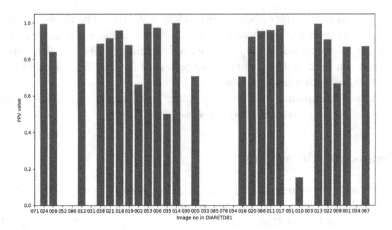

Fig. 8. Results of candidate aggregation

6 Conclusion and Future Prospects

The proposed method has been very effective in exudate detection. The algorithm has a good precision on images which have large no of exudates. The development of such an automated system can be used to reduce the burden on ophthalmologists.

We have found that morphological operations on images are effective but less consistent. The models based on morphology are very sensitive to nature of images. The methods which employ both morphological operations and machine learning techniques tend to work better. The current method has a lot of potential as it incorporates most of exudates pixels in its candidates and gives out actual pixels after classification. This method is different from works which provide regions in which exudates can be found. It attempts to exactly segment out exudates. By generating different candidates, it takes care of all the factors which may cause a group of pixels look like exudates. Future work can be based on improving the sensitivity of algorithm and addition of new features to get better classification results on the candidate images. Also extensiveness of method can be realised by testing it on various other datasets namely STARE, DIARETDB0 and MESSIDOR.

References

1. Sopharak, A., Uyyanonvara, B., Barman, S., Williamson, T.H.: Automatic detection of diabetic retinopathy exudates from non-dilated retinal images using mathematical morphology methods. Comput. Med. Imaging Graph. **32**(8), 720–727 (2008)
2. Welfer, D., Scharcanski, J., Marinho, D.R.: A coarse-to-fine strategy for automatically detecting exudates in color eye fundus images. Comput. Med. Imaging Graph. **34**(3), 228–235 (2010)
3. Jaafar, H.F., Nandi, A.K., Al-Nuaimy, W.: Detection of exudates in retinal images using a pure splitting technique. In: 2010 Annual International Conference of the IEEE Engineering in Medicine and Biology Society (EMBC), pp. 6745–6748. IEEE, August 2010

4. Karegowda, A.G., Nasiha, A., Jayaram, M.A., Manjunath, A.S.: Exudates detection in retinal images using back propagation neural network. Int. J. Comput. Appl. **25**(3), 25–31 (2011)
5. Kumar, P.S., Kumar, R.R., Sathar, A., Sahasranamam, V.: Automatic detection of exudates in retinal images using histogram analysis. In: 2013 IEEE Recent Advances in Intelligent Computational Systems (RAICS), pp. 277–281. IEEE, December 2013
6. Luangruangrong, W., Kulkasem, P., Rasmequan, S., Rodtook, A., Chinnasarn, K.: Automatic exudates detection in retinal images using efficient integrated approaches. In: 2014 Annual Summit and Conference on Asia-Pacific Signal and Information Processing Association (APSIPA), pp. 1–5. IEEE, December 2014
7. Ram, K., Sivaswamy, J.: Multi-space clustering for segmentation of exudates in retinal color photographs. In: Annual International Conference of the IEEE Engineering in Medicine and Biology Society, EMBC 2009, pp. 1437–1440. IEEE, September 2009
8. Araújo, F., Silva, R., Macedo, A., Aires, K., Veras, R.: Automatic identification of diabetic retinopathy in retinal images using ensemble learning. In: Workshop de Informática Médica, Maceió, Alagoas, Brasil (2013)
9. Kauppi, T., et al.: The DIARETDB1 Diabetic Retinopathy Database and Evaluation Protocol. In: BMVC, pp. 1–10, September 2007
10. Vision Impairment and Blindness: World Health Organization. www.who.int/mediacentre/factsheets/fs282/en/
11. Harangi, B., Lazar, I., Hajdu, A.: Automatic exudate detection using active contour model and region wise classification. In: 2012 Annual International Conference of the IEEE Engineering in Medicine and Biology Society (EMBC), pp. 5951–5954. IEEE, August 2012

Using Lucas-Kanade Algorithms to Measure Human Movement

Yao Mi[1], Prakash Kumar Bipin[2], and Rajeev Kumar Shah[3(✉)]

[1] Chengdu Neusoft University, Chengdu, China
Yao.Mi@foxmail.com
[2] Wuhan University of Technology, Wuhan, China
prakash_bpn@yahoo.com
[3] University of Electronic Science and Technology of China, Chengdu, China
rajeevshah97@yahoo.com

Abstract. As an important part of clinical studies, Motion estimation knowledge is widely used to gather useful movement information for medical professionals to find out the best treatment for chronic pain. The purpose of this project is to develop a program to analyze patients' movements and therefore to improve the treatment of patients. Initially, the basic Luca-Kanade algorithm was implemented. And this program was primarily improved upon by setting a threshold to decrease the noise, and then by selecting feature points to process. Additionally, the resizing method was adopted to further improve the whole system. The solution successfully meets the project aims as the system performs much better than the original one with higher accuracy and speed, while the motion trail can be represented clearly by multiple optical flow fields and the useful information can be detected from the video through all the improved implementations.

Keywords: Motion estimation · Lucas-Kanade · Edge detector ·
Optical flow field

1 Introduction

This paper described the life cycle of the whole project, including the preliminary study of motion estimation, the basic implementation of Lucas-Kanade algorithm, the original testing results of Lucas-Kanade algorithm, the testing results of Lucas-Kanade algorithm after improving, the output of improved algorithm, and the evaluation, as well as analysis, of final data.

1.1 Motion Estimation

As an important field of today's society for its' wide application, motion estimation can be applied to numerous aspects, including surveillance, like the surveillance of a parking lot, control applications, such as an interface to games, analysis like diagnostics of patients or athletes to understand and improve their performance (Moeslund et al. 2006), and so on.

© Springer Nature Singapore Pte Ltd. 2019
S. Minz et al. (Eds.): ICICCT 2018, CCIS 835, pp. 118–130, 2019.
https://doi.org/10.1007/978-981-13-5992-7_10

In general, motion estimation can be regarded as a technology of video coding and video processing (Wang et al. 2013). More specifically, motion estimation tries to determine motion vectors by processing adjacent frames in a video sequence (Lu and Liou 1997).

The most common motion estimation technique is to solve the optical flow constraint equation, which is a concept used to describe one object's movement (Gibson 1994).

$$\nabla I \cdot v = -I_t. \tag{1}$$

Where $\nabla I = (I_x, I_y)$ is the spatial intensity gradient, $v = (u, v)$ is the image velocity, and I_t is the change of intensity with respect to time (Beauchemin and Barron 1995).

Optical flow refers to the movement speed of each pixel in the image. In order to calculate the optical flow, the intensity of each object is assumed to be constant, thus, given that point $A(x, y)$ moves to $B(x + dx, y + dy)$ on dt, the intensity of this point is uniform. Therefore,

$$I(x, y, t) = I(x + dx, y + dy, t + dt). \tag{2}$$

Where $I(x, y, t)$ is the intensity of point $A(x, y)$ on time t, $I(x + dx, y + dy, t + dt)$ it the intensity of this point on time $t + dt$, while dx and dy stand for the displacement of this point on horizontal and vertical aspects respectively.

Moreover, according to Taylor expansion,

$$I(x + dx, y + dy, t + dt) = I(x, y, t) + \frac{\partial I}{\partial x} dx + \frac{\partial I}{\partial y} dy + \frac{\partial I}{\partial t} dt + H.O.T. \tag{3}$$

If the displacement of the point and the time are sufficiently small, H.O.T (Higher Order Derivative) can be ignored. Therefore,

$$\frac{\partial I}{\partial x} dx + \frac{\partial I}{\partial y} dy + \frac{\partial I}{\partial t} dt = 0. \tag{4}$$

$$\frac{\partial I}{\partial x} \frac{dx}{dt} + \frac{\partial I}{\partial y} \frac{dy}{dt} + \frac{\partial I}{\partial t} = 0. \tag{5}$$

$$I_x u + I_y v + I_t = 0. \tag{6}$$

$$I_x u + I_y v = -I_t. \tag{7}$$

Under this assumption, an optical flow, which maps the approximated motion between two frames of a video, can be drawn onto a 2D plane.

However, this is an ill-posed equation, since there are two unknowns in one equation. And many researchers try to solve this problem, and finally, come up with solutions to deal with this problem. More specifically, methods to solve optical flow computation can be further divided into the local method, also known as Lucas-Kanade technique or Bigun's structure tensor method, and global method, including Hom/Schunck approach and its extensions (Bruhn et al. 2005).

1.2 Lucas-Kanade Algorithm

Proposed by Lucas and Kanade (1981), Lucas-Kanade method is widely used to solve Eq. (1). With the assumption that the flow is essentially constant in a local neighborhood of the target pixel, the basic optical flow equations for all the pixels in that neighborhood can be solved by the least squares criterion (Lucas and Kanade 1981). And the inherent ambiguity of the optical flow equation can be solved by combining data from several nearby pixels under Lucas-Kanade method (Baker and Matthews 2004). Therefore, the Lucas-Kanade method is less sensitive to image noise than pointwise methods (Bruhn et al. 2005). However, as a purely local method, Lucas-Kanade method cannot provide flow information in the interior of the image's uniform regions (Bruhn et al. 2005).

Additionally, as this algorithm assumes that the optical flow of all the pixels is the same in a certain area, therefore, according to the optical flow constraint equation Eq. (1), the pixels in this area can be represented as:

$$
\left|
\begin{array}{l}
I_{x_1} u_x + I_{y_1} u_y = -I_{t_1} \\
I_{x_2} u_x + I_{y_2} u_y = -I_{t_2} \\
\quad \cdots \\
I_{x_m} u_x + I_{y_m} u_y = -I_m
\end{array}
\right.
\tag{8}
$$

Change these equations as matrix is:

$$
\begin{pmatrix}
I_{x1} & I_{y1} \\
I_{x2} & I_{y2} \\
\cdot & \cdot \\
\cdot & \cdot \\
I_{x_m} & I_{y_m}
\end{pmatrix}
\begin{pmatrix}
u_x \\
u_y
\end{pmatrix}
= -
\begin{pmatrix}
I_{t_1} \\
I_{t_2} \\
\cdot \\
\cdot \\
I_{t_m}
\end{pmatrix}.
\tag{9}
$$

Simplify this matrix, then we can get:

$$
Av = b.
\tag{10}
$$

Applied the least squares method to solve this overdetermined equation, thus:

$$
A^T A v = A^T b.
\tag{11}
$$

$$
v = (A^T A)^{-1} A^T b.
\tag{12}
$$

1.3   Optical Flow Field

An optical flow field is a box with arrows, and each arrow is used to show the moving speed and direction of each pixel between two frames (Iwata and Kikuta 2000). For example, Fig. 1(c) shows the optical flow field for the cube rotating, shown in Figs. 1 (a) and (b).

(a)   (b)   (c)

Fig. 1. Optical flow field (c) displaying box rotation to the right from (a) to (b)

2   Related Work

2.1   Improvements About Motion Estimation

In order to solve the problems about the motion of the camera and the correspondence of all pixels, Irani and Anandan (1999) proposed a direct method, which can collect all the information of the pixels in the image, to measure the target's movement. However, a direct method is sensitive to natural noises, and will cost a long time to compute (Zisserman 1999). To improve the processing speed, Nguyen and Tan (2004) proposed a series of fast block-matching algorithms (BMAs), which is used to limit the number of search locations or to simplify the measure of match between two blocks under comparison.

However, fast block-matching algorithms (BMAs) method cannot accurately figure out the global motion in other camera motion, like scaling or rotating. To solve this problem, Huang and Hsieh (2004) come up with a feature-based method. Additionally, Niu et al. (2014) also proposed a fast and robust local method, based on the Lucas-Kanade paradigm, to process large image formats by removing false feature point.

2.2   Improvements About Decreasing Noises

Noise refers to any entity that negatively affects the purpose of image processing, and it would cause complex influence on image signal phase. Therefore, how to smooth out noise while keeping the details of the image is the major task of image filtering (Alex and Wahi 2014). And threshold segmentation performs well in terms of decreasing noise (Alex and Wahi 2014).

2.3 Edge Detector

Many researchers adopt feature points to improve the accuracy and processing speed of motion estimation, and one common method to figure out suitable feature points is the edge detector. Researchers proposed many methods of edge detector, including Canny, Nalwa-Binford, Sarkar-Boyer, and Sobel detector (Heath et al. 1998). Among all these edge detectors, Canny detector, which is a common method used to locate sharp intensity changes and to find project boundaries, seems to get the best performance (Ding and Goshtasby 2001). Heath (1998) also pointed out that Canny detector is less sensitive to noises while it can detect the weak edge more specifically.

2.4 Image Resizing

To further improve the processing speed, researchers apply the image-resizing method to manipulate the image in advance. According to Shen (2000), resizing leads to better visual quality for a low motion sequence, and it also leads to a trade-off between spatial resolution and the temporal resolution for fast motion sequences.

2.5 Displaying Method

To present the outcomes of motion estimation better, some reviews about methods of motion display had been done.

Generally, there are two main methods to display results. One is to use optical flow field to represent motion in the image: several arrows are used to show the motion, and each arrow represents the movement of one pixel. Using this method, the motion vector can be visualized directly and people can get a good perception of physical motion intuitively, but this method requires for a relatively clean display of sample.

The other one is to use a color visualization map, which is proposed by Bouthemy and Kervrann (2015), to show the magnitude of motion. Although it is hard for unprofessional users to understand the result presented by this method, it provides a better visual perception in terms of subtle differences between neighbor motion vectors, and a dense visualization of the flow field (Fortun et al. 2015).

3 Solution

3.1 Tools

Matlab was used to implement the algorithm and draw the optical flow field according to the outputs, because, as a widely used method in image processing and video manipulation area, Matlab is a clear language and can be documented easily (Gonzalez et al. 2006). Additionally, the agile approach was adopted in this project, as, compared with other methods, like waterfall module, it can be changed or modified easily (Cao and Ramesh 2008).

Moreover, the source of the videos used in this project were taken from Medtronic study, and the videos were created under a lab setting using the Kinect. Additionally, four different types of videos (video_1 – before painkillers with crutches, video_2 – before painkillers without crutches, video_3 – after painkillers with crutches, video_4 – after painkillers without crutches), which show a man with chronic pain walking a few yards, turning around and walking back, have been analyzed.

3.2 Specification and Design

1. Load the Image Sequence

The way to analyze the videos is to process each frame in the video, so the first step of analyzing is to read the image sequence in the folder. TIFFs are widely used in image manipulation, and this method enables users to select the folder of image sequences and to cut out a part of them to process.

2. Image Preparation

When analyzing the frame, this method only needs the information about pixel's intensity, thus the hue and saturation can be ignored. Therefore, to improve the speed of calculation, the RGB images can be transferred into grayscale image to process. Additionally, to have a more accurate result, the intensity needs to be represented from 0 to 1 (double) instead of 0 to 255 (integer). Matlab provides the function, rgb2gray() and im2double(), to meet this requirement.

Moreover, this algorithm asks for the information of partial derivatives of each pixel to process the frames, while each pixel is discrete, thus convolution can approximately replace the partial derivatives. Matlab provides the function, conv2() for convolution operation:

conv2(image1,[-1 1; -1 1]) to represent the partial of intensity on horizontal direction

conv2(image1, [-1-1; 1 1]) to represent the partial of intensity on vertical direction

Besides, the partial of intensity on time can be represented by the difference of intensity between two frames:

It = conv2(image2, [1 1;1 1]) - conv2(image2, [1 1;1 1]);

Where It is the partial of intensity on time image1 is the previous frame and image2 is the next frame.

3. Basic Lucas-Kanade Algorithm

The first step to implement the basic Lucas-Kanade algorithm is to set the window size, and, according to the theory of Lucas-Kanade algorithm, the motion of all the pixels in that window is assumed to be the same.

The next step is to construct Eq. 12. in Matlab and then to get the direction and speed of all the pixels in the image. The pseudo-code below shows how to implement the basic Lucas-Kanade algorithm (Fig. 2).

Basic Lucas-Kanade algorithm
1: Create a 2D matrix [u,v] to store the speed of horizontal and vertical for all pixel and make the default value as 0
2: For each the pixels (i,j) in the image
3: Get the window where (i,j) is in the center of this window
4: Get the convolution of all the pixels in this window and stored them in Ix Iy and It
5: Transfer the Ix, Iy, It from 2D matrix to 1D matrix
6: Combine the Ix, Iy to a 2D matrix as A
7: Let nu = (pinv(A'*A))*A'*(-It) to get the speed of this pixel, where nu(1) is the speed on horizontal and nu(2) is the speed on vertical
8: Let u(i,j) = nu(1) and v(i,j) = nu(2)

Fig. 2. Pseudo-code for basic Lucas-Kanade algorithm

4. Lucas-Kanade Algorithm with Threshold

As the Lucas-Kanade algorithm method is to compute all the pixels between each other in essence, there would be numerous noises in the outcome. Setting a threshold to filter some noises is a good way to solve this problem, thus only the speed faster than the threshold would be captured, and the speed less than the threshold would be ignored.

5. Lucas-Kanade Algorithm with Feature Point

Another way to improve the accuracy and speed of Lucas-Kanade algorithm is to compute the feature points rather than all the pixels in the image. In this project, the core task is to estimate human motion, therefore taking the edge of human body as feature points can help to improve accuracy and speed. To accomplish this function, use the edge() function in Matlab to figure out the feature points to process. Moreover, this function would come up with a binary image, in which value 1 refers to detected edge points. And then, use the find() function to get the coordinate of all edge points.

Also, Canny detection algorithm method was adopted in this project as it is less sensitive to noise and using this method enables the system to find out the precise edge of the human body (Heath et al. 1998).

6. Lucas-Kanade Algorithm with Resizing the Image

To decrease the feature points and to maintain the accuracy level at the same time, shrinking the image was adopted to decrease the total pixels in the image. Moreover, shrinking the image would not affect the outline of people in the image. The imresize() function provided by Matlab was adopted to shrink the image.

7. Draw the Optical Flow Field

The optical flow field can be represented as a plot of arrows, and these arrows can be drawn by the function, quiver (x, y, u, v) from Matlab. More specifically, x and y are the start point of the arrows, while u and v stand for direction and length of the arrows respectively. Under this system, the optical flow field will be drawn on the first frame, and the output of each frame would be recorded on the same picture by optical flow field, therefore, the motion trail of the patient can be displayed.

3.3   Verification and Validation

Numerous tests have been done throughout the whole developing process. In each test, only two frames would be analyzed to test the accuracy and speed of improved algorithm. After that, an image sequence would be processed to evaluate the performance of this improved algorithm. And then, this algorithm would be applied to process four different types of video.

4   Results

4.1   Comparison of Different Implementation

One intuitive way to evaluate the program is to compare the outcome of different implementations. The figures below show the optical flow field of two frames after processing by different implementations with the default window size of 10 and the threshold of 1.

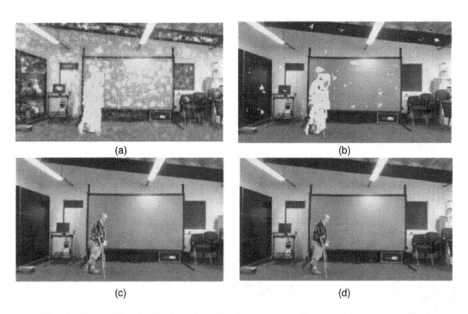

(a)   (b)

(c)   (d)

Fig. 3. Lucas-Kanade display of motion between two frames without autoscaling

Figure 3 displays the outcome of the basic Lucas-Kanade implementation, the Lucas-Kanade implementation with a threshold, Lucas-Kanade implementation with feature points (edges) and threshold, and Lucas-Kanade implementation with feature points and threshold after resizing, respectively. It can be seen that there are many noises in Fig. 3(a) and that the noises decreased significantly after introducing threshold. Moreover, almost no noises are there in Fig. 3(c) and (d).

In terms of patients' movement, Fig. 3(a) and (b) cannot show the moving trail clearly, while Fig. 3(c) and (d) give a clear moving trail. Comparing with Figs. 3(c) and (d) has fewer arrows, while it can also display the movement trail effectively.

In addition, processing speed is another indicator to evaluate the whole system. Table 1 shows the average magnitude of different algorithms.

Table 1. The processing speed for computing two frames

Implementation	Average magnitude (pixel/frames)	Time cost for processing each frame (second)
Basic Lucas-Kanade	0.27723	38.7
Lucas-Kanade with threshold	1.9358	38.2
Lucas-Kanade with feature points and threshold	1.8514	5.5
Lucas-Kanade with feature points, threshold and resizing	2.679	0.15

From this table, it can be seen that, after applying feature points, threshold, and resizing method, the time cost for processing each frame decreased significantly.

4.2 User Interface

As the main purpose of this project is to develop a program to analyze patients' movements and therefore to help to improve the treatment of patients, a simple but clear user interface is crucial for unprofessional users. Figure 4 displays the interface of this project.

Fig. 4. User interface

In this interface, users can simply choose one implementation and then set the parameter according to their needs. After clicking 'OK' button, the outcome, including the motion trial and related data would be displayed on the screen directly.

Table 2. Average magnitude of movement in frames

	Video_1 (before painkillers, w/crutches)	Video_2 (before painkillers, w/o crutches)	Video_3 (after painkillers, w/crutches)	Video_4 (after painkillers, w/o crutches)
v, vertical (pixels/frames)	0.60625	0.54983	0.87883	0.60425
u, horizontal (pixels)	2.3833	2.7747	2.4153	2.8784
Max magnitude on vertical	1.9696	2.3838	2.4072	2.9041
Max magnitude on horizontal	2.8549	3.6397	2.8732	3.7075
Average magnitude (pixels)	3.0857	3.569	3.3487	4.0513

4.3   Comparison of Four Videos

Lucas-Kanade implementation with feature points, threshold and resizing method, is selected to process the videos, as, compared with the other three methods, it provide the best optical flow field with the fastest processing speed and fewest noises.

Table 2 summarizes the data that is useful for analyzing the effect of painkillers and crutches on patient's movement, who is walking a few yards, turning around and walking back. Moreover, all the data is generated through Lucas-Kanade algorithm method with feature points, threshold and resizing under the frames' number of 60, a window size of 10, and a threshold of 1.

Effect of Painkillers: By comparing video_1 with video_3, and video_2 with video_4, the effect of painkillers on patients' movement can be evaluated. Obviously, the man can walk much faster after taking painkillers, as the data shows that the man walks approximately 13% faster after taking painkillers without crutches. Moreover, from the aspect of horizontal motion, he also moves faster after taking painkillers.

Effect of Crutches: By comparing video_1 with video_2, and video_3 with video_4, the effect of using crutches on patients' movement can be evaluated. Obviously, without crutches, the man can walk faster and is able to make more movement upwards. For example, on average, the man walks up to 20% times faster without using crutches. Secondly, the man is able to make more movement upwards without using crutches, since the max magnitude on the horizontal is significant bigger when walking without crutches.

5 Evaluation

Just as previous analysis in Sect. 4, all the project aims, including functional and non-functional aims have been met, thus, generally, the solution is successful. However, to further evaluate the system and for future use, the strengths, limitations, and approach of this project would be examined in this section.

5.1 Strengths of Solution

Based on the testing outcomes of implementing the four types Lucas-Kanade algorithm, the last one, Lucas-Kanade implementation with feature points, threshold and resizing, was the most efficient method developed. This method was faster than others with a processing speed of around 0.1 s, as it firstly resizes the image and then finds feature points to process. Therefore, One of the biggest strength of this system is that it can be used in real-time for its fast processing speed. Additionally, the idea behind this project can be used in other tasks, such as detecting the speed of blood flow (Huang et al. 2013).

Another benefit to this implementation is that much other useful information, like the average and max magnitude on vertical and horizontal aspects, can be gathered at the same time through this method. And all of these data are easily understandable for general users.

Also, this system is flexible and users can control it simply because there are not any hard-coded parameters, users can easily set the parameters to adapt his or her needs. For example, users can set the length of the image sequence to process by doing setting related parameters in the user interface. Also, users can set threshold and window size to decide the number of optical flow fields in the output.

The system is also consistent and reliable, as the output, as well as the time of processing, is constant when processing the same image sequence under same parameters. For example, the deviation of processing time is around 0.02 s for the same parameters, like the image sequence, window size and the value of the threshold. Additionally, the same result can be generated each time. And, according to the optical flow field, most of the displayed arrows located around the moving human, thus the output data are reliable.

5.2 Limitation of Solution

Although there are many advantages of this system, there are still some limitations. The first is that, rather than specific movements of one part, like the man's hair or hand, this system can only detect the whole movements of the man in the video.

Also, the implementations were written to be optimal for these videos because the goal of this project was to analyze the four specific videos. Therefore, the system has strict requirements for the videos need to be processed. For example, for the videos in which there are two people walking, this system can only come up with the average moving speed of the two people rather than showing two people motion result separately.

There are also limitations related to analyzing the videos. Firstly, this system can only process one video at a time. In addition, there might be other variables that affect man's movement, causing some deviation to the result.

6 Conclusions

6.1 Project Overview

During this project, a system using basic Lucas-Kanade algorithm and its three improvements was developed. And, due to the accuracy and speed, Lucas-Kanade implementation with feature points, threshold and resizing was chosen to analyze the four videos. In addition, a simple but clear interface has been developed for general users, and the output would be transformed into easily understandable data to users.

6.2 Main Findings

All the project aims, including all functional and non-functional aims, have been accomplished. Through applying feature points, a threshold and resizing method, the basic Lucas-Kanade implementation has been improved significantly in terms of accuracy and processing speed.

Additionally, this system provides many ways to display the data, including optical flow field and indicators of speed. And according to the results, the man can walk much faster after taking painkillers, and the man can also walk much faster without crutches. Moreover, the man can make more upward motion without crutches.

Moreover, considering that different users have different preferences and requirements, this project develops a system for users to set the parameters according to his or her needs.

6.3 Further Work

Researches about computer vision and motion estimation is on-going and becoming increasingly important. And other approaches, like frame difference method, have been proposed to make motion estimation (Nishu 2014).

In future work, not only the optical flow based but also the frame difference based method will be implemented to compare which one can meet various demands better. Moreover, in the future, the pyramidal Lucas-Kanade algorithm (Niu et al. 2014) can be employed to enable the system to process motion information more precisely. Also, adaptive multi-motion model in the joint detection and tracking (JDT) framework (Wang et al. 2013) can be adopted to detect the information of multiple objects' motion separately.

References

Alex, D.S., Wahi, A.: BSFD Background subtraction frame difference algorithm for moving object detection and extraction. J. Theor. Appl. Inf. Technol. **60**(3), 623–628 (2014)

Baker, S., Matthews, I.: Lucas-Kanade 20 years on: a unifying framework. Int. J. Comput. Vis. **56**(3), 221–255 (2004)

Bruhn, A., Weickert, J., Schnörr, C.: Lucas/Kanade meets horn/Schunck: combining local and global optic flow methods. Int. J. Comput. Vis. **61**(3), 1–21 (2005)

Cao, L., Ramesh, B.: Agile requirements engineering practices: an empirical study. IEEE Softw. **25**(1), 60–67 (2008)

Ding, L., Goshtasby, A.: On the canny edge detector. Pattern Recogn. **34**(3), 721–725 (2001)

Fortun, D., Bouthemy, P., Kervrann, C.: Optical flow modelling and computation: a survey. Comput. Vis. Image Underst. **134**, 1–21 (2015)

Gibson, J.J.: The visual perception of objective motion and subjective movement. Psychol. Rev. **101**(2), 318–323 (1994)

Gonzalez, R.C., Woods, R.E., Eddins, S.L.: Digital image processing using MATLAB. Dorling Kindersley Pvt, India (2006)

Heath, M., Sarkar, S., Sanocki, T., Bowyer, K.: Comparison of edge detectors. Comput. Vis. Image Underst. **69**(1), 38–54 (1998)

Huang, J.-C., Hsieh, W.-S.: Automatic feature-based global motion estimation in video sequences. IEEE Trans. Consum. Electron. **50**(3), 911–915 (2004)

Huang, T.-C., Chang, C.-K., Liao, C.-H., Ho, Y.J.: Quantification of blood flow in internal cerebral artery by optical flow method on digital subtraction angiography in comparison with time-of flight magnetic resonance angiography. PLoS ONE **8**(1), e54678 (2013)

Irani, M., Anandan, P.: About direct methods. In: Triggs, B., Zisserman, A., Szeliski, R. (eds.) IWVA 1999. LNCS, vol. 1883, pp. 267–277. Springer, Heidelberg (2000). https://doi.org/10.1007/3-540-44480-7_18

Iwata, K., Kikuta, H.: Measurement of dynamic flow field by optical computed tomography with shearing interferometers. Opt. Rev. **7**(5), 415–419 (2000)

Ko, B., Kim, S., Nam, J.: Image resizing using saliency strength map and seam carving for white blood cell analysis. Biomed. Eng. Online **9**(1), 54 (2010)

Lucas, B.D., Kanade, T.: An iterative image registration technique with an application to stereo vision. In: IJCAI, pp. 674–679 (1981)

Lu, J., Liou, M.L.: A simple and efficient search algorithm for block-matching motion estimation. IEEE Trans. Circ. Syst. Video Technol. **7**(2), 429–433 (1997)

Moeslund, T.B., Hilton, A., Krüger, V.: A survey of advances in vision-based human motion capture and analysis. Comput. Vis. Image Underst. **104**(2–3), 90–126 (2006)

Nguyen, V.A., Tan, Y.: Fast block-based motion estimation using integral frames. IEEE Signal Process. Lett. **11**(9), 744–747 (2004)

Niu, Y., Xu, Z., Che, X.: Dynamically removing false features in pyramidal Lucas-Kanade registration. IEEE Trans. Image Process. **23**(8), 3535–3544 (2014)

Torr, P.H.S., Zisserman, A.: Feature based methods for structure and motion estimation. In: Triggs, B., Zisserman, A., Szeliski, R. (eds.) IWVA 1999. LNCS, vol. 1883, pp. 278–294. Springer, Heidelberg (2000). https://doi.org/10.1007/3-540-44480-7_19

Singla, N.: Motion detection based on frame difference method. Int. J. Inf. Comput. Technol. **4** (0974–2239), 1559–1565 (2014)

Wang, Z., Ben Salah, M., Zhang, H.: Object joint detection and tracking using adaptive multiple motion models. Vis. Comput. **30**(2), 173–187 (2013)

An Innovative Method of Feature Extraction for Text Classification Using PART Classifier

Ankita Dhar[1]([⊠]) (iD), Niladri Sekhar Dash[2] (iD), and Kaushik Roy[1] (iD)

[1] Department of Computer Science,
West Bengal State University, Kolkata, India
ankita.ankie@gmail.com, kaushik.mrg@gmail.com
[2] Linguistic Research Unit, Indian Statistical Institute, Kolkata, India
ns_dash@yahoo.com

Abstract. With the advent of technology and thrust to create machines with human intelligence, the frontiers in machine learning are being stretched incessantly. With the increasing number of digital information in recent scenario, text classification has gained importance in machine learning task which needs to study texts thoroughly to achieve success. It is a task of assigning a random document to its predefined text class. This paper aims at presenting a methodology for developing an automatic system for solving the problem of classifying Bangla text document into their respective text categories. It introduces a hybrid approach (i.e., PART) for classification of Bangla text documents based on 'term association' and 'term aggregation' as baseline feature extraction methods. Comparison of results with other classification algorithms shows that this approach can elicit better results than the existing methods.

Keywords: Text classification · Feature · Term association · Term aggregation · PART · Classifier

1 Introduction

In recent time, Internet has become the most popular way of communication media for which, there is an increase in vast amount of users using the texts as well as the availability of number of online text documents. Since, the amount of text documents and users continues to increase, tasks for automatic text document categorization or text document classification have become an essential method for helping people to find, organize, and manage the huge amount of digital text data.

The automatic text classification system is based on the analysis of content automatically to allocate a text document into its pre-determined category. Generally, various researches have been carried out in different languages for classifying a text document to its appropriate text class (genre) based on the contents but very few works have been carried out in Bangla. For this study, nearly 8000 Bangla text documents with contents from eight text domains: Business, Entertainment, Food, Medicine, Science & Technology, Sports, State and Travel have been extracted from online news corpus as well as from other online sources. These are used as a trial dataset for the

© Springer Nature Singapore Pte Ltd. 2019
S. Minz et al. (Eds.): ICICCT 2018, CCIS 835, pp. 131–138, 2019.
https://doi.org/10.1007/978-981-13-5992-7_11

experiment to be carried out by using the rule based classification algorithm based on term association and term aggregation feature selection approaches.

The remaining portion is assembled as follows. Some recent works on text classification have been discussed in Sect. 2; Sect. 3 cast lights on the proposed model describing dataset being used and the feature extraction and selection methods employed for the experiment; Sect. 4 presents results by discussing the classifier being used; and the paper is concluded in Sect. 5.

2   Related Works

From the literature survey being carried out, it is observed that researchers have paid great attention on text classification for English and Arabic but very few works have been employed on Indian languages. For instance, DeySarkar *et al.* [1] used clustering based approach as feature selection method on 13 datasets and classified those using Naive Bayes. Guru and Suhil [2] introduce Term_Class relevance as feature values on 20Newsgroup and as classifiers SVM and KNN were used. Jin *et al.* [3] used bag-of-embeddings model with SGD classification algorithm on Reuters21578 and 20Newsgroups datasets. Wang and Zhang [4] introduced two new approaches: tf.icf and icf-based in their work as feature extraction schemes.

In case of Arabic text classification, a system has been developed using rule based classifier for classifying medical documents [14]. Haralambous *et al.* [15] used light stemming and rootification along with TFIDF and dependency grammar properties for classifying text documents extracted from Kalimat corpus. Ali and Ijaz [16] worked with some statistical properties of the lexicon extracted from crude corpus which was analyzed by Zipf's and Heaps Law for Urdu text classification.

Gupta and Gupta [5] classified Punjabi text documents using hybrid approach which combines Naive Bayes and Ontological Based classification over 184 Punjabi text documents obtained from news articles covering seven sub classes of Sports namely Cricket, Hockey, Kabaddi, Football, Tennis, Badminton and Olympics. ArunaDevi and Saveeth [10] developed compound features from CIIL and Mozhi corpus for classifying Tamil text documents. Swamy and Thappa [11] classified 100 text documents each for Kannada, Tamil and Telugu based on Zipf's law, Vector Space Model, TF-IDF weighting scheme using Decision Tree (J48), Naive Bayes (NB) and KNN.

For Bangla text classification, the author in [6] used n-gram technique for categorizing newspaper text corpus extracted from *Pratham Alo* newspaper. Mandal and Sen shows the comparison of four classifiers namely; SVM, NB, DT (C4.5) and KNN and obtained an accuracy of 89.14%, 85.22%, 80.65% and 74.24% respectively for categorizing 1000 labeled news web documents into five categories discussed in [20]. Kabir *et al.* [7] implemented SGD classifier for classifying Bangla text documents from 9 domains and achieved accuracy of 93.85%. Different types of classification methods for classifying Bangla text document were studied and the observations were presented in the work of Islam *et al.* [8]. In another work of Islam *et al.* [9], the application of TFIDF weighting scheme along with SVM classifier is shown and an accuracy of 92.57% have been achieved for classifying Bangla text documents covering twelve text categories.

Sarmah *et al.* [17] and Mohanty *et al.* [18] used language specific Wordnet for classifying Assamese and Sanskrit text documents respectively. In work of [17] they have considered four categories such as News, Sports, Science and Arts and the proposed method outcomes with a result of accuracy 90.27% for classifying Assamese text documents. For Marathi text classification, Patil and Bogiri [12] introduce LINGO clustering algorithm on 200 Marathi news text documents. Bolaj and Govilkar [13] used Marathi dictionary for computing the feature vector and classifying the text documents using Multinomial Naive Bayes, SVM, Modified KNN, and ontology based classification.

3   Proposed Method

An outline of the proposed work is presented in the Fig. 1. The methodology incorporating the development of the datasets along with the generation of the feature sets based on 'term association' and 'term aggregation' to train the model classifier which is a rule based classifier (PART) is also detailed in the following subsections.

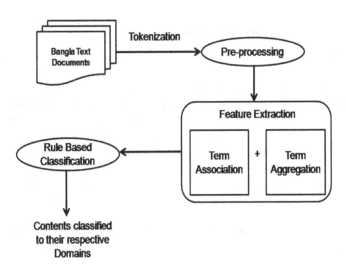

Fig. 1. Outline of the proposed work.

3.1   Data Collection

Data collection plays a significant part in the output of any experiment. While building a dataset much attention is to be needed so that errors cannot creep in the upcoming processes. For this experiment, total 8000 Bangla text documents have been considered covering eight categories such as Business (B), Entertainment (E), Food (F), Medical (M), State news (P), Sports (SP), Science & Technology (ST), and Travel (T). For each domain, 1000 Bangla text documents have been considered. The text documents have been extracted from online news corpuses, various web pages and some Bangla online magazines as presented in [20].

3.2 Pre-processing

Prior to the application of various feature extraction and selection approaches, one must need to go through tokenization and stopwords removal stages. In text classification task, the tokens are commonly used as features to train the model. Since, each text document consists of sentences including a series of characters or words or phrases, so it needs to be segmented into tokens or words to get the features. The method of segmenting the sentences into such lexical units is called tokenization and the unit is called token. In text classification process, tokens are segmented based on some set of delimiters. Here, in this experiment, each sentence is tokenized using 'space' as the delimiter to get the individual words or tokens. After tokenization, the total number of tokens retrieved from all the text documents results in **23,36,821** tokens. Since all the tokens in the text document are not relevant enough to retain in the feature set, removal of stopwords is required to reduce the dimension as well as to increase the accuracy of the outcome. After performing stopwords removal task that includes removal of punctuations, special characters, postpositions, interjections, numerals, some adverbs, pronouns, and English terms which results in **10,91,960** tokens.

3.3 Feature Extraction and Selection

The main focus of interest for quite some time is the approaches for extracting and selecting features, and with the construction of large databases and the need for good machine learning techniques, new approaches to feature extraction and selection are in great demand. While dealing with huge dataset, if the irrelevant or redundant features are not removed beforehand, training model might not produce desirable outcomes. Reducing the number of these unwanted features immensely decreases the running time of a training algorithm and helps the researchers in gaining a better perception about the underlying notion of a real-world classification problem.

Hence we have tried to incorporate two weighting schemes based on term association (TA_1) and term aggregation (TA_2) as our feature extraction and selection approaches for the experiment.

TA_1(t_i) is the count of the terms associated with the contents of each domain of each text documents. It is calculated in respect to each text documents by using Eq. 1.

$$TA\_1(t_i) = \frac{O(t_i) + n\_domain}{\sum O(t_i)} \tag{1}$$

$O(t_i)$ gives occurrence count of term t_i in a particular text. n_{domain} is the occurrence count of t_i in a particular domain of a text document. $\sum O(t_i)$ is the total frequencies of all the terms in a text document.

TA_2(t_j) is the summation of all the occurrences of a term together with the occurrence count of a term occurring in the domain of the total dataset. It is computed based on the dataset considered by using the Eq. (2) stated below.

$$\mathrm{TA\_2}(t_j) = \frac{W(t_j) + F(t_j)}{N} \tag{2}$$

$W(t_j)$ is the total occurrences count of term $\mathbf{t_j}$ in total documents. Here, summation has been taken over all documents. $F(t_j)$ counts the presence of term t_j in domains of all the text documents along with its individual number of occurrence. $\mathbf{N}$ denotes the dataset. $W(t_j)$ and $F(t_j)$ is estimated using the equations (Eqs. 3 and 4). In both the cases normalized values between 0 and 1 have been selected as features to train the model classifier.

$$W(t_j) = \sum_{j=1}^{N} O(t_j) \tag{3}$$

$$F(t_j) = O(t_j) + \sum N_{n\_domain} \tag{4}$$

4   Result Analysis

Classification is a prime task of data mining problems. For a given set of labeled training features, the classification task builds a classifier. A classifier in text classification sense is a comprehensive model applied to assume the class index for the documents that are unlabeled. Many approaches have already been proposed for the classification task. Here, in our experiment, we have used a hybrid approach called PART, a rule based classification algorithm for the classification purpose.

Rule based classification approach evaluate the performance based on simple "If-Then" knowledge in order to decide the applicability of the text documents to their respective categories. PART uses separate-and-conquer process. It creates a partial decision tree from all the iterations and considers the suitable leaf into a rule. Weka [19] tools have been used for the classification task. The confidence factor is set to 0.25 and for reduced-error pruning the number of folds is set to be 5. One fold is used for pruning purpose and the remaining for developing more rules. The number of instances per rule is 5. It is seen that with increasing number of instances per rule, the accuracy get reduced.

In the experiment, 5 Fold cross-validation is performed on the dataset and achieved accuracy of 96.83% for PART classification algorithm. The classification accuracy has been considered here for the result, which is computed of how well a text document is correctly classified into its respective category. It is simply calculated using the following Eq. (5). The domain-wise accuracy for hybrid approach (PART) classification algorithm is presented in Fig. 2.

$$\mathrm{Accuracy} = \frac{\text{No. of Correctly Classified Text Documents}}{\text{Total no. of Text Documents}} * 100\% \tag{5}$$

We compare the results of PART classifier with some other commonly used rule based classification algorithm namely Decision Table, OneR, and RIPPER along with

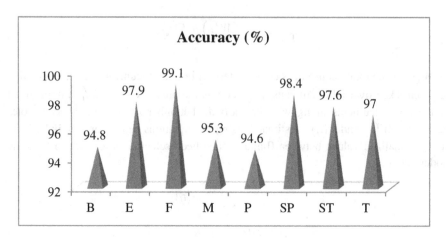

Fig. 2. Domain-wise accuracy for PART classifier.

Bayesian classification algorithms such as Naive Bayes Multinomial (NBM) and Naive Bayes (NB) because of its use in many text classification tasks [1, 5, 7, 8, 12, 14]. The accuracy achieved for various classifiers is displayed in a line chart in Fig. 3. The results obtained from the comparison are also illustrated through the following Table 1.

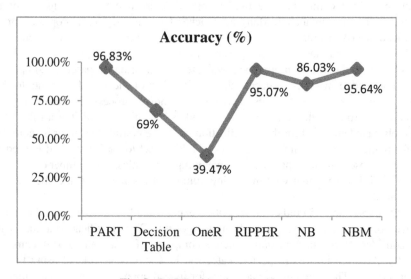

Fig. 3. PART with other classifiers.

The PART classifier outperforms other algorithms; in fact, the average rank is the highest: Rank 1 (Table 2), and the Friedman test [1] validates the statistical significance. To compare the results, this test is employed because it does not require any assumption about the model being used here. It can be observed from Table 2, that

Table 1. Different performance measures for classification.

Classifiers	Precision	Recall	F-measure
PART	0.968	0.968	0.968
Decision table	0.686	0.686	0.686
OneR	0.394	0.394	0.394
RIPPER	0.950	0.950	0.950
NB	0.860	0.860	0.860
NBM	0.956	0.956	0.956

PART obtain a better mean rank (rank is assigned in ascending order i.e. top rank: 1.00 and last rank: 6.00) compare to other five classifiers. The mean ranks for the classifiers are presented in Table 2. The details of the test statistics of the Friedman rank sum test is also provided here in Table 3 where N is the dataset; df is the degree of freedom; and Asymp. Sig. is the significance level.

Table 2. Obtained mean rank.

Algorithms	Mean rank
PART	1.00
Decision table	5.00
OneR	6.00
RIPPER	2.60
NM	4.00
NBM	2.40

Table 3. Test statistics of Friedman test.

N	5
Chi-Square	24.657
Df	5
Asymp. Sig.	0.05

5   Conclusion

This paper presents two weighting schemes for extraction and selection of the features to classify Bangla text documents from eight different domains. In future this experiment can be expanded in number of text documents consisting of contents from few more domains. Also some standard feature selection methods as well as new hybrid approaches can be introduced for classifying the contents to their pre-determined categories. From this experiment it can also be observed that among the three rule based classification algorithm (PART, RIPPER, Decision Table and OneR), PART performs better followed by RIPPER for classifying Bangla text documents with multiple domain.

Acknowledgement. One of the authors thanks DST for their support.

References

1. DeySarkar, S., Goswami, S., Agarwal, A., Akhtar, J.: A novel feature selection technique for text classification using naive bayes. In: International Scholarly Research Notices, vol. 2014, p. 10 (2014)
2. Guru, D.S., Suhil, M.: A novel term_class relevance measure for text categorization. In: Proceedings of ICACTA, pp. 13–22 (2015)
3. Jin, P., Zhang, Y., Chen, X., Xia, Y.: Bag-of-embeddings for text classification. In: Proceedings of IJCAI, pp. 2824–2830. (2016)
4. Wang, D., Zhang, H.: Inverse-category-frequency based supervised term weighting schemes for text categorization. J. Inf. Sci. Eng. **29**, 209–225 (2013)
5. Gupta, N., Gupta, V.: Punjabi text classification using naive bayes, centroid and hybrid approach. In: Proceedings of SANLP, pp. 109–122 (2012)
6. Mansur, M., UzZaman, N., Khan, M.: Analysis of N-gram based text categorization for bangla in a newspaper corpus. In: Proceedings of ICCIT, p. 08 (2006)
7. Kabir, F., Siddique, S., Kotwal, M.R.A., Huda, M.N.: Bangla text document categorization using stochastic gradient descent (SGD) classifier. In: Proceedings of CCIP, pp. 1–4 (2015)
8. Islam, Md.S., Jubayer, F.E.Md., Ahmed, S.I.: A comparative study on different types of approaches to Bengali document categorization. In: Proceedings of ICERIE, p. 6 (2017)
9. Islam, Md.S., Jubayer, F.E.Md., Ahmed, S.I.: A support vector machine mixed with TF-IDF algorithm to categorize Bengali document. In: Proceedings of ICECCE, pp. 191–196 (2017)
10. ArunaDevi, K., Saveeth, R.: A novel approach on tamil text classification using C-feature. Int. J. Sci. Res. Develop. **02**, 343–345 (2014)
11. Swamy, M.N., Thappa, M.H.: Indian language text representation and categorization using supervised learning algorithm. Int. J. Data Min. Tech. Appl. **02**, 251–257 (2013)
12. Patil, J.J., Bogiri, N.: Automatic text categorization marathi documents. Int. J. Adv. Res. Comput. Sci. Manage. Stud. **03**, 280–287 (2015)
13. Bolaj, P., Govilkar, S.: Text classification for Marathi documents using supervised learning methods. Int. J. Comput. Appl. **155**, 6–10 (2016)
14. Al-Radaideh, Q.A., Al-Khateeb, S.S.: An associative rule-based classifier for Arabic medical text. Int. J. Knowl. Eng. Data Min. **03**, 255–273 (2015)
15. Haralambous, Y., Elidrissi, Y., Lenca, P.: Arabic language text classification using dependency syntax-based feature selection. In: Proceedings of ICALP, p. 10 (2014)
16. Ali, A.R., Ijaz, M.: Urdu text classification. In: Proceedings of FIT, pp. 21–27 (2009)
17. Sarmah, J., Saharia, N., Sarma, S.K.: A novel approach for document classification using Assamese WordNet. In: Proceedings of ICGW, pp. 324–329 (2012)
18. Mohanty, S., Santi, P.K., Mishra, R., Mohapatra, R.N., Swain, S.: Semantic-based text classification using WordNets: Indian language perspective. In: Proceedings of ICGW, pp. 321–324 (2006)
19. Hall, M., Frank, E., Holmes, G., Pfahringer, B., Reutemann, P., Witten, I.H.: The WEKA data mining software: an update. SIGKDD Explor. **11**, 10–18 (2009)
20. Dhar, A., Dash, N.S., Roy, K.: Classification of text documents through distance measurement: an experiment with multi-domain bangla text documents. In: Proceedings of ICACCA, pp. 1–6 (2017)

An Adaptive Frequency Based Steganography Technique

Sonam Chhikara$^{(\boxtimes)}$ⓘ and Rajeev Kumarⓘ

School of Computer and System Sciences, Jawaharlal Nehru University,
New Delhi, India
`chhikara05@gmail.com`, `rajeevkumar.cse@gmail.com`

Abstract. Steganography is an art of embedding data in an imperceptible way. Steganography technique has two category based on transformation: spatial and frquency domain transformation based techniques. The requirements of steganography are capacity, quality and imperceptibility. This paper works on capacity and quality simultaneously by embedding data in transformed domain at selected locations. Here, secret message bits are embedded in middle frequency, few low frequency and high frequency components at alternate position of discrete cosine transformed image. By this method, secret message bits will less affect the cover image's information part. Analyses of this method and other DCT based methods over same image data set shows that proposed work has good PSNR value and high embedding capacity.

Keywords: Steganography · Data hiding · Security · DCT

1 Introduction

In digital communication knowledge developed world, the main concern is to make hard for unintended user to access the secret information hidden inside the communication. Several methods have been developed to secure personal information like cryptography, watermarking, steganography etc. Cryptography is the science of exchanging information in secret codes by encryption and decryption. It is the ancient technique for transferring secret information securely over unsecure channel [1]. Drawback of using cryptography is, even if it adds security in communication but the encrypted data format attracts third party attention as encrypted message is in unreadable and scrambled form which in itself again breaks the security. To overcome this, various more powerful techniques have developed, one of them is watermarking. Watermarking is a way of embedding information on host signal [2]. Watermarking is generally used for copyright and authenticity. This way of embedding is used when the information which is to be hidden and the channel which will hide the data, both are associated with each other. It is one-to-many technique for transferring secret information. Steganography is another advanced way for providing security. Steganography is an art of embedding secret message inside another multimedia channel like

S. Minz et al. (Eds.): ICICCT 2018, CCIS 835, pp. 139–149, 2019.
https://doi.org/10.1007/978-981-13-5992-7_12

image, text, video etc. in an imperceptible way [3]. Here, the file which is to be protected need not to be associated with the cover file. It is one-to-one communication technique. Steganography is further categorized into two parts: linguistic steganography and technical steganography. Technical part is further divided as: digital image, video, audio, text. Figure 1 shows the security system diagram.

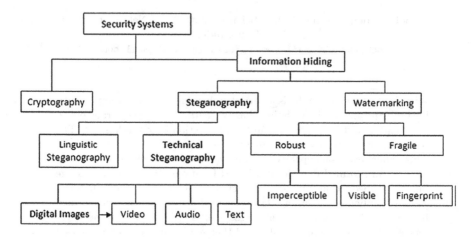

Fig. 1. Security system diagram.

This paper will focus on digital image steganography. Digital image steganography is divided further on domain based as: Spatial steganography and Frequency domain based steganography technique. First one is also called pixel based steganography. Here, secret data is embedded into actual pixel of the image by varying the value of pixels slightly so that unintended user unable to detect the difference between cover and stego image. Most popular spatial domain method is LSB. Spatial domain method is further divided as: sequential embedding and random embedding method. In sequential embedding method, data will be hidden in sequence i.e. from left to right, from first bit of the cover image [4,5]. In random embedding method, data will be embedded in a scattered way over the cover image i.e. random pixels will be selected from the image and then embed the secret data inside it [6,7]. LSB based steganography technique has advantages as: It is simple to implement in comparison to other methods. Secondly, it doesn't require much change in cover image and is less suspicious. Third, it can be blended with other embedding technique for more security. Some disadvantages are: If stego image go under some filtering technique then it will destroy the secret information. Secondly, scaling, rotation, translation, cropping etc. introduce extra noise which further destroys the secret information. These limitations can be overcome by frequency domain based steganography.

In Frequency domain based embedding technique, first original image is transformed from time to frequency components then embed the secret message in transformed components. DWT, DFT and DCT are used in frequency domain based steganography. In DCT based steganography technique, original image media is divided into same size chunks and DCT is applied on each chunk from the intensity value of each pixel. Next, quantization is used to make these coefficients as whole numbers using standard table. Figure 2 shows the jpeg process which used DCT:

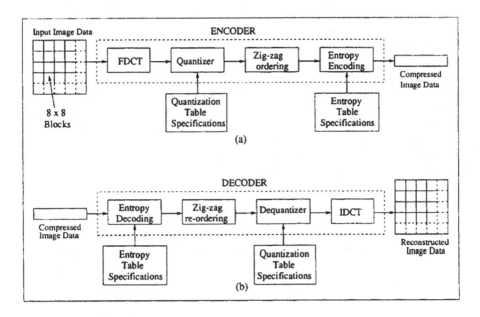

Fig. 2. Detailed JPEG process using DCT [8].

DFT and DWT based methods are similar to DCT, instead of hiding data in DCT coefficients, DFT and DWT coefficients will be used for embedding the information [9,10]. Frequency domain based steganography is less perceptible in comparison to spatial methods but the capacity for hiding is less in frequency domain based methods and these are also complicated to implement. Spatial domain based techniques allow more capacity and frequency based techniques give good quality.

This paper is divided into five parts: first is introduction. Second section is literature survey which will brief all the related work. Next, proposed work of this paper. After that, experimental results will be elaborated and last section is for concluding the work.

2 Literature Survey

Lot of research has been done in DCT part of steganography, two valuable initiatives were J-steg and JPHide [11]. J-steg embeds the data bits in LSB of cosine transformed components after quantization. JPHide modifies the 2 LSBs of DCT coefficients for embedding 2 secret message bits. It increases the capacity by compromising quality of image. Outguess [12] uses the PRNG for generating location for embedding message bit randomly over whole cover image non non-uniformlly. F5 [13] steganographic algorithm is introduced which work same as outguess but for embedding message bit decrease the selected coefficient value by one. YASS [14] divides the image into big blocks and uses a key which randomly select a host 8×8 block for performing DCT on all blocks. Error correction codes are used for encoding the message then apply inverse DCT to the selected host block and finally get compressed image.

Raja et al. [15] introduced an hybrid steganography by combining LSB and DCT on image cover media which makes secret message more secure by double security and maintains image quality. First, secret bits embedded by replacing LSBs of the cover media after that resultant image is passed for DCT in order to get final stego image. For enhancing security, quantization followed by coding algorithm compressed the resultant stego image.

Raftari et al. [16] used IWT and DCT for embedding an secret image into frequency components of cover image by using Munkre's algorithm which preserve image quality with the help of horizontal, diagonal and vertical detailed bands of DCT components. This technique gives good visual quality stego image with security.

Chang et al. [17] presented their proposal of hiding in JPEG images by dividing into 8×8 blocks. For improving visual quality of the image, middle quantized DCT components are used for embedding. Modified Quantization table sets the pixels in middle frequency region to 1. Secret data is then hidden into the two LSB of each middle frequency part.

Subsequently, Sakai et al. [18] introduced a steganographic technique where noisy region blocks are not used for hiding purpose. Blocks are divided into smooth and noisy. Smooth part of the image is selected by using DC component of the neighboring blocks. This method makes detection difficult by hiding in smooth region only.

Almohammad et al. [19] introduced 16×16 block based embedding technique and correspondingly use the quantized matrix of 16×16 matrix by using the same technique as used in [15]. By modifying the size of block from 8×8 to 16×16 hiding capacity of data increased and the computational time is less than the above method.

Natee Vongurai's work [20] modified the previous work by further increasing the block size to 32×132 and corresponding quantization matrix size from 16×16 to 32×32 by cubic interpolation technique which further increased the embedding capacity and reduced the computational time. But increasing in size of quantization table also increased the number of cover image DCT coefficients for embedding which affected the quality of image and made the algorithm more complex.

DCT-M3 [21] embedded the message in an image by considering modulus-3 as base factor instead of modulus-2, i.e., In each 8×8 block, only 2 bits of secret message are embedded by computing modulus 3 of the difference of two non-overlapping AC components from the selected random series and then embed the 2-bit of compressed secret information accordingly in the source image. This increased the embedding rate by maintaining minimum perceptibility and produced stego image with less entropy which means less manipulation required which improves the quality.

3   Proposed Work

In the present paper, DCT technique is used to embed text information in a digital image. As explained above, DCT technique has low frequency, high frequency and middle frequency components. Each frequency part has some information about the image. So, embedding secret information in these frequency components may change the original information of the image. To keep the original image information secure with the secret message, embedding should be less perceptible with more capacity. If low frequency components are selected for embedding data then image quality will be ruined as it contains more information about the image. If data will be hidden in high frequency part then the coding technique will be affected. So, in the present paper, last two row of low frequency, first two rows of high frequency and middle frequency components diagonally are selected for embedding. Figure 3 shows the embedding flow diagram:

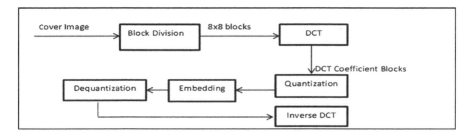

Fig. 3. Embedding process.

3.1   Embedding Process

Gray and colored images are used as cover files for embedding secret message. For embedding, first the image will be divided into 8×8 blocks and if padding requires it will be applied to the last block of the image. Second step is to apply DCT and quantization then embed the message bits at selected positions, i.e. last two row of low frequency component, middle frequency component and first two row of high frequency component at alternate coefficients (Fig. 4).

Algorithm 1. Embedding Algorithm

Input: Secret text file (M) and the Original Image (I_c)
Output: Steg Image (I_s)

1. Divide Original image into non-overlapping 8×8 chunks.
2. Apply DCT on each 8×8 chunk from top left to bottom right.
3. Quantization of each DCT coefficient by using standard 8×8 quantization table values.
4. Instead of embedding in every pixel, embed the information into selected quantized components of each chunk and selection of these positions is highlighted in figure 4:

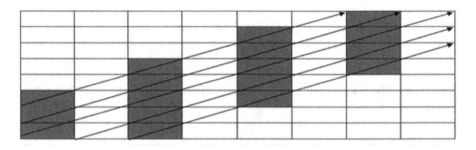

Fig. 4. Embedding positions in a block.

5. Alternate pixels are used for embedding as:

$$x = f(x) = \begin{cases} x+1, & 0 \le x < 1; \quad \text{extract } s == 1 \\ x-1, & 0 \le x < 1; \quad \text{extract } s == 0 \\ x-0.5, & x < 0; \quad \text{else } x+0.5 \end{cases} \tag{1}$$

Here, s is secret message bit. x and xx are DCT coefficients before hiding and after hiding correspondingly.
6. Apply dequantization on the resultant block by multiplying it with quantization table.
7. Apply inverse DCT on each block and finally stego-image (I_s) will be obtained.

3.2 Extraction Process

Extraction procedure is reverse of the hiding process. The extraction algorithm is described as:

Algorithm 2. Extraction Algorithm

Input: Steg Image (I_s).
Output: Extracted secret text file (M) and the original Image (I_c).

1. Divide suspicious image (I_s) into non-overlapping 8×8 blocks.
2. Apply DCT on each 8×8 block from top left to bottom right.
3. Quantization of each DCT coefficient by using standard 8×8 quantization table values.
4. Extract the information from the selected positions from each block as:

$$x = f(x) = \begin{cases} x - 1, & 1 \leq x < 2; & \text{extract } s == 1 \\ x + 1, & -1 \leq x < 0; & \text{extract } s == 0 \\ x + 0.5, & x < 0.5; & \text{else } x - 0.5 \end{cases} \tag{2}$$

5. Dequantize the blocks and apply inverse DCT to get the hidden data (M) and original image (I_c) back.

---

4 Experimental Result

This section will give simulation and experimental results. The proposed method, Sakai's method and Chang's method are Experimented with data set of four images shown in Fig. 6(a–h) with their stego image. Experiments are done on MATLAB 2012a windows 7, CPU core i7 with 10 GB of RAM. For analysis, data set of 4 images is used and all methods are evaluated with these '$m \times n$' cover images as 'C' and 'S' as stego image over 3 parameters:

(1) PSNR. (2) Mean Squared Error (MSE). (3) Capacity.

PSNR is a quality matric which distinguish cover and stego image. PSNR value and quality are directly proportional. It varies from 0 to 1. Poor quality is indicated by 0 and high quality by 1. For a good steganography technique, PSNR should approach to 1. Table 1 shows the PSNR of all the three methods and Fig. 5(a) shows this comparison by plot.

$$PSNR = 10 \log_{10} \left(\frac{max_i^2}{MSE} \right) = 20 \log_{10} \left(\frac{max_i}{\sqrt{MSE}} \right) \tag{3}$$

Table 1. Comparison of PSNR(db).

Methods	Images			
	Lena	Baboon	Forest	Autumn
Chang et al.	44.4	40.9	48.8	41.4
Sakai's	50.56	48.6	55.1	43.6
Our method	60.18	64.8	55.8	49.9

MSE is an average of the squares of errors. MSE indicates upper bound of the errors acceptable in an algorithm. For good embedding technique it should be as less as it can be. Table 2 shows MSE of all the three methods and Fig. 5(b) shows this comparison by plot.

$$MSE = \frac{1}{mn} \sum_{0 \leq i \leq m-1} \sum_{0 \leq j \leq n-1} \|S(i,j) - C(i,j)\|^2 \tag{4}$$

Table 2. Comparison of MSE.

Methods	Images			
	Lena	Baboon	Forest	Autumn
Chang et al.	0.0099	0.0082	0.0096	0.0094
Sakai's	0.0099	0.0087	0.0102	0.0087
Our method	0.0095	0.0070	0.0096	0.0090

Hiding capacity of a cover file is one of the major matric for evaluating a Steganography technique. It is measured as number of bits of cover image used for embedding. During embedding data, one of necessary requirement is having more capacity for data to transfer securely in an imperceptible way. Table 3 shows the comparison of PSNR of all the three methods and Fig. 5(c) shows this comparison by plot.

Table 3. Comparison of capacity (bits).

Methods	Images			
	Lena	Baboon	Forest	Autumn
Chang et al.	20800	20800	10806	5677
Sakai's	1538	1538	1495	1773
Our method	90086	90086	46776	23001

All the comparison showed that the proposed technique has good capacity with better quality, which is requirement of a good steganography technique.

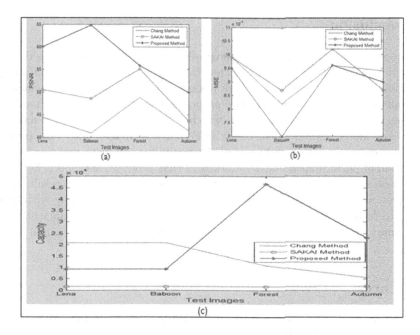

Fig. 5. Comparison of existing method with proposed method.

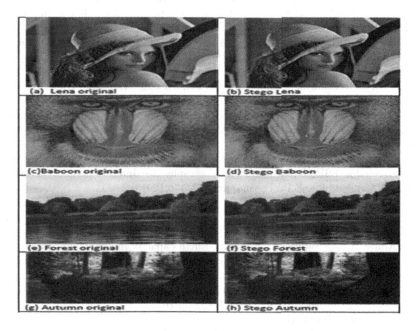

Fig. 6. Image data set for analysis.

5   Conclusion

This proposed frequency based steganography technique embeds secret data in DCT components of the image. Selected Coefficients for hiding are only from the middle frequency, two rows of high frequency and low frequency coefficients diagonally at alternate locations. The proposed algorithm will either modify or keep the DCT coefficients value same which will depend on the secret message bits. Cover image should be of larger size than the hidden file. This process will be repeated for all 8×8 blocks of the image for complete message length. Evaluation of performance matrices indicates that proposed method is better in comparison to Sakai's method and Chang's method. Experimental result shows that given method has more hiding capacity than the existing one with good PSNR. In future, this work can be extended by changing the coefficient value up to some extend and find out some threshold value for high capacity and better quality.

References

1. Anderson, R.J., Petitcolas, F.A.P.: On the limits of steganography. IEEE J. Sel. A. Commun. **16**, 474–481 (2006)
2. Cox, I., Miller, M., Bloom, J., Fridrich, J., Kalker, T.: Digital Water-marking and Steganography. Morgan Kaufmann Pub-lishers Inc., San Francisco (2008)
3. Petitcolas, F.A.P., Anderson, R.J., Kuhn, M.G.: Information hiding-a survey. Proc. IEEE **87**, 1062–1078 (1999)
4. Celik, M.U., Sharma, G., Tekalp, A.M., Saber, E.: Reversible data hiding. In: Proceedings of the International Conference on Image Processing, vol. 2, pp. 157–160 (2002)
5. Ker, A.D.: Steganalysis of embedding in two least-signicant bits. IEEE Trans. Inf. Forensics Secur. **2**, 46–54 (2007)
6. Yu, L., Zhao, Y., Ni, R., Li, T.: Improved adaptive LSB steganography based on chaos and genetic algorithm. EURASIP J. Adv. Signal Process. **2010**, 876–946 (2010)
7. Shreelekshmi, R., Wilscy , M., Madhavan, C.E.V.: Cover image preprocessing for more reliable LSB re-placement steganography. In: International Conference on Signal Acquisition and Processing, pp. 153–156 (2010)
8. Acharya, T., Tsai, P.-S.: JPEG2000 Standard for Image Compression: Concepts, Algorithms and VLSI Architectures. Wiley Interscience, New York (2004). ISBN. 0471484229
9. Al Ataby, A., Al Naima, F.: A modified high capacity image steganography technique based on wavelet transform. Int. Arab J. Inf. Technol. **7**, 358–364 (2010)
10. Naoum, R., Shihab, A., Al Hamouz, S.: Enhanced image steganography system based on discrete wavelet transformation and resilient back propagation. Int. J. Comput. Sci. Network Secur. **16**, 114–122 (2016)
11. Allan Latham. Jphide (2008)
12. Provos, N.: Software OutGuess (2001). www.outguess.org
13. Westfeld, A.: F5—a steganographic algorithm. In: Moskowitz, I.S. (ed.) IH 2001. LNCS, vol. 2137, pp. 289–302. Springer, Heidelberg (2001). https://doi.org/10.1007/3-540-45496-9_21

14. Solanki, K., Sarkar, A., Manjunath, B.S.: YASS: yet another steganographic scheme that resists blind steganalysis. In: Furon, T., Cayre, F., Doërr, G., Bas, P. (eds.) IH 2007. LNCS, vol. 4567, pp. 16–31. Springer, Heidelberg (2007). https://doi.org/10.1007/978-3-540-77370-2_2

15. Raja, K.B., Chowdary, C.R.: A secure image steganography using lSB, DCT and compression techniques on raw images. In: Proceedings of the IEEE 3rd International Conference on Intelligent Sensing and Information Processing 2005 (ICISIP), pp. 170–176 (2005)

16. Raftari, N., Moghadam, A.M.E.: Digital image steganography based on assignment algorithm and combination of DCT-IWT. In: 2012 Fourth International Conference on Computational Intelligence, Communication Systems and Networks (CICSyN), pp. 295–300. IEEE (2012)

17. Chang, C.-C., Chen, T.-S., Chung, L.-Z.: A steganographic method based upon JPEG and quantization table modification. Inf. Sci. **141**, 123–138 (2002)

18. Sakai, H., Kuribayashi, M., Mori, M.: Adaptive reversible data hiding for JPEG images. In: International Symposium on Information Theory and Its Applications, pp. 1–6 (2008)

19. Almohammad, A., Hierons, R.M., Ghinea, G.: High capacity steganographic method based upon JPEG. In: Third International Conference on Availability, Reliability and Security, pp. 544–549 (2008)

20. Vongurai, N., Phimoltares, S.: Frequency-based steganography using 32×32 interpolated quantization table and discrete cosine transform. In: Fourth International Conference on Computational Intelligence, Modelling and Simulation, pp. 249–253 (2012)

21. AwadAttaby, A., Mursi Ahmed, M.F.M., Alsammak, A.K.: Data hiding inside JPEG images with high resistance to steganalysis using a novel technique: DCT-M3. Ain Shams Eng. J. **9**(4), 1–10 (2017)

A Machine Learning Based Approach to Driver Drowsiness Detection

Swapnil Misal[1](✉) [ID] and Binoy B. Nair[2] [ID]

[1] Department of Electronics and Communication Engineering,
Amrita School of Engineering, Amrita Vishwa Vidyapeetham, Coimbatore, India
swapnilmisal001@gmail.com
[2] SIERS Research Laboratory,
Department of Electronics and Communication Engineering,
Amrita School of Engineering, Amrita Vishwa Vidyapeetham, Coimbatore, India
b_binoy@cb.amrita.edu

Abstract. Drowsy driving is a major cause of road accidents around the globe. A driver fatigue detection system that can alert the drowsy driver in a timely manner will therefore be of great help in improving road safety. This paper provides a non-invasive, camera-based innovative technique for detection of driver drowsiness based on eye blinking and mouth movement. A camera is mounted on the car dashboard facing the driver. First, face, eye and mouth of the driver are extracted from the images captured by the camera. Next, features for eyes and mouth are extracted and a classifier based detection system identifies if the driver is fatigued. Results demonstrate that the proposed system can efficiently identify indications of drowsiness on the drivers face.

Keywords: Yawning · Eye PERCLOS · Fatigue

1 Introduction

Driver response time is affected due to fatigue which significantly increases the chances of an accident. Monotony on free-flow traffic highway, night-time driving, sleep deprivation, lighting situations, medication or alcohol leads to drowsiness. India's National Crime Records Bureau (NCRB) has recorded that 44–65% of all fatal road accidents are due to drinking and driving [1] and 72% of accidents are on state and national highways. National Highway Traffic Safety Administration (NHTSA) also recorded yearly 886 fatal crashes and approximate 37,000 injury [2].

In many cases, the driver himself/herself cannot recognize their fatigue level, which is a very important issue that needs to be considered. Therefore use of a driver assistance system for drowsiness detection is extremely important. In this paper, a machine learning based fatigue detection system is proposed. A dashboard mounted camera is used for continuously monitoring the driver. Driver's face is first detected using Viola-Jones algorithm, features of eyes and mouth are then extracted and a classifier is then used to detect the presence or absence of fatigue. Remainder of this paper is organized as follows: Sect. 2 presents survey of literature in the area, proposed technique is discussed in Sect. 3, results and analysis are in Sect. 4, with the final conclusions presented in Sect. 5.

© Springer Nature Singapore Pte Ltd. 2019
S. Minz et al. (Eds.): ICICCT 2018, CCIS 835, pp. 150–159, 2019.
https://doi.org/10.1007/978-981-13-5992-7_13

2   Literature Survey

Following are the parameters which when monitored can be used for drowsiness detection:

- Methods based on driver's current state:
  (A) Visual features:
    - Eye PRECLOS [3]
    - Eye Blinking rate [4]
    - Yawing
    - Head nodding
    - Distance between steering wheel and driver
  (B) Non-visual features:
    - Heart rate variability
    - Electrocardiogram
    - Electroencephalogram
    - Electromyogram
    - Electro-oculogram
    - Photoplethysmography

- Methods based on driver performance:
    - Vehicle Speed Monitoring
    - Steering wheel sensor [5]
    - Monitoring frequency of brake
    - Distance between Vehicles

Some other techniques include [6] Methods based on driver performance do not always provide advance information about drowsiness, as performance is measured after driver has been experiencing fatigue for certain amount of time. Also, driver discomfort needs to be taken into account and hence, a non-contact/non-invasive technique for driver drowsiness (and hence, fatigue) detection using camera based detection of facial features is proposed. The proposed system provides good trade-off between accuracy of detection and comfort of driver.

There have been studies involving camera-based detection of facial features. Qiao et al. proposed an android based smartphone application for detecting drowsiness [7]. Geometrical location of eyes and mouth after detecting face is used for defining ROI. Variance in black pixels in current and previous frame is then used to predict drowsiness. Convolution Neural Network has been employed in [8] to detect drowsiness using eye features. Features extracted from eye region of the person's image to detect fatigue have also been used in [9]. Detection of mouth movement for detection of yawning as an indication of drowsiness is presented in [10]. Head movement (nodding) tracked with the help of depth imaging can also be used for fatigue detection, as in [11].

It is observed from the surveyed literature that most important features for non-invasive/non-contact fatigue (drowsiness) detection is to track eyes and mouth. Tracking head movements in addition can improve accuracy but includes depth imaging which leads to costly hardware usage. Hence, in the present study, features extracted from both eyes and mouth are considered for drowsiness detection.

3 Methodology

Following are the steps involved in the proposed drowsiness detection system:

(a) Capture video sequence
(b) Face detection and extraction
(c) Eye and Mouth region extraction
(d) Detection of drowsy state

Overall functioning of the system is presented in Fig. 1.

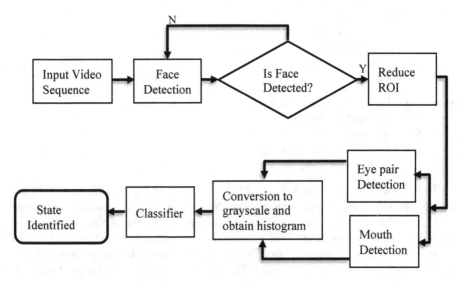

Fig. 1. Proposed system block diagram

3.1 Capture Video Sequence

Camera is placed on the car dashboard to capture videos at 30 fps. The images are resized to 640 × 480 for further processing. Figure 2 shows the camera setup for video capturing.

Fig. 2. Camera setup for video input

3.2 Face Detection and Extraction

Machine learning based approach is used for detection of the face from the captured images [12]. The technique employed in the present study is Viola-Jones framework [13]. Steps in algorithm are given below:

Haar Features. Classification based on features is faster compared to working with pixels. So, Haar features are selected for face detection. These are extracted by using a set of kernels as shown in Fig. 3. These kernels with varying sizes are convolved with image sub-windows of fixed size e.g. 24 × 24 and generate 180000+ Haar features. But all the features extracted are not required for successful detection of faces. Hence most important features with respect to face detection are selected using a boosting algorithm. Viola-Jones framework employs Adaboost [14] algorithm.

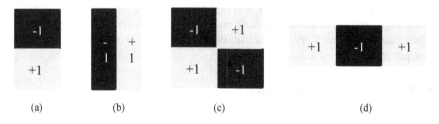

Fig. 3. Haar features

AdaBoost [14] Algorithm. Viola-Jones algorithm uses AdaBoost technique for selection of both effective features which have significant variety and a small set of good classification functions for particular classifiers. This is the process during training of model. Following are steps in AdaBoost algorithm:

(i)   Assign same weights to training examples
(ii)   Find weighted error for each input feature and select the best
(iii) Re-assign the weights as follows:

> Wrongly classified => more weight
> Correctly classified => less weight

(iv)   Final classifier is combination of the weak ones, weighted according to error

Cascade Classifier. The classifiers and threshold values obtained from boosting technique are then used in cascade manner to reduce computational time on negative images. Consider 3 stage cascade classifier with 33 features as shown in Fig. 4.

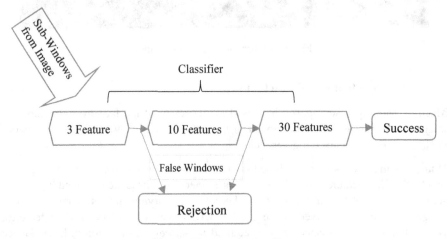

Fig. 4. Three stage classifier

Detection rate per stage is 100% and rejection increases with stage, consider 50% for first stage, second stage will be 80% and third will be 98%. This cumulative false positive rate is used as a criteria for AdaBoost algorithm for selection of weak classifiers per stage.

3.3   Eye and Mouth Region Extraction

After extraction of face from image, face area is again divided in two partitions to reduce image size to detect Eye and Mouth region using Viola-Jones framework. Figure 5 provides an example of regions detected for further processing.

Eye and Mouth region extracted from face are converted to grayscale. Distribution of intensity for grey scaled images is obtained using histogram plot with 10 bins. These bins serve as features for a classification algorithm detecting drowsiness condition (Fig. 6).

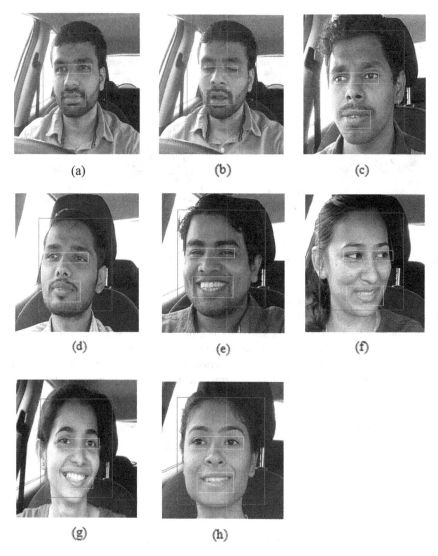

Fig. 5. Face, Mouth and Eyes Detection and marking with bounding boxes under (a) normal driving and (b) drowsy driving and (c), (d), (e), (f), (g), (h) are samples of test subjects

3.4 Identifying Drowsy State

Yawning is a sure sign of drowsiness. It is observed that during yawning, the eyes get closed while the mouth is simultaneously open. Hence, in this study, the one of the main criterion for drowsiness is defined as:

IF eyes = closed AND mouth = Open THEN CLASS = Drowsy
Else
CLASS = Not Drowsy

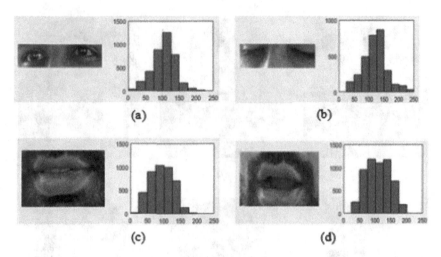

Fig. 6. Histogram plot for (a) Eyes open, (b) Eyes closed, (c) Mouth closed, (d) Mouth open

This detection of drowsiness based on closing and opening of mouth is detected using the change in the number of pixels in the bins of eye and mouth histograms using machine learning. A decision tree classifier is employed. Decision tree is most widely used in supervised learning, with most promising attribute as root. The attribute selection is done using information gain criterion. The attribute with highest gain value is selected as the splitting attribute to grow the tree at that partition. This process continues till leaf nodes are reached i.e. categories. Consider p_i is probability of sample in D belongs to a particular class and attribute A is used to split D into v partitions to classify D, Eqs. (1), (2) and (3) used for selection of feature as head at every level.

$$Info(D) = -\sum\nolimits_{i=1}^{n} p_i log_2(p_i) \tag{1}$$

$$Info_A(D) = \sum\nolimits_{i=1}^{v} \frac{|D_i|}{|D|} * Info(D_i) \tag{2}$$

$$Gain(A) = Info(D) - Info_A(D) \tag{3}$$

Using features discussed in Sect. 3.3 and obtaining samples with same features, a decision tree model is trained, which is used to classify drowsy condition. An example of a decision tree generated as the result is presented in Fig. 7. In the figure, the two classes are Drowsy and Not_Drowsy. The mouth features (10 histogram bins for the mouth) are represented as **MouthX,** where **X** is the bin number. Similarly, the eye features (10 histogram bins for the eye) are represented as **EyeX,** where **X** is the bin number.

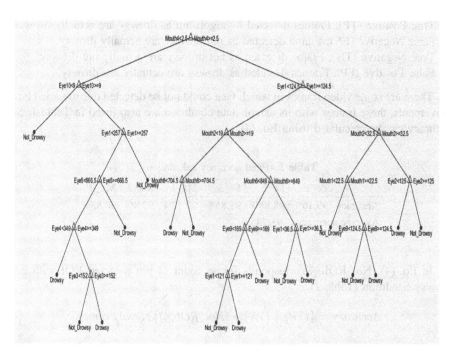

Fig. 7. Example of decision tree used for the third female (Fe_3) test subject mentioned in results

4   Result and Analysis

The proposed system is evaluated on six subjects (three male (Ma_1-Ma_3) and three female (Fe_1-Fe_3)) [18]. Table 1 below provides the details of detection per subject. Following are some terms to be known for further understanding.

Table 1. Detailed analysis of algorithm performance on six different persons

Subjects	Total frames	Drowsy frames		Not drowsy frames		ROI not detected frames	
		TP	FN	TN	FP	Not drowsy	Drowsy
Fe_1	1068	249	4	747	5	63	0
Fe_2	1163	179	4	808	9	163	0
Fe_3	1391	128	3	1158	4	89	9
Ma_1	1705	322	7	1300	5	69	2
Ma_2	1273	159	13	1064	15	22	0
Ma_3	874	40	0	696	10	128	0

True Positive (TP): Frames detected by algorithm as drowsy are actually drowsy.
False Negative (FN): Frame detected as not drowsy are actually drowsy.
True Negative (TN): Frame detected as not drowsy are actually not drowsy.
False Positive (FP): Frames detected as drowsy are actually not drowsy.

There are some video frames in which face could not be detected due to varied head movements, these frames with its actual state condition are also listed in Table 1. So, accuracy can be calculated using Eq. (4).

Table 2. Final accuracy calculations

	Fe_1	Fe_2	Fe_3	Ma_1	Ma_2	Ma_3
Accuracy	99.16%	98.88%	98.85%	99.17%	97.8%	98.85%
Average accuracy = 98.785%						

In Eq. (4), Not_ROI_{ND} corresponds frame count of not detected ROI with not-drowsy condition (Table 2).

$$Accuracy = \{(TP) + (TN) + (Not\_ROI_{ND})\}/Total\,Frames \qquad (4)$$

5 Conclusions

This paper presents an effective non-contact/non-invasive solution to detect driver drowsiness (fatigue). The system uses Viola-Jones framework for detection of eye and mouth from the image of drivers face. The extracted features from eye and mouth are used to identify drowsy/non-drowsy state using a decision tree based classifier. The system tested on six different subjects (three male and three female) performs detection with overall accuracy of 98.78% for a total of 7474 frames considered. Some of the issues that need to be addressed include effective detection of eye open/close condition while wearing spectacles. Future enhancements could involve application of deep learning algorithms [16] to further speed up the detection process.

Acknowledgement. The authors like to thank the persons who readily accepted to be part of performance evaluation of system proposed in this paper.

References

1. National Crime Records Bureau (NCRB), Traffic Accidents in India (2014). http://ncrb.nic.in/StatPublications/ADSI/ADSI2014/chapter-1A%20traffic%20accidents.pdf
2. National Highway Traffic Safety Administration (NHTSA), Drowsy Driving. https://www.nhtsa.gov/risky-driving/drowsy-driving
3. Leng, L.B., Giin, L.B., Chung, W.-Y.: Wearable driver drowsiness detection system based on biomedical and motion sensors. In: IEEE SENSORS, pp. 1–4. IEEE (2015)

4. Drutarovský, T: Driver's Microsleep Detection. Bachelor thesis, Faculty of Informatics and Information Technologies, Slovak University of Technology, Bratislava (2014)
5. Ramesh, M.V., Nair, A.K., Kunnathu, A.T.: Real-time automated multiplexed sensor system for driver drowsiness detection. In: 2011 7th International Conference on Wireless Communications, Networking and Mobile Computing (WiCOM), pp. 1–4. IEEE, September 2011
6. Jia, W., Peng, H., Ruan, N., Tang, Z., Zhao, W.: WiFind: driver fatigue detection with fine-grained Wi-Fi signal features. IEEE Trans. Big Data. https://doi.org/10.1109/TBDATA. 2018.2848969
7. Qiao, Y., Zeng, K., Xu, L., Yin, X.: A smartphone-based driver fatigue detection using fusion of multiple real-time facial features. In: 2016 13th IEEE Annual Consumer Communications & Networking Conference (CCNC), pp. 230–235. IEEE, January 2016
8. Zhang, F., Su, J., Geng, L., Xiao, Z.: Driver fatigue detection based on eye state recognition. In: International Conference on Machine Vision and Information Technology (CMVIT), pp. 105–110. IEEE, February 2017
9. Harisanker, M., Shanmugha Sundaram, R.: Development of a nonintrusive driver drowsiness monitoring system. In: Jain, L.C., Patnaik, S., Ichalkaranje, N. (eds.) Intelligent Computing, Communication and Devices. AISC, vol. 308, pp. 737–743. Springer, New Delhi (2015). https://doi.org/10.1007/978-81-322-2012-1_79
10. Akrout, B., Mahdi, W.: Yawning detection by the analysis of variational descriptor for monitoring driver drowsiness. In: 2016 International Image Processing, Applications and Systems (IPAS), pp. 1–5. IEEE. November 2016
11. Wongphanngam, J., Pumrin, S.: Fatigue warning system for driver nodding off using depth image from Kinect. In: 2016 13th International Conference on Electrical Engineering/ Electronics, Computer, Telecommunications and Information Technology (ECTI-CON), pp. 1–6. IEEE, June 2016
12. Martin, S., Tawari, A., Trivedi, M.M: Balancing privacy and safety: protecting driver identity in naturalistic driving video data. In: 6th International Conference on Automotive User Interfaces and Interactive Vehicular Applications, pp. 1–7. ACM, September 2014
13. Viola, P., Jones, M.: Rapid object detection using a boosted cascade of simple features. In: Proceedings of the 2001 IEEE Computer Society Conference on Computer Vision and Pattern Recognition, CVPR 2001, vol. 1, pp. I-511–I-518. IEEE (2001)
14. Freund, Y., Schapire, R.E.: A desicion-theoretic generalization of on-line learning and an application to boosting. In: Vitányi, P. (ed.) EuroCOLT 1995. LNCS, vol. 904, pp. 23–37. Springer, Heidelberg (1995). https://doi.org/10.1007/3-540-59119-2_166
15. Test Subject Dataset. https://drive.google.com/open?id=1hTkOi27CcYw4Q9rOOci6e D6lGADs4a-m
16. Saeed, A.: Deep Physiological Arousal Detection in a Driving Simulator. Master thesis: MSc Computer Science, August 2017
17. Wetzel, L., et al.: Glycosyltransferase homologs prevent promiscuous cell aggregation and promote multicellular development in the choanoflagellate S. rosetta, bioRxiv 384453 (2018). https://doi.org/10.1101/384453

A Hybrid Framework for Detecting Non-basic Emotions in Text

Abid Hussain Wani$^{(\boxtimes)}$ ⓘ and Rana Hashmy

Department of Computer Science, University of Kashmir, Srinagar, J&K, India
`abid.wani@uok.edu.in`

Abstract. The task of Emotion Detection from Text has received substantial attention in the recent years. Although most of the work in this field has been conducted considering only the basic set of six emotions, yet there are a number of applications wherein the importance of non-basic emotions (like interest, engagement, confusion, frustration, disappointment, boredom, hopefulness, satisfaction) is paramount. A number of applications like student feedback analysis, online forum analysis and product manual evaluation require the identification of non-basic emotions to suggest improvements and enhancements. In this study, we propose a hybrid framework for the detection and classification of such non-basic emotions from text. Our framework principally uses Support Vector Machine to detect non-basic emotions. The emotions which go undetected in supervised learning are attempted to be detected by using the lexical and semantic information from word2vec predictive model. The results obtained utilizing this framework are quite encouraging and comparable to state-of-the-art techniques available.

Keywords: Emotion detection · Non-basic emotions · Text classification · Hybrid framework · Human Computer Interaction

1 Introduction

Emotions form an inherent and natural ingredient of human behavior. In response to various external and internal processes we express our emotions through written text, verbal communications as well as through facial expressions and body language. With the growing emphasis on the use of computing technologies for carrying out tasks which otherwise are not easily manageable for humans and often prone to errors, automatic emotion detection from text has received substantial attention in natural language processing. The recent advancements in Human-Computer-Interaction field have given a boost to work in this area.

The recognition of affect is critical to a number of applications and interfaces because an interface or application can never respond to users' affective states if it not in a position to sense and detect their affective states [1]. A number of studies have been carried out for emotion detection from facial expressions [2, 3] and written text [4–6]. Most of the work that has been carried out for the detection of emotions in text embarks upon recognition of only a set a six basic emotions proposed by Ekman [7], however, many applications in essence require detection of a larger set of emotions for

© Springer Nature Singapore Pte Ltd. 2019
S. Minz et al. (Eds.): ICICCT 2018, CCIS 835, pp. 160–166, 2019.
https://doi.org/10.1007/978-981-13-5992-7_14

more their effectiveness. Applications like student feedback analysis, online forum analysis and product manual evaluation require the identification of non-basic emotions to suggest improvements and enhancements. In fact in one study [8], it is suggested that engagement non-basic emotions like boredom, confusion, and frustration figured at five times the rate that of basic emotions. We attempt to detect set of eight non- basic emotions i.e., interest, engagement, confusion, frustration, disappointment, boredom, hopefulness, satisfaction in text by employing a hybrid framework comprising principally of Support Vector Machine to classify and k-means algorithm propelled by word2vec to fine tune the classification by extract semantically similar words from sentences.

2   Hybrid Framework

The problem of detecting affect from text has been approached by a number of ways. Most common approaches to emotion recognition include keyword spotting, machine learning-based (supervised, unsupervised or hybrid) and knowledge-based techniques. Although each approach has its own strengths and weaknesses yet there is lot of scope for improving upon them for most of them to robustly sense the affect in text and are able to achieve a fine-grained emotion classification [9]. Considering the fundamental fact that statistical Natural Language Processing techniques often require a good number of sentences or corpus as input to achieve reasonable accuracy as they are inherently semantically weaker.

We propose a hybrid framework for the detection of eight non-basic emotions from text which principally uses both Support Vector Machine and semantic information from word2vec to classify the sentences as per the emotion expressed in the sentence. In our experiments we found that a good number of sentences were classified as neutral by our supervised algorithm although they actually conveyed some affect sense. In order to deal with this issue we employed lexical resources like WordNet and Oxford Dictionary to retrieve the similar words for all emotion categories i.e., interest, engagement, confusion, frustration, disappointment, boredom, hopefulness, satisfaction. We then employed this lexical information to retrieve word-vectors for all entries in each of our emotion-wordsets. Utilizing word2vec enabled us to get the semantic information about words which we then used to arrive at final emotion label for a sentence. As our approach models affect at the sentence level and takes into account both lexical and semantic information, therefore there are less chances of it being tricked by structural features like ambiguity and negation at the word-level. Figure 1 depicts the proposed framework.

2.1   Supervised Classification of Sentences

In our study we used the student feedback dataset from extended Oza's dataset [10] which comprises of the students feedback for different lecture series. As the proposed framework utilizes supervised learning (SVM) to detect affect from the textual student responses we annotated each response with an emotion label among the eight emotions (interest, engagement, confusion, frustration, disappointment, boredom, hopefulness,

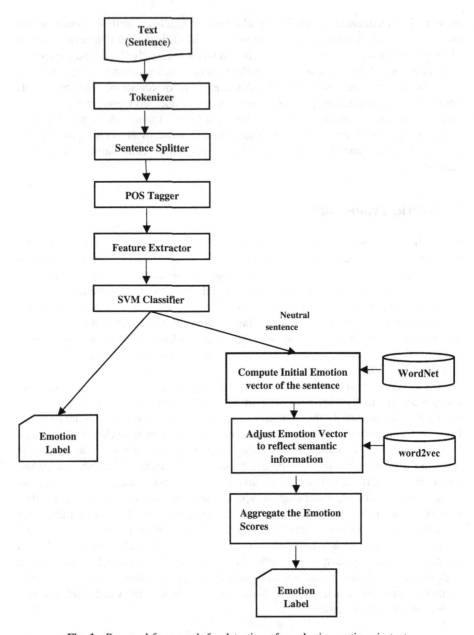

Fig. 1. Proposed framework for detection of non-basic emotions in text

satisfaction). This set of non-basic emotions is clearly more relevant in the given setup. To conduct our experiment for the same, four annotators labeled this data by providing relevant emotion label for each response or annotating the sentence as neutral if it does not convey any affect sense. The feedback from students being received as sentences, our focus is on the sentence-level analysis.

The interpretation and sensing of affect varies from one person to another. This interpretation, particularly for written text is profoundly subjective [11], and therefore the annotation for feedback responses can subtly vary between different judges, therefore annotation was carried out by four judges in our study. To compare inter-annotator agreement we used Cohen's kappa. The average inter-annotator agreement was 0.78. Table 1 depicts the pair-wise inter-annotator agreement in emotional categories.

Table 1. Inter-annotator agreement for non-basic emotions

Category	J1↔J2	J1↔J3	J1↔J4	Average
Interest	0.78	0.64	0.74	0.72
Engagement	0.56	0.58	0.68	0.60
Confusion	0.81	0.87	0.89	0.85
Frustration	0.80	0.75	0.71	0.75
Disappointment	0.68	0.54	0.55	0.59
Boredom	0.75	0.65	0.69	0.69
Hopefulness	0.71	0.72	0.68	0.70
Satisfaction	0.86	0.81	0.88	0.85

As is evident from the results of the inter-annotation agreement, there is a variation in agreement among the human judges. The results show that among all emotion categories, the annotators mostly agree in identifying instances of confusion and satisfaction.

2.2 Unsupervised Classification of Left-Over Sentences

While classifying sentences for non-basic emotions using Support Vector Machine, we found that a majority (47%) of the sentences were classified as neutral. In order to classify these leftover sentences we employed lexical resources such as WordNet and Oxford Dictionary and word2vec to classify the leftover corpus. Words which are lexically and semantically connected to each other were put into separate files; one for each emotion category. Each entry of the file contains two fields: the word itself and its weight. Theses weights are the used to populate the emotion vector. We use WordNet to capture the lexical relatedness and word2vec to capture the semantic affinity. The emotion vector is first populated by the weights assigned to the words in each wordset. The weights assigned in this study are as under:

WordNet weight (w_{wn}): Words extracted for each emotion category from WordNet which essentially represent the synonyms are assigned a weight of 0.9.

word2vec weight (w_{wv}): We train the word2vec model using Wikipedia text dump. Words in the vector for each category are assigned a weight of 0.7.

One exceptional case to handle is if a word appears in more than wordset-file. In order to deal with duplication of word in different wordset- files, we keep only the word which has highest weight and remove all of its other duplications. All the above weights have been assigned empirically.

2.3   Computation of Emotion Vector

In order to assign a specific emotion label to a sentence, we computed the emotion vector. The emotion vector is computed at two levels: word and sentence level. The emotion vector for each word contained in a sentence is computed by summing the weight of word from both the associated weights. Suppose w_l is the weight from this weighted lexicon then we have,

$$w = w_{wn} + w_{wv} \tag{1}$$

To calculate the emotion vector of whole sentence, we take the summation of all affect words, as shown in (2).

$$\alpha_s = \sum\nolimits_{k=1}^{n} w_k \tag{2}$$

where n is the total number of words, with stop-words dropped.

Once the emotion vector of a sentence is calculated, if the highest score is more than a threshold value t, the sentence is labeled with that very emotion otherwise it qualifies as neutral. The final emotion label L_S is computed as

$$L_S = \begin{cases} E_k & \text{if } \alpha_S > t \\ Neutral & otherwise \end{cases} \tag{3}$$

3   Evaluation and Results

We evaluated our framework for emotion detection and classification by employing Leave-one-out cross validation, in which N separate times, the classifier (SVM) is trained on all the data except for one point and a SVM output is generated for that point. The highest accuracy achieved in our experiments was 81.25%. In our experiments, the replacement of slangs (e.g. "yass" with "yes") and orthographic features (e.g. "sooo fruuustrating") has not been handled. Moreover the utility of domain-specific knowledge has not been investigated, which is likely to improve our results. In future experiments, we will work in these areas to better gauge the emotion expressed in student feedback (Table 2).

The results were compared using the standard measures of Precision, Recall and F1-score. The results obtained that using our framework on Luo's dataset [12] best classification accuracy were achieved for "confusion" and "satisfaction". For Oza's dataset, best results were achieved for satisfaction, confusion and interest.

Table 2. Precision, Recall and F1-measure.

Emotion category	Luo's dataset			Oza's dataset		
	P	R	F1	P	R	F1
Interest	61.14	63.78	62.43	63.22	59.25	61.17
Engagement	65.62	54.57	59.59	58.75	55.52	57.09
Confusion	71.33	78.12	74.57	68.20	65.98	67.07
Frustration	65.25	61.27	57.28	56.20	62.25	59.07
Disappointment	63.65	69.33	66.37	63.25	55.25	58.98
Boredom	66.23	75.45	70.54	51.33	56.55	53.81
Hopefulness	69.30	60.45	64.57	49.56	55.75	52.47
Satisfaction	78.25	71.25	74.59	74.27	72.03	73.13

4 Conclusion

This paper introduced a novel hybrid framework for the recognition and classification of non-basic emotions from text. Both supervised and unsupervised techniques were used to identify the emotions in text. The recognition of non-basic emotions with reasonable accuracy was achieved which essentially finds applications in a number of areas.

References

1. Calvo, R.A., D'Mello, S.: Affect detection: an interdisciplinary review of models, methods, and their applications. IEEE Trans. Affect. Comput. **1**, 18–37 (2010)
2. Kahou, S.E., et al.: EmoNets: multimodal deep learning approaches for emotion recognition in video. J. Multimodal User Interfaces **10**, 99–111 (2016)
3. Soleymani, M., Asghari-Esfeden, S., Fu, Y., Pantic, M.: Analysis of EEG signals and facial expressions for continuous emotion detection. IEEE Trans. Affect. Comput. **7**, 17–28 (2016)
4. Aman, S., Szpakowicz, S.: Identifying expressions of emotion in text. In: Matoušek, V., Mautner, P. (eds.) TSD 2007. LNCS (LNAI), vol. 4629, pp. 196–205. Springer, Heidelberg (2007). https://doi.org/10.1007/978-3-540-74628-7_27
5. Balahur, A., Tanev, H.: Detecting implicit expressions of affect from text using semantic knowledge on common concept properties. In: Tenth International Conference on Language Resources and Evaluation, LREC 2016, pp. 1165–1170 (2016)
6. Canales, L., Strapparava, C., Boldrini, E., Martnez-Barco, P.: Exploiting a bootstrapping approach for automatic annotation of emotions in texts. In: Proceedings - 3rd IEEE International Conference on Data Science and Advanced Analytics, DSAA 2016, pp. 726–734 (2016)
7. Ekman, P.: An argument for basic emotions. Cogn. Emot. **6**(3–4), 169–200 (1992)
8. D'Mello, S., Calvo, R.A.: Beyond the basic emotions. In: CHI 2013 Extended Abstracts on Human Factors in Computing Systems on - CHI EA 2013, p. 2287. ACM Press, New York (2013)

9. Wani, A., Hashmy, R.: An unsupervised common sense-based learning framework for emotion detection and classification in textual social data. J. Artif. Intell. Res. Adv. **4**, 49–56 (2017)
10. Oza, K.S., Kamat, R.K., Naik, P.G.: Student feedback analysis: a neural network approach. Presented at the 25 March 2017
11. Binali, H., Wu, C., Potdar, V.: Computational approaches for emotion detection in text. In: 4th IEEE International Conference on Digital Ecosystems and Technologies, pp. 172–177. IEEE (2010)
12. Luo, W., Liu, F., Liu, Z., Litman, D.: Automatic summarization of student course feedback. In: Proceedings of the 2016 Conference of the North American Chapter of the Association for Computational Linguistics: Human Language Technologies, pp. 80–85 (2016)

A Novel Feature Selection Method Based on Genetic Algorithm for Opinion Mining of Social Media Reviews

Savita Sangam$^{(\boxtimes)}$ ⓘ and Subhash Shinde

University of Mumbai, Mumbai, India
savita.sangam@gmail.com

Abstract. Use of social media for sharing the opinions about the products or the services by individuals or business organizations is becoming very common nowadays. Consumers are keen to share their views on certain products or commodities. This leads to the generation of large amount of unstructured social media data. Thus text data is being formed gradually in many areas like automated business, education, health care, show business and so on. Opinion mining, the sub field of text mining, deals with mining of review text and classifying the opinions or the sentiments of that text as positive or negative. The work in this paper develops a framework for opinion mining. It includes a novel feature selection method called Most Persistent Feature Selection (MPFS) for feature selection and a genetic algorithm (GA) based optimization technique for optimizing the feature set. MPFS method uses information gain of the features in the review documents. The feature set thus produced is optimized using GA technique to get the most effective feature set for sentiment classification. Then a Support Vector Machine (SVM) algorithm is used for classifying the sentiments of reviews expressed in text with the proposed feature selection and optimization method. The classifier models generated show the acceptable performance in terms of accuracy when compared with the other existing models.

Keywords: Feature selection · Genetic algorithm · Opinion mining · Sentiment classification

1 Introduction

The review data produced by the social media applications may not be in a proper structure and may require lot of processing in order to make it usable. In order to process these reviews, data models need to be constructed. The focus of this research work is to process and analyze the opinions or the sentiments of the social media reviews by applying some data mining techniques. According to Liu [1], the study of analyzing opinions in written language, is termed as opinion mining. According to Pang and Lee [2, 3] "the task of analyzing the opinion, sentiment, and subjectivity computationally is known as opinion mining and it is also called as Sentiment Analysis (SA)". Decision makers rely on SA for making their decisions. For example various shopping sites like Amazon, Flipkart etc. take feedback from the customers which will help them to take proper decisions for improving the quality of their services. SA

© Springer Nature Singapore Pte Ltd. 2019
S. Minz et al. (Eds.): ICICCT 2018, CCIS 835, pp. 167–175, 2019.
https://doi.org/10.1007/978-981-13-5992-7_15

techniques have been applied widely in many areas like business, entertainment, medicine, politics etc. Sentiment Classification (SC) process classifies the sentiments of the text reviews into negative or positive or sometimes neutral. The two main approaches for sentiment classification are; Lexicon Based approach and Machine Learning approach [2, 10]. In Lexicon based approach, a sentiment score is calculated using a lexicon of negative and positive words. A value is assigned to each word to indicate the positivity or the negativity of that word. The overall sentiment of the text is sum or average or any other function of all the words. This approach is domain specific and gives low recall.

The Machine Learning algorithm uses data sets that are labeled to perform the classification task. The classifier gets trained on training data in the form of features which are the words or phrases in the text. It then classifies the unseen test data based on its training. Naïve Bayes (NB), Support Vector Machine (SVM), and Maximum Entropy (MAXENT) are some of the machine learning systems mentioned by the researchers for the sentiment classification work. Different feature selection mechanisms to select the features in the text and in depth analysis of the sentences as a whole are the points that are to be considered for the accurate sentiment classification.

We have proposed a new method for feature selection and a feature optimization technique to prove that the popular machine learning techniques like SVM when trained using the features produced by our method generate good enough classification accuracy of up to 96%. The classifier is also trained using simple unigrams, bigrams and trigrams features, and their performance is compared with our model. The results produced with the proposed method are found to be satisfactory and are discussed in detail in result analysis section.

The remaining part of the paper is arranged as: Sect. 2 includes related work, proposed framework for the opinion mining is given in Sect. 3, experimental result and its analysis are given in Sect. 4, and we conclude in Sect. 5.

2 Related Work

A huge amount of research work is going on in opinion mining in recent times. Researchers are working on classifying the sentiments of the reviewers for different domains like restaurant reviews, product reviews, and movie reviews etc. Sentiment classification task has been done using machine learning approach, lexicon approach or the combination of both the approaches which will produce a hybrid approach. It can be performed at three levels; document level, sentence level and feature level [4]. NB and SVM algorithms are normally referred as baselines for new systems developed for text labeling and sentiment analysis study [5]. Pang and Lee [6] first used these classification methods in their experiments to classify movie reviews. A lexicon based approach uses the sentiment gain of the terms in general [7]. This approach is mentioned by Hu and Liu for the first time for feature level and classification at the sentence level. Sentiment classification at the sentence level is analogous to sentiment classification at document level since sentences are part of the documents [8]. But this task is difficult as sentences are less informative when compared to the entire document. There are different types of sentences like direct sentence (e.g. the movie is superb) and indirect sentences (e.g. Golmal 2 is almost like its previous version) which require more understanding of the problem. Feature level classification tries to determine the sentiment on certain aspects in the text reviews.

The words, terms or the phrases present in the text passage which contribute in finding the polarity of the sentiment of the text passage are called as features. The machine learning systems first get trained on these features and then classify the unseen text. By selecting the best features we can get better accuracy of the classifier. There are several approaches mentioned in the literature for finding out the finest features [9–11].

Opinions can be expressed in any language. Many researchers have worked on multilingual data. The work usually translates data from one language to another and then finds the sentiments of the original data. Cross-language sentiment classifiers are built for various languages like Chinese, Spanish, and Arabic etc. by many researchers achieving comparable results with the monolingual ones [12, 13]. The authors of the paper [14] have combined SVM and Artificial Neural Network (ANN) for sentiment classification of movie reviews data. Nurulhuda and Ali [15] have mentioned three different weighting schemes to generate the word vectors which are Term Frequency-Inverse Document Frequency, binary Occurrence and term Occurrence. In [16], the authors showed that Naive Bayes with binarized features seems to work better for several text classification tasks. In [17], the authors proposed a method using gini index for selecting the features. Ouyang et al. [18] introduced word embedding features based on deep learning technology for optimizing the accuracy of their proposed model to carry out attribute-level sentiment analysis. In [19], the authors have proposed an approach to maintain the corpus of texts for emotion classification using genetic algorithm. They showed that balancing the corpus would increase the performance of the classifier up to 86.14% from 76.58% with the imbalanced corpus. The authors of the paper [20] used an optimization algorithm based on genetic algorithm to get better F1 score of the classifier. The SVM, MAXENT and stochastic gradient descent (SGD) classification algorithms were used to find the classification models for different datasets. With the selected features they achieved 97% accuracy as the best case.

Many researchers have developed feature selection algorithms which lack in finding the most informative features that are needed for the machine learning algorithms to produce accurate results. Single words or unigrams are considered as best features but they require more space and time for processing. Hence in this study, most persistent bigrams and trigrams are selected as informative features and further due to optimization of these informative features using genetic algorithm, a better performance is achieved in classifying the sentiments of the text reviews.

3   Framework for Opinion Mining

The machine learning approaches require a set of useful features for sentiment classification. So a novel feature selection method called Most Persistent Feature Selection (MPFS) that make use of information gain of the features in the text is proposed here. MPFS method is applied on bigram and trigram features in the documents. The feature set is further optimized using a genetic algorithm based technique. Most of the existing work shows that SVM is the perfect machine learning classifier in sentiment classification. So this classifier is used as the base classifier in our approach. The short depiction of the proposed structure is given in Algorithm A. Algorithm B is for the MPFS method and feature optimization method using GA is as presented in Algorithm C.

Algorithm A. Proposed framework

> For each document d in the data set
>> do {
>>> Preprocessing (d)
>>> Extract features (d)
>>> Select Most persistent features (d)
>> }
>> Generate Most persistent feature set()
>> Optimize the feature set using genetic algorithm()
>> Train the model using SVM classifier
>> Evaluate the performance of the model

Algorithm B. Feature Selection

> Input: movie reviews documents
> Output: review documents classified as positive or negative

> Step 1: Preprocessing of the review documents is carried out to filter out
>> punctuations, stop words and special characters.
> Step 2: The preprocessed documents are tokenized into bigrams (trigrams)
>> features.
> Step 3: Features with minimum occurrence of three or more times are selected.
> Step 4: for each feature f_i in document d_i feature score is calculated
>> using chi square scoring function.
> Step 5: for each document d_i
>> for each feature f_i
>>> if feature score is not less than 0.5
>>>> select f_i as most persistent feature
>>> else reject the feature.
>>> end if
>> end for (//feature)
> end for (//document)
> Step 6: The selected most persistent feature set is then given as input to sentiment
>> classifier for classification.

Algorithm C. Feature Optimization

Step 1: All the features selected from MPF selection algorithm are considered in the initial population.

Step 2: The accuracy of the new model is considered as the assessment for fitness function.

Step 3: The value of the fitness function is used to select individuals from a population for later breeding.

Step 4: Out of 't' total features, each individual feature has a probability of 1/t for mutation.

Step 5: Step 2-4 are repeated generating new models with different combination of features till no more new models.

The skeleton of the work is revealed in Fig. 1.

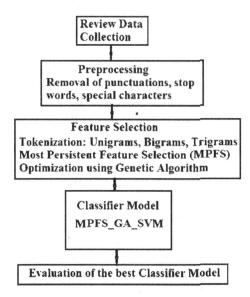

Fig. 1. Proposed system architecture

The detailed description of the above figure is explained as follows.

3.1   Review Data Collection

The review data can be collected from web which contains the social media data like Facebook, Twitter and blogs etc. Several review datasets of movies, products, restaurants etc. are available for sentiment classification task. The dataset used in this work is movie reviews dataset developed by Pang and Lee [3]. It contains 2000 processed affirmative and negative text files. The reviews on the movies are considered because they contain range of emotions or sentiments.

3.2 Preprocessing

The activities involved here are:

- Removal of punctuations marks (".", ":", "?" etc.)
- Filtering out natural language specific stop words (in, on, an etc.)
- Elimination of special characters ("@,", "$", "#" etc.).
- Discarding repetitive characters like in okkkk, gooo, noooo etc.

3.3 Feature Selection

Feature selection methods are used to identify and eliminate unrelated and unnecessary features to reduce the burden of training of the classifier. Several combinations can be made for selecting features which involves lots of effort. Therefore, sophisticated methods are required to perform feature selection in practice. The MPFS method is applied here to find the most relevant features in the review documents.

3.4 MPFS Method

The MPFS method proposed here tries to find out the most persistent features in the documents. Initially the feature set consists of all the bigrams like "movie is", "is very", "very beautiful" etc. Instead of considering all the bigrams, only useful bigrams like "very beautiful" which contributes mainly in finding the sentiment, can be considered. This requires the information gain or the bigram score of the features. This score is calculated using the chi square statistic. The bigram features with the score of 0.5 or above are taken as the most persistent features. Similar to bigrams, trigrams (e.g. "not so good") are also considered here for the experimentation purpose.

3.5 Optimization Using Genetic Algorithm

The authors of the article [21] mention that genetic algorithm is one of the most superior algorithms for selecting features. The features from MPFS method are further optimized using genetic algorithm approach. The initial population here consists of the feature set produced by MPFS method. An example of a chromosome with the header which stores the number of movie review documents and the presence of most persistent features in each document is shown in Table 1. The presence of the feature is indicated by 1 and absence by 0.

Table 1. Example chromosome with the header

Documents	Features				
	F1	F2	F3	...	Ft
D1	0	1	1	...	1
D2	1	0	0	...	1
D3	0	0	1	...	0
...	...	...	...	...	
Dt	0	1	0	...	0

4 Results

We conducted the experiments on Intel core i3 processor with 32/64 bit operating system. Python 3.5.2 with NLTK 3.2.1 version is used for programming purpose. The experiments are performed on various size of movie reviews dataset. The movie reviews polarity dataset used in this work contains a folder named movie_reviews. In this folder there are subdirectories called 'pos' and 'neg' which contain 1000 affirmative and 1000 negative text files respectively. The performance is evaluated by tenfold cross validation (CV) method. Depending on the feature set selected (MPBFS-most persistent bigram feature selection, MPTFS- most persistent trigram feature selection, MPBF_GA- MPBF Genetic Algorithm) and the classifier used, different classifier models are generated. The graphical illustration for the comparison of the performances of classifier models in terms of accuracy is shown in Fig. 2.

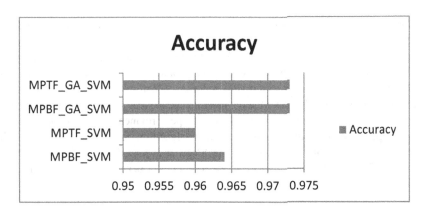

Fig. 2. Performance of the proposed classifier models

4.1 Result Analysis

The accuracies of the classifier models with unigram, bigram and trigram features are compared with the accuracies produced using proposed MPBF, MPTF, MPBF_GA and MPTF_GA. It can be noticed that the proposed MPBFS and MPTFS method work

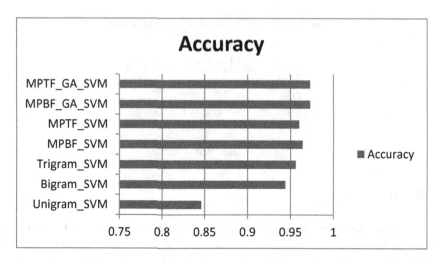

Fig. 3. Performance of the various classifier models

slightly better than SVM with all the trigrams. The result is further enhanced by applying GA technique yielding 97% with both MPBF and MPTF. Figure 3 shows graphically the performance of SVM using unigram features (UGF), bigram features (BGF), trigram features (TGF), MPBF, MPTF, MPBF_GA and MPTF_GA.

5   Conclusion

A novel feature selection method and a feature optimization technique based on genetic algorithm are proposed here for sentiment classification of movie review documents. The SVM classifier is trained on those selected features and testing is done with tenfold cross validation method. The use of most persistent and optimized features set make the classifier model perform better in terms of accuracy which is the main objective of this work. The results show that SVM with the most persistent features show better performance when compared to other models. The performance is further improved by applying optimization technique using genetic algorithm for feature selection. The different combination of the classifiers like SVM and Neural Network to generate a hybrid classifier model can be a future scope to get better performance of the sentiment categorization.

References

1. Liu, B.: Sentiment Analysis and Opinion Mining, vol. 5, no. 1. Morgan & Claypool Publishers, San Rafael, May 2012
2. Pang, B., Lee, L.: Opinion mining and sentiment analysis (2008)
3. Pang, B., Lee, L.: A sentimental education: sentiment analysis using subjectivity summarization based on minimum cuts. In: Proceedings of ACL (2004)

4. Hu, M., Liu, B.: Mining and summarizing customer reviews. In: Proceedings ACM SIGKDD, pp. 168–177 (2004)
5. Wang, S., Manning, C.D.: Baselines and bigrams: simple, good sentiment and topic classification. In: Proceedings of the 50th Annual Meeting of the Association for Computational Linguistics, pp. 90–94, Jeju, Republic of Korea, 8–14 July 2012
6. Pang, B., Lee, L., Vaithyanathan, S.: Thumbs up? sentiment classification using machine learning techniques. In: Proceedings of EMNLP, pp. 79–86 (2002)
7. Jurek, A., Mulvenna, M.D., Bi, Y.: Improved lexicon-based sentiment analysis for social media analytics. Secur. Inform. 4(1), 9 (2015)
8. Fu, G., Wang, X.: Chinese Sentence-Level Sentiment Classification Based on Fuzzy Sets, Coling 2010: Poster Volume, pp. 312–319, Beijing, August 2010
9. Fang, X., Zhan, J.: Sentiment analysis using product review data. J. Big Data 2(1), 5 (2015)
10. Tripathy, A., Anand, A., Rath, S.K.: Classification of sentiment reviews using N-gram machine learning approach. Expert Syst. Appl. 57, 117–126 (2016)
11. Sohail, S.S., Siddiqui, J., Ali, R.: Feature extraction and analysis of online reviews for the recommendation of books using opinion mining technique. Perspect. Sci. 8, 754–756 (2016)
12. Zhou, X., Wan, X., Xiao, J.: CL opinion miner: opinion target extraction in a cross-language scenario. In: IEEE/ACM Transactions on Audio, Speech, and Language Processing, vol. 23, no. 4, April 2015
13. Tartir, S., Nabi, I.A.: Semantic sentiment analysis in arabic social media. J. King Saud Univ. Comput. Inf. Sci. 29, 229–233 (2017)
14. Tripathy, A., Anand, A., Rath, S.K.: Document-level sentiment classification using hybrid machine learning approach. Knowl. Inf. Syst. 53, 805 (2017)
15. Zainuddin, N., Selamat, A.: Sentiment Analysis Using Support Vector Machine, IEEE I4CT, Langkawi, Kedah, Malaysia, pp. 333–337 (2014)
16. Jurafsky, D., Martin, J.H.: Naive Bayes and Sentiment Classification, Speech and Language Processing, 7 November 2016
17. Manek, A.S., Shenoy, P.D., Mohan, M.C., Venugopal, K.: Aspect term extraction for sentiment analysis in large movie reviews using Gini Index feature selection method and SVM classifier. world wide web 20(2), 135–154 (2016)
18. Chunping, O., Yongbin, L., Shuqing, Z., Xiaohua, Y.: Opinion objects identification and sentiment analysis. Int. J. Database Theor. Appl. 8(6), 1–12 (2015)
19. Ferreira, L.C., Dosciatti, M.M., Nievola, J.C., Paraiso, E.C.: Using a genetic algorithm approach to study the impact of imbalanced corpora in sentiment analysis. In: Proceedings of the Twenty-Eighth International Florida Artificial Intelligence Research Society Conference
20. Catak, F., Bilgem, T.: Genetic algorithm based feature selection in high dimensional text dataset classification. WSEAS Trans. Inf. Sci. Appl. 12(1), 290–296 (2015)
21. Gómez, F., Quesada, A.: Genetic algorithms for feature selection in data analytics. www. neuraldesigner.com. Artelnics

Mean Distance Parameter Based Facial Expression Recognition System

Pushpa Kesarwani[1(✉)], Akhilesh Kumar Choudhary[3],
and Arun Kumar Misra[2]

[1] Department of Information Technology, G.L. Bajaj Institute of Technology
and Management, Greater Noida, India
pushpak2728@gmail.com
[2] Faculty of Computer Science and Engineering, Motilal Nehru National
Institute of Technology, Allahabad, India
akm@mnnit.ac.in
[3] Department of Mobile Services,
Bharat Sanchar Nigam Limited, Ghaziabad, India
choudhary.akhilesh@gmail.com

Abstract. Human-like facial expression recognition is the ultimate goal of all automatic facial expression recognition system. Facial expression recognition is mostly achieved by comparing the test image of a person with his/her neutral image. In this paper, "mean distance parameter" (MDP) has been proposed, and is used to recognize the facial expression. In this proposed methodology, database is not required to train the system for expression recognition, but neutral images from the database have been used only once for calculating the mean distance parameter. After establishment of the mean distance parameter based on region of interest (ROI) height, action units (AUs) have been detected by comparing it with the test image's fiducial point distance. Facial expression recognition has been performed based on these detected AUs in the test image, and recognition rate of 96.66% has been achieved for Cohn-Kanade database.

Keywords: Facial expressions recognition · Facial action coding system · Action units · Mean distance parameter

1 Introduction

Facial expressions are the consequences of changes in emotion or mental state of a person due to many reasons e.g. during communication between two persons due to changes in topics, circumstances and intensions. Facial expressions convey non-verbal clues, which play an important role in interpersonal relations and human behavior. Automatic facial expression recognition is applied in behavioral science, clinical practice, lie-detection, intelligent environments, pain assessment and related fields. Constructing an automatic expression recognition system depends on the sense of facial expression. Anger, Disgust, Fear, Happy, Sad, and Surprise are the six basic facial expressions that are common among all humans, despite the cultural or other differences. Other than these six expressions there can be many more expressions that are

S. Minz et al. (Eds.): ICICCT 2018, CCIS 835, pp. 176–191, 2019.
https://doi.org/10.1007/978-981-13-5992-7_16

specific to a region, culture, and person or even to a situation. In this paper, a method is proposed which is able to detect and measure these six facial expressions and few others which are combinations of these. The relationships between the measured facial deformations and the mathematical description of the corresponding action units (AUs) and rules required for identification of expressions have been used.

1.1 Database Used

For experimentation purposes, the extended Cohn-Kanade (CK+) dataset has been used, which consists of 210 adults facial behavior, 18 to 50 years old participants, 69% female, 81% Euro-American, 13% Afro-American, and 6% other groups. Participants of the database were trained to perform a series of 23 facial expressions which included single AUs and combinations of AUs. The image size of all the faces are 640 × 480 pixel of 8-bit gray-scale.

1.2 AdaBoost Detection Principles

In proposed method, AdaBoost detection principle [12] has been adapted for face detection process, to get the advantage of the low computational cost associated with Haar-like features set. It is due to following reasons:

(a) Lack of significant structural information about the facial components as compared to the whole face. When the detected face resolution is low then the structure of the facial components is less detectable.
(b) Due to variations in the shape of the components, e.g. eyes, there is difference in the expressions conveyed by the same or different people. This problem also arises in high resolution face images.

To cater above mentioned extended Haar-like features sets [12] have been used, which are simple and inexpensive.

The rectangular feature value (F) is calculated as follows [12, 13]:

$$F = \left\{ \sum (pixels\ in\ white\ area) - \sum (pixels\ in\ shaded\ area) \right\}$$

Rectangular feature set of facial component are shown as in Fig. 1(c).

$$left\ eye = area(A) - area(B)$$
$$right\ eye = area(A') - area(B')$$
$$nose = area(C) + area(E) - area(D)$$
$$mouth = area(F) + area(H) - area(G)$$

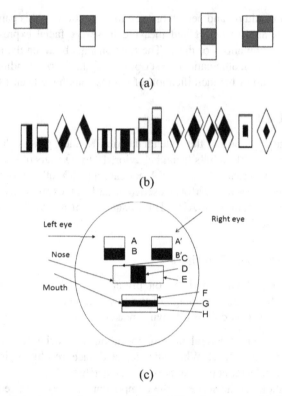

(a)

(b)

(c)

Fig. 1. (a) Five basic types of rectangular Haar–like feature set (b) Fourteen extended rectangular Haar-like feature set [12] (c) Facial component detection by rectangular feature set

Face detection in an image has been calculated with the help of rectangular region as follows.

> **If F > threshold value then**
> **Face**
> **else**
>   **Non- face**

Initially five basic rectangular Haar-like features set [12] have been used in face detection processes as shown in Fig. 1(a). Some of the features have been added in the basic rectangular Haar-like features set, which are 45° rotated rectangle features set and center-surround features set [12] as shown in Fig. 1(b). The additional features are more representative for different shapes than the basic Haar-feature set. Due to the addition of these features, the performance of detection has increased.

1.3   Facial Action Coding System

The contraction of each facial muscle (single and in combination with other muscles) was determined [3] which changes the appearance of the face. A set of Action Units (AUs) are developed that refer to the various movements of the facial muscles. In the proposed system, the set of 44 AUs has been used which divide the whole face into two parts, upper face AUs and lower face AUs, as shown in Table 1 (basic upper and lower face AUs). FACS can describe any facial behavior related to universal expressions. Out of these 44 AUs only a few are used for the expression detection.

Table 1. Basic upper and lower face action units of FACS system (from http://www.pinterest. com)

Upper Face Action Units					
AU 1	AU 2	AU 4	AU 5	AU 6	AU 7
Inner Brow Raiser	Outer Brow Raiser	Brow Lowerer	Upper Lid Raiser	Cheek Raiser	Lid Tightener
*AU 41	*AU 42	*AU 43	AU 44	AU 45	AU 46
Lid Droop	Slit	Eyes Closed	Squint	Blink	Wink
Lower Face Action Units					
AU 9	AU 10	AU 11	AU 12	AU 13	AU 14
Nose Wrinkler	Upper Lip Raiser	Nasolabial Deepener	Lip Corner Puller	Cheek Puffer	Dimpler
AU 15	AU 16	AU 17	AU 18	AU 20	AU 22
Lip Corner Depressor	Lower Lip Depressor	Chin Raiser	Lip Puckerer	Lip Stretcher	Lip Funneler
AU 23	AU 24	*AU 25	*AU 26	*AU 27	AU 28
Lip Tightener	Lip Pressor	Lips Part	Jaw Drop	Mouth Stretch	Lip Suck

2   Proposed Method

Facial expression recognition is mostly achieved by comparing the test image of a person with his/her neutral image, which is already stored in the data base. In the proposed method, database is not required to train the system for expression recognition, but neutral images from the database has been used only once for calculating the proposed mean distance parameter. The steps involved in the proposed method are shown in Fig. 2 and are as follows:

Step1: Face area has been detected and localized from input image or video by conventional Viola-Jones AdaBoost method [12, 13].

Step 2: Facial components i.e. nose, mouth, eyes, and eyebrows are located within the detected face area.

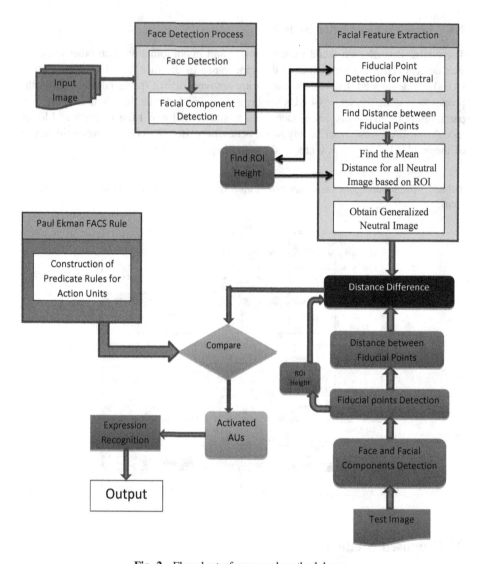

Fig. 2. Flowchart of proposed methodology

Step 3: Now positions of the 22 fiducial points are approximated based on the bounding box of the detected facial components [11]. It is assumed that the actual fiducial points are localized within an M × M neighborhood of the approximated fiducial point's position, where M is determined by the size of facial components.

The working process of these three steps is shown in Fig. 3.

Step 4: Cohn-Kanade database has been used in this proposed method. 22 fiducial points have been calculated for all neutral images of this database as depicted in Fig. 4.

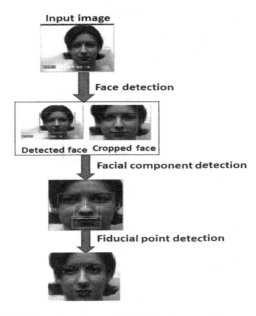

Fig. 3. Face detection and fiducial point extraction process

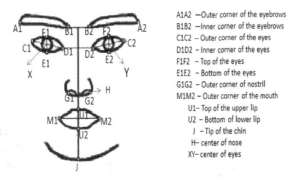

Fig. 4. Fiducial point's position on face

Step 5: As human face size varies with physical location and climate condition as well as age of person so fiducial point's positions also vary. To design such system, which is applicable for all type of faces, first face size have been calculated. It is not the whole face size. Instead it is a region of interest (ROI) height (vertical middle line of face). ROI height has been calculated by triangulation (which is constructed from the outer corners of the eyebrows and the tip of the chin), as shown in Fig. 5. In this step region of interest (ROI) height has been calculated for all neutral image of this database, which will be used to categorize the neutral images, into different categories of equal ROI height.

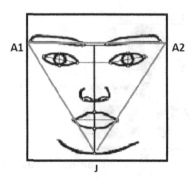

Fig. 5. Triangulation is used to estimate the size of face

ROI height calculation: Let P is the middle point between fiducial points A_1 and A_2 then

$$P(x,y) = \left[x_p, y_p\right]$$
$$= \left[\frac{(x_{A1} + x_{A2})}{2}, \frac{(y_{A1} + y_{A2})}{2}\right]$$

And ROI height is given by the distance between P(x, y) and J(x, y) which represents the tip of chin.

$$\text{ROI height} = \sqrt{\left\{(x_P - x_J)^2 + (y_P - y_J)^2\right\}}$$

Step 6: Face categorization of the neutral images have been done based on the ROI height as shown in Fig. 6.

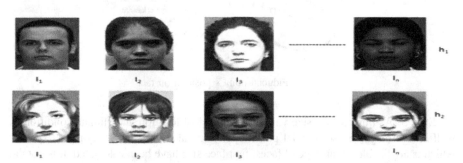

Fig. 6. Examples of neutral images from Cohn-Kanade database which describes the categorization of face based on ROI height

Step 7: After calculating the ROI height, distance between few fiducial points has been calculated for all neutral images of Cohn-Kanade (CK+) database which contains 210 adult's images i.e. A1C1, A2C2, B1D1, B2D2, F1E1, F2E2, D1M1, D2M2, HM1, HM2, U1U2, M1M2, and HJ as shown in Fig. 7.

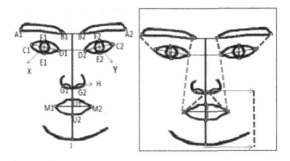

Fig. 7. Dotted lines of face represents distance between fiducial points which is used to defines rules for AUs

These are thirteen distances and henceforth represented as D_1, D_2... D_{13} i.e. D_j j = 1 to 13. For A1C1, A2C2, B1D1, B2D2, F1E1, F2E2, D1M1, D2M2, HM1, HM2, U1U2, M1M2, and HJ respectively.

Step 8: In this step, mean distance parameter has been calculated for each dotted line of neutral images based on the ROI height (h_1, h2 etc.). Pseudo code for calculating the mean distance parameter is as follows:

Mean_distance_parameter ()
  {

$$D_1 = Distance(A1C1)$$
$$= \sqrt{\left\{(x_{A1} - x_{C1})^2 + (y_{A1} - y_{C1})^2\right\}},$$

$$D_2 = Distance(A2C2)$$
$$= \sqrt{\left\{(x_{A2} - x_{C2})^2 + (y_{A2} - y_{C2})^2\right\}}$$

/* Similarly D_3, D_4... D_{13} has been calculated for each pair of fiducial points of a neutral image i.e. B1D1, B2D2, F1E1, F2E2, D1M1, D2M2, HM1, HM2, U1U2, M1M2, and HJ*/

$$Mean(A1C1) = Mean(D1)$$
$$= \sum_{I=1}^{n} \frac{(D_1)_I}{n},$$

$$Mean(A2C2) = Mean(D2)$$
$$= \sum_{I=1}^{n} \frac{(D_2)_I}{n}$$

(Where I is the number of neutral images i.e. I_1, I_2 ... I_n as shown in Fig. 6)

/* similarly Mean(D3), Mean(D4) ... Mean(D13) has been calculated for each pair of fiducial points. */

}

If ROI_height $==$ h_1 THEN

Mean_distance_parameter ();

else if ROI_height $==$ h_2 THEN

Mean _distance_parameter ();

...

else if ROI_height $==$ h_n THEN

Mean _distance_parameter ();

End

In the above code, h_1, h_2 ... h_n are ROI height values of n neutral images and Mean_distance_parameter () is a function to calculate the mean distance of fiducial points of all neutral images based on ROI height.

Step 9: In this step, generalized neutral images have been obtained based on ROI height i.e. h_1, h_2 ... h_n. Further, the database is used only once to establish the mean distance parameter and it has not been used to train the system for expression recognition.

Step 10: For the test image repeat steps 1 to 5, for calculating the ROI height and step 7 to calculate the fiducial point's distances. Step 6 is not required because no categorization is required for test image. Similarly fiducial point's distances have been calculated for the test image also i.e. A1C1, A2C2, B1D1, B2D2, F1E1, F2E2, D1M1, D2M2, HM1, HM2, U1U2, M1M2, and HJ, and these thirteen distances represented as d_1, d_2... d_{13} i.e. d_k k = 1 to 13.

$$d_1 = Distance(A1C1)$$
$$= \sqrt{\left\{(x_{A1} - x_{C1})^2 + (y_{A1} - y_{C1})^2\right\}}$$

Similarly d_2, d_3... d_{13} has been calculated for the test image.

Step 11: In this step, difference between generalized neutral image fiducial point's distances and test image fiducial points distances has been calculated as follows

$$diff(D_i) = MD_i - d_i$$

Where i = 1, 2, 3...13 and MD is mean fiducial point distance in obtained neutral image and d is fiducial point distance in test image.

If $diff(D_i)$ = 0, then the test image is same as the neutral image.

If $diff(D_i)$ > 0 or $diff(D_i)$ < 0, then it will be used in identification of action units and the facial expression.

Step 12: In this step, predicate rules for AUs have been constructed based on facial action coding system (FACS). And the differences between fiducial point's distance of generalized neutral image and the test image calculated in step 11. The rules are as shown in Table 2.

Table 2. The description of Aus and related rules with distance differences for particular AUs

AU	Distance between fiducial points	Description of AUs and related rules
AU1	B1D1, B2D2	**Raised inner portion of the eyebrow(s)** IF diff (B1D1) < 0 OR diff (B2D2) < 0 THEN AU1
AU2	A1C1, A2C2	**Raised outer portion of the eyebrow(s)** IF diff (A1C1) < 0 OR diff (A2C2) < 0 THEN AU2
AU4	B1B2	**Eyebrows pulled closer together (frown)** IF diff (B1B2) > 0 THEN AU4
AU5	F1E1, F2E2	**Raised upper eyelid(s)** IF diff (F1E1) < 0 OR diff (F2E2) < 0 THEN AU5
AU6	HM1, HM2	**Cheek Raised** IF diff (HM1) < 0 AND diff (HM2) < 0 THEN AU6
AU7	F1E1, F2E2	**Lid tightened** IF diff (F1E1) > 0 OR diff (F2E2) > 0 THEN AU7
AU10	HU1	**Upper Lip Raiser** IF diff (HU1) > 0 THEN AU10
AU12	M1M2, D1M1, D2M2	**Lip Corner Puller** IF diff (M1M2) < 0 AND diff (D1M1) > 0 AND diff (D2M2) > 0 THEN AU12
AU15	D1M1, D2M2	**Lip Corner Depressor** diff (D1M1) < 0 AND diff (D2M2) < 0 THEN AU12
AU16	HU2	**Lower Lip Depressor** IF diff (HU2) < 0 THEN AU16
AU20	M1M2, D1M1, D2M2	**Lip stretcher** IF diff (M1M2) < 0 AND diff (D1M1) < 0 AND diff (D2M2) < 0 THEN AU20
AU22	U1U2, M1M2	**Lip Funneled** IF diff (U1U2) < 0 AND diff (M1M2) < 0 THEN AU22
AU23	U1U2, M1M2, M1D1, M2D2	**Lip Tightened** IF diff (U1U2) > 0 AND diff (M1M2) < 0 AND diff (M1D1) ≥ 0 AND diff (M2D2) ≥ 0 THEN AU23
AU24	U1U2	**Lip Presser** IF diff (U1U2) > 0 AND diff (M1M2) > 0 THEN AU24
AU25	A1U2	**Lips part** IF diff (U1U2) < 0 THEN AU25
AU26	JU2	**Jaw Drop** IF diff (JU2) < 0 THEN AU26
AU27	M1M2, U1U2	**Mouth Stretch** IF diff (M1M2) > 0 AND diff (U1U2) < 0 THEN AU27

3 Detection of AUs in the Test Image

Contractions of facial muscles produce changes in the shape and location of the facial features, which in turn changes in the position of the fiducial points. Contractions of facial muscles can be observed from the fiducial point's distances as shown in Fig. 7. Changes in the position of the fiducial points have been represented in terms of AUs and for each facial expression, AUs and/or their combinations have been illustrated in Table 3 [3]. Facial expressions of a person will be recognized, only if the AUs are active in the test image.

Table 3. AUs that compose a particular facial expression

Input Image	AUs used	Output
	AU7+ AU12 or AU13	Happy
	AU1+AU4+AU15	Sad
	AU2+AU4+AU10	Disgust
	AU4+AU5 OR AU7 + AU22 or AU23 or AU24	Anger
	AU1+AU2+AU4+AU5 +AU7+AU20+AU26	Fear
	AU1+AU2+AU5+AU27	Surprise

A direct-chain based method has been utilized in this proposed method that encodes AUs occurring alone or in a combination in the test image. To recognize the facial expressions all the active AUs are detected first and out of these, only those AUs are selected which have maximum variation. In this system, six basic expressions have been analyzed based on related rules of AUs i.e., Happy, Sad, Angry, Disgust, Fear, Surprise (Fig. 8).

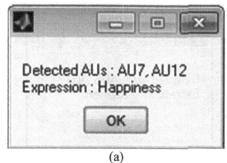

(a)

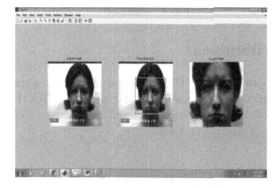

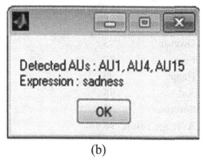

(b)

Fig. 8. (a) Facial expressions of happiness, (b) Facial expressions of sadness and, (c) Facial expressions of happiness (Image taken from Webcam)

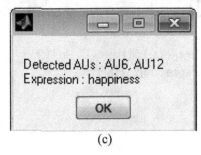

(c)

Fig. 8. (*continued*)

4   Results and Discussion

The results have been tested on CK+ database as well as some personal images obtained with the help of a web cam (real time image), on MATLAB 2013 version. Recognition rates of facial expression achieved as tested on Cohn-Kanade (CK+) database is 96.66% as reported in Table 4.

Table 4. Facial expression recognition rate

Expression	Recognition rate (%)
Anger	98
Disgust	93
Fear	97
Happy	99
Sad	98
Surprise	95
Average result	**96.66**

Table 5 presents a brief comparison between proposed method and six other expression recognition systems available in the literature [14]. From Table 5, it can be observed that the accuracy of our method never falls below 93% for any facial expression and average recognition rate of our system is higher than other expression recognition systems.

Table 5. Comparison of the proposed mean distance parameter recognition system with other system taken from Ilbeygi et al. (2012)

Expression	DP [14] %	HMM (Zhou 2004) %	CBR (Khanum 2009) %	FRBS (Khanum 2009) %	FCBR (Khanum 2009) %	FS (Ilbeygi 2012) %	Proposed method %
Anger	87.50	36.11	95	70	100	92.75	98
Disgust	4.16	41.67	80	100	82	91.30	93
Fear	79.16	63.89	75	90	80	94.20	97
Happy	91.66	96.66	76	100	95	98.55	99
Sad	8.33	27.78	95	70	85	92.75	98
Surprise	91.66	66.66	80	95	100	94.20	95
Average result	**60.41**	**55.46**	**70.83**	**87.50**	**90.33**	**93.96**	**96.66**

It can also be observed from Table 5 that the image databases by other six facial expression recognition algorithms [14] are different from the image database (CK+) used by the proposed method in terms of size, expression and color etc. Since each method reports its accuracy for facial expression recognition with a specific image database and as such the exact comparison is never possible. Therefore, no benchmark database is available for evaluating the accuracy of facial expression recognition systems.

To show the strength of the proposed system, it has been compared with Starostenko et al. [15].

Starostenko et al. [15] used 19 fiducial points and 15 distances between these points. They also require neutral image of a person whose expression is to be recognized, for comparing with test image. However, in the proposed method, 22 fiducial points and the distances between these fiducial points based on the action units of expression have been used as described in Table 2. Further, the proposed method introduces the concept of mean distance parameter for facial expression recognition. This parameter helps in recognition even if neutral image of the person whose expression is to be recognized is not stored in the database, because it is a mean (average) distance parameter of all neutral images available in the database based on ROI height. ROI height helps to categories person's face category as shown in Fig. 6. This system also works for real time images for expression recognition. Because in this system, neutral image of that person is not required whose recognition is to be done, where as Starostenko's [15] system does not work for real time images. Further, fuzzy logic with ontology editor protégé for establishment of rules has been used in [15] whereas in the proposed method a simple direct- chain method based rules have been used and implemented in MATLAB 2013.

5 Conclusion

In the proposed method, a concept of mean distance parameter has been introduced for facial expression recognition system and successfully implemented which results in achieving a recognition rate of 96.66% for CK+ (Cohn-Kanade) database. (i) It is to be noted that neutral image of the person whose expression is to be recognized is not required to be present in the database. The method is also tested for smaller set of real time images. (ii) It is to be noted that the recognition rate is better than Dynamic Programming **(DP)**, Hidden Markov Model **(HMM)**, Case Based Reasoning **(CBR)**, Fuzzy Based Reasoning System **(FBRS)**, Fuzzy Case Based Reasoning **(FBRS)**, and Fuzzy System **(FS)** by approximately **36.25%, 41.20%, 25.83%, 9.16%, 6.33%**, and **2.70%** respectively.

References

1. Ahonen, T., Hadid, A., Pietikainen, M.: Face description with local binary patterns: application to face recognition. IEEE Trans. Pattern Anal. Mach. Intell. **12**, 2037–2041 (2006)
2. Mase, K.: Recognition of facial expression from optical flow. IEICE Trans. (E) **74**, 3474–3483 (1991)
3. Friesen, E., Ekman, P.: Facial action coding system: a technique for the measurement of facial movement. Palo Alto (1978)
4. Bartlett, M.S., Hager, J.C., Ekman, P., Sejnowski, T.J.: Measuring facial expressions by computer image analysis. Psychophysiology **36**(2), 253–263 (1999)
5. Donato, G., Bartlett, M.S., Hager, J.C., Ekman, P., Sejnowski, T.J.: Classifying facial actions. IEEE Trans. Pattern Anal. Mach. Intell. **21**(10), 974 (1999)
6. Dasari, S.D., Dasari, S.: Face recognition using Tchebichef moments. Int. J. Inf. Netw. Secur. **1**(4), 243 (2012)
7. Atta, R., Ghanbari, M.: Face recognition based on DCT pyramid feature extraction. In: 2010 3rd International Congress on Image and Signal Processing (CISP), vol. 2, pp. 934–938. IEEE, October 2010
8. Bettadapura, V.: Face expression recognition and analysis: the state of the art. arXiv preprint arXiv:1203.6722 (2012)
9. Fox, E., et al.: Facial expressions of emotion: are angry faces detected more efficiently? Cogn. Emot. **14**(1), 61–92 (2000)
10. Matsumoto, D., et al.: Facial expressions of emotion. In: Lewis, M., Haviland-Jones, J.M., Barrett, L.F. (eds.) Handbook of Emotions, 3rd edn, pp. 211–234. Macmillan, New York (2008)
11. Choi, J.Y., Ro, Y.M., Plataniotis, K.N.: Boosting color feature selection for color faces recognition. IEEE Trans. Image Process. **20**(5), 1425–1434 (2011)
12. Hamm, J., et al.: Automated facial action coding system for dynamic analysis of facial expressions in neuropsychiatric disorders. J. Neurosci. Methods **200**(2), 237–256 (2011)

13. Harris, C., Stephens, M.: A combined corner and edge detector. In: Alvey Vision Conference, vol. 15, no. 50, pp. 10–5244, August 1988
14. Cohen, I.: Automatic facial expression recognition from video sequences using temporal information. MS thesis. University of Illinois at Urbana-Champaign (2000)
15. Starostenko, O., Cortés, X., Sánchez, J.A., Alarcon-Aquino, V.: Unobtrusive emotion sensing and interpretation in smart environment. J. Ambient Intell. Smart Environ. 7(1), 59–83 (2015)

Variation of Stability Factor of MSERs for Text Detection and Localization in Natural Scene Image Using Naive Bayes Classifier

Rituraj Soni[1(✉)] , Bijendra Kumar[1] , and Satish Chand[2]

[1] Department of Computer Engineering,
Netaji Subhas Institute of Technology, New Delhi, India
`rituraj.soni@gmail.com`
[2] School of Computer and Systems Science,
Jawaharlal Nehru University, New Delhi, India

Abstract. The process of extracting textual regions from the scene images is a significant matter in the field of image processing & computer vision. It is very challenging due to different fonts, variable font size, illumination conditions and complex background etc. In last decade, image segmentation using Maximal Stable Extremal Regions (MSERs) played an important role in this area due to its various advantages. The generation of MSERs is controlled by variation of stability factor delta in deciding the promising stable areas. The aim of this paper is to study the effect of parameter delta and calculate the optimal delta on the different versions of MSER for detection and localization of text in scene images. Four different features Stroke Width Heterogeneity, Perpetual Color Contrast, Histogram of Oriented Gradients at Edges, Occupy Rate are used to evaluate the probability of text using naive Bayes Model for each version of MSERs. The Training is accomplished on the ICDAR 2013 training dataset and experiments for testing our method are carried out on ICDAR datasets to show the importance of delta (optimal value) parameter of MSER in providing the optimum results expressed as f-measure, recall and precision.

Keywords: Text region extraction · Natural scene images · Delta · MSERs · Naive bayesian

1 Introduction

Detection & localization of text in the scene (natural) images serve as an appreciable contribution in the real-world applications like robot navigation, scene understanding, assistance to blind people, driving vehicles etc. over the last decade [1–3]. Its main aim is to find and locate text constituents accurately in scene images as well as to assemble them into text regions leaving non-text aside. The salient information about images is present in the form of text that can be extracted by detecting and localization of text regions that can be used in various applications. The complexities present in natural scene images [1, 3] like a variety of font, size, and style of text, color, occlusion, texture, complex background, uneven lighting and image resolutions are few barriers that needs to be solved to increase efficient detection and localization. MSER [4] based

© Springer Nature Singapore Pte Ltd. 2019
S. Minz et al. (Eds.): ICICCT 2018, CCIS 835, pp. 192–206, 2019.
https://doi.org/10.1007/978-981-13-5992-7_17

segmentation methods play a decisive role in determining the possible candidate regions and emerge as best segmentation method over the years. The delta Δ parameter of MSERs [5] controls the calculation of stability and thereby helps in determining the stable regions (possible text components) in images.

The focus in this paper is to analyze, study the effect and obtain the optimal value of delta parameter in the different versions of MSER algorithm using four features for finding the presence of the text and its position in the blurred images. The original algorithm of MSER [4], contrast-enhanced MSER [6], Edge-preserving MSER [7] and combination of contrast-enhanced edge preservation MSER is applied on ICDAR 2013 benchmark dataset for different values of delta (1 to 20) as a pre-processing step. Thereafter, component filtering rules are applied to each version of MSER to remove non-text constituents. The, four text-specific features are calculated on remaining possible text constituents and probability of text is calculated using Naive Bayes to calculate the existence of text in the image. Finally, labeling of non-text and text constituents is performed by energy minimization and graph cut [8], followed by clustering using mean-shift for grouping of the texts.

The rest of the paper is coordinated as follows: Introduction is described in Sect. 1, Sect. 2 explores related work. Section 3 describes the version of MSERs and stability factor. Working of the proposed system is explained in Sect. 4. Experiments & results are examined in Sect. 5 and Sect. 6 concludes the paper.

2 Related Work

As per the researchers over the years, the text regions are detected and localized i.e. extracted from the scene images by following different types of methods namely, connected-component (cc), region, & hybrid based. The methods based on region [1, 9] uses sliding window to detect the text elements in multi-scale images followed by classification to spot the text. Such methods are slow and extremely sensitive to the alignment, but effective for images having dense characters.

Connected-component (CC) based methods [10–12] use color similarity, spatial layout, edge detection for segmentation of possible text components and have smaller computation cost [1]. They are slow and require prior knowledge of text position and scale in components. MSERs [13] based methods are considered under CC category and are known for generating stable regions against a range of thresholds. They are robust to rotation, scale, and affine transformation but sensitive to blur and low contrast images. Hybrid methods combine advantages of both CC and region based methods to achieve better results.

Neumann et al. [11] propose to extract character candidate by using extremal regions (ERs) [4] in intensity, red, green and blue channels of pixel values. It is not robust to small character sizes, blurred text, and low resolution. Neumann et al. [12] discuss a low memory and less time-consuming method to test all Extremal regions in real-time-based using novel features to attain good character detection results. Merino-Gracia et al. [14] discuss an image segmentation approach based on hierarchical MSERs to find more stable region using the combination of MSER+ and MSER−.

Chen et al. [15] propose edge-enhanced MSERs to extract character and uses width of the stroke as a feature is used to find the presence of textual regions in the images. It fails on blurred and low-contrast characters. Tsai et al. [16] discuss two-stage hypothesis based method by fine-tuning the different parameters of MSER. Li and Lu [6] discuss method based on contrast-enhanced MSER by enhancing the contrast between characters and background to reduce the effect of blurriness.

Li et al. [7] discuss an edge-preserving MSER to remove the effect of blurriness caused by mixed pixels around the edges. Tian et al. [17] discuss a multi-level MSER method in the different color channels to detect text candidates using four text specific features. Zamberletti et al. [18] discuss Fast Feature Pyramid based method that generates text confidence map and uses multi-resolution MSERs to discard false-positive detection from the map.

Gomex and Karatzas [19] discuss a method of text region grouping using MSER, based on optimal clustering feature space. Guan and Chu et al. [20] uses mutual verification and integration for classification of text extracted by SWT and MSER. Ghanei and Faez [21] use robust MSER detector for low luminance contrast images by exploiting the delta Δ parameter of MSER. The work in [2, 16, 17, 21] also discuss the effect of Δ parameter of MSER algorithm. In our earlier work [22] we used five features to enhance the accuracy of text detection process using a single fixed value of delta.

In this paper we examine the effect of the Δ parameter of MSER on four different versions of MSERs in scene text localization to determine the optimal value of Δ for each version of MSERs.

3   Variation of MSER and its Δ Parameter

3.1   Original MSER (OMSER)

There are certain regions in images that own properties of invariance and stability due to which they can be detected with high repeatability and are termed as distinguished regions (DRs) [4] Those distinguished regions in which all pixels inside the regions have either lower or higher intensity as compared to the pixels on its exterior boundary are known as extremal regions (ERs). Those extremal regions for which intensity variation remains stable across a span of thresholds are termed as the Maximally Stable Extremal Region (MSER) [4]. ERs depend on the intensity function on its outer boundaries and the inside region. The stable regions are extracted from the given image by taking into account the variation in the area by considering the modification regarding the intensity of components governed by thresholding the given image for a gray level. The stability criteria of MSERs (explained in Sect. 3.4) is defined as the difference of area normalized by connected component's area. Properties of MSERs [4] such as stability, assist in multi-scale detection, In-variance to affine transformation, detected in linear time make them useful in the area of text detection and localization methods [11, 12, 23].

3.2   Contrast Enhanced MSER (CONMSER)

The original MSERs suffers from the problems of low-resolution and blurriness in images. To overcome this issue, contrast-enhanced MSER is proposed by Li and Lu [6] by increasing the contrast between text and its background. For an given input image I, an intensity image $I_n = (I_r + I_g + I_b)/3$ is calculated in HSI color space. Thereafter, an intensity gradient check (at pixel(j, k)) is applied using $I_n(j + 1, k)–I_n(j–1, k) > T_1$, if it is true then contrast-enhanced image is obtained as $I_c (j \pm 1, k) = I_c (j \pm 1, k) + T_2$ where $c \in (R, G, B)$ $(T_1 = 30, T_2 = 50)$. Then on the resultant contrast-enhanced Image [6] original MSER is applied and thereby it reduces the problem of blurriness to a certain extent and thus increases the performance as compared to original MSER.

3.3   Edge Smoothing MSER (ESMSER)

The method [6] reduces the effect of blurriness on natural scene images, but still; some mixed pixels around the edge boundary create the problem in identifying the characters separately. Li et al. [7] propose an edge preserving MSER on images for dealing with blurriness in images. The edge smoothing process is assisted by the guided filter [24].

3.4   Stability Factor (Δ) of MSER

The formulation of MSERs are determined by a sole parameter Δ and its stability [5] is the inverse of the corresponding area variation (AV) of the region ER as the intensity amount is raised by Δ. The area variation [5] of region ER_i is defined as

$$AV = \frac{|ER_{i+\Delta} - ER_{i-\Delta}|}{|ER_i|} \tag{1}$$

Where, |.| is the area of the Extremal Region ER, i intensity and Δ is the augment in intensity. For any Extremal region ER_i, if Eq. 1 has local minimum then it is considered as Maximum Stable Extremal Region. Therefore it means that the Extremal regions having lower difference than the regions Δ level below & above are termed as Maximum Stable Extremal regions. Thus, Delta Δ monitors the stability of a region. As exhibited in Fig. 1 the input image is processed through original MSER for different values of Δ ranging from 1 to 20 and as evident from the Fig. 1 that the text part merges with adjacent text/non-text components for smaller values[1] from (1–4), text part remain stable and appear prominently for medium Δ values (5–13), whereas for higher values of Δ from (14–20), the text part starts mixing with the image background. This happens due to images having different illumination and varying contrasting backgrounds. Since the images in natural scene images have varied illumination and contrast, therefore a fixed value [16, 17] of delta cannot be used in images to perceive the existence of text.

---

[1] {$\Delta = 2$ is skipped due space limitation. It is almost similar to $\Delta = 1$.}

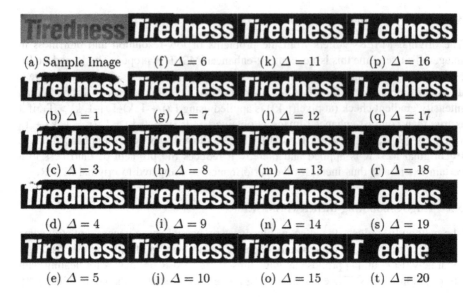

Fig. 1. Generation of region using OMSER (a) Sample Image (b) Regions at different Δ

Motivation: The motivation comes from the fact that in [4, 16, 17] Δ parameter of MSERs act as an important factor in deciding the stability for text components in the scene images. This motivate us to study behavior and discover the optimal value of Δ for different versions of MSER that gives best outcomes concerning precision, recall and f-measure for each version of MSER algorithms.

4 Proposed System

As mentioned in above section that Δ governs the stability of the text regions in the scene images so, in current work, we discuss the variation of stability factor Δ and find its optimal value for the different version of MSERs in the domain of text detection & localization in natural images. The different versions of MSERs considered in this work are Original MSER (OMSER) [4] Contrast Enhanced MSER (CONMSER) [6], Edge Smoothing MSER (ESMSER) [7] and (CONESMSER) Contrast Enhanced Edge Smoothing MSER (proposed). The training is performed on the ICDAR 2013 [25] training dataset of text segmentation task using four features of the text & non-text constituents. Our method along with the range of values (1–20) of the Δ parameter on the different versions of MSERs is applied on ICDAR (2013, 2011) test datasets.

4.1   Contrast Enhanced Edge Smoothing MSER (CONESMSER)

The OMSER suffers from the problem of blurriness, due to which the edges of characters cannot be distinguished properly, therefore, to deal with blurriness problem in images we use contrast enhancement and then edge smoothing followed by MSER, which is as follows:

Algorithm 1. CONESMSER-Contrast Enhanced Edge Smoothing MSER
Require: Colored Image I
Ensure: Possible Text Components
1: For Color Image I, Intensity I_n is calculated as $I_n=(I_r+I_g+I_b)/3$.
2: for every pixel at (s,t) in the image do
3: If $I_n(s+1,t)$ - $I_n(s-1,t)$ > T_1 then
4: $I_c (s\pm1,t) = I_c (s\pm1,t) + T_2$
5: end if
6: end for
7: Convert Contrast Enhanced Image I_c into intensity image I_i using HSI model.
8: Smooth I_i using the guided Filter [24] and Get contrast enhanced edge smoothened Image I_{ces}.
9: Perform MSER algorithm on contrast enhanced smoothed image I_{ces}.

The parameter T_1 and T2 [6] are 30 and 50 respectively. As shown in Fig. 2d, characters are properly separated (obtained by applying Algorithm 1 (CONESMSER) as compared to characters in Fig. 2(b) and (c). Heuristics filtering rules are applied on output components of each version of MSER to remove false positives (bricks, windows, leaves etc.)

(a) Sample Image   (b) OMSER   (c) CONMSER   (d) CONESMSER

Fig. 2. Well separated characters in (d) CONESMSER as compared to (b) and (c)

4.2   Text Specific Features and Probability of Text (PT$_{ver}$)

We propose four text specific attributed (features) to discern text & non-text components. The components obtained from each version of MSER undergoes feature extraction process needed for determining probability of text (PT$_{ver}$).

(a) **Stroke Width Heterogeneity (SWH):** The text parts of an image contain almost constant stroke width l_{sw} that discerns them from the non-text parts. Stroke Width Transform [6, 7, 10] can be defined as the straight line with unvarying width between across edge pixels in the perpendicular direction [10]. The non-text parts do not possess uniform stroke width across the structure. Stroke Width Heterogeneity for a region(r) is defined as:

$$SWH(r) = \frac{Variance(l_{sw})}{mean(l_{sw})^2} \qquad (2)$$

(b) **Histogram of Oriented Gradient at Edges:** The gradient magnitude and its direction at edges of a component calculated by HOG feature (Histogram of Oriented Gradient) [7, 26] is applied to discriminate text as well as non-text components. It relies on the concept that edges of the text areas forms a connected boundary and has corresponding pixels in opposite orientation. We calculate the gradient orientation of edges in four different quadrants for determining the text components. It is invariant to transformations; rotations and can attain the gradient properties at the edges effectively in scene images that are subject to different illumination & taken at various camera orientations. HOGE feature for region r is given as:

$$HOGE(r) = \frac{\sqrt{\sum_{i=1}^{2} k_i}}{\sum_{i=1}^{4} n_i(r)} \qquad (3)$$

here $k_i = (n_i (r) - n_{i+2} (r))^2$ for i = 1 to 2 and the count of edge pixels in bin i for any region r is defined by $n_i(r)$. The expression $\sum_{i=1}^{4} n_i(r)$ is to preserve scale invariance [7]. The character component edges have all different types of edge points [34] as it has closed boundaries but edges of non-text components do not contains four types of corresponding points and therefore rejected.

(c) **Perpetual Color Contrast (PCC):** In natural scene images there is always some difference in color of the text regions and its surrounding, therefore Perpetual Color Contrast (PCC) is explained as the difference between color of the text and its adjoining areas. Jensen-Shannon Divergence (JSD) [27] may be applied to judge color difference between two regions. The PCC of a region X as compared to its surrounding X^*, is given by:

$$PCC(r) = \sum_{L,A,B} SQRT \sum_{i=1}^{B} JSD((CH_i(X)||CH_i(X^*)) \qquad (4)$$

CH(X) is color histogram of X and CH(X*) is color histogram of X* in LAB space. Here X* is the region exterior to the region X, but within rectangle surrounding the region X, B denotes the histogram bins. JSD(X)||(X*) is the Jensen-Shanon Divergence [27] between regions X and X*.

(d) **Occupy Rate (O_R):** The Occupy Rate (O_R) [28, 29] is explained as the ratio of the count of foreground pixel and region's bounding box area. The non-text components are too long or too short in structure, whereas the true text components possess compact structure.

Probability of Text: All the four features are distinct to each other; therefore be used to evaluate the probability of a component c as a text (t_c) in following manner:

$$PT_{ver}(t_c|\lambda) = \frac{p(t_c)\Pi_{f_r\epsilon\lambda}p(f_r|t_c)}{\sum_{j\epsilon\{t_c,nt_c\}}p(j)\Pi_{f_r\epsilon\lambda}p(f_r|j)} \tag{5}$$

Where λ = (SWG, HOGE, PCC,OR), f_r stands for features, ver stands for different version of MSER, and p(nt_c) indicates prior probability of non-text and p(t_c) indicates prior probability of text. They can be estimated with the help of relative frequency during training process. The feasibility p($f_r|$ nt_c) and p($f_r|$ t_c) by calculating features on non-text & text components respectively is modeled by training process on ICDAR 2013 dataset as follows:

Training Process: The distribution of features on non-text & text constituents for training purpose is computed on ICDAR training 2013 dataset [25] which contains 229 images from natural scene images in following way:

(1) The ground truth (pixel level information) from ICDAR 2013 training dataset is used to calculate the distribution of four features on text constituents.
(2) For non-text constituents respective versions of MSER is applied to training images to obtain feasible candidate constituents. Then, by using pixel level information the text constituents are removed from them and four fetures are extracted on remaining non-text areas.

4.3 Labeling and Grouping

For classification in text and non-text constituents properly, we use graph cut model [8] that applies label (1) to text and label (0) to non-text. For this $G_I = (V_I \ E_I)$ is designed as a graph model with respect to an image I in which, vertex set $V_I = \{v_i\}$ consists of possible text regions and edge set $E_I = \{e_i\}$ consists of the interaction between vertexes. Non-text & text can be separated using optimization of Q = $\{q_i\}$ (labeling of text), where qϵ {0, 1} with the help of energy minimization [8] for Eq. 6.

$$E(Q) = \sum_i u_i(q_i) + \sum_{i,j\epsilon E_I} v_{ij}(q_i, q_j) \tag{6}$$

Unary Potential: Probability of text for each version of MSER PT_{ver} in equation 5 is same as unary potential for the region as:

$$u_i(q_i) = \begin{cases} PT_{ver}(q_i|\lambda), & q_i = 1 \\ 1 - PT_{ver}(q_i|\lambda), & q_i = 0 \end{cases} \tag{7}$$

Pair Wise Potential: The distance feature and color distance feature are implemented to express similarity between regions. Color Distance Feature CD_f [7] is the color distance (using L2 norm in LAB model) between two regions trg_i, trg_j. Distance Feature (Euclidean distance) D_f (trg_i, trg_j) amidst the centroids of possible text components(regions) trg_i, trg_j. So, the pairwise potential is:

$$v_{ij}\left(q_i, q_j\right) = \begin{cases} 0, & otherwise \\ \left(1 - \tanh\left(JD\left(q_i, q_j\right)\right)\right), & q_i \neq q_j \end{cases} \tag{8}$$

Where, The joint difference JD [7] can be estimated as:

$$JD\left(trg_i, trg_j\right) = \gamma D_f\left(trg_i, trg_j\right) + (1 - \gamma)CD_f\left(trg_i, trg_j\right) \tag{9}$$

Where $\gamma = 0.5$ defines the weight assign to D_f and CD_f. The labeled text components are grouped into text line using mean-shift clustering.

5   Results and Discussions

5.1   Performance Estimation and Dataset(S)

We have implemented our method on two datasets namely, ICDAR 2013 [25] & ICDAR 2011 [30]. ICDAR 2011 has 255(testing) & 229(training) images, whereas ICDAR 2013 has 233(testing) and 229(training) images. The performance is estimated with the help of three different measures namely recall (r), precision & f (harmonic mean [31] of r & p). The p, r, f is estimated with the help of the deteval tool, that uses detected bounding box and ground truth bounding boxes for many-to-one, one-to-one matches and one-to-many matches.

5.2   Effect of Stability Factor Δ on Different Versions of MSERs

The delta parameter Δ plays a significant role in the MSER algorithm. In our experiments which are performed on Matlab using vlfeat toolbox [5] (for MSERs), we varied the value of Δ from 1 to 20 for four versions of MSERs namely, OMSER, CONMSER, ESMSER, CONESMSER. For each case of MSER, there is the single value of Δ (where f-measure is optimal) that is chosen as the optimal Δ value. On such optimal value, the system gives the best performance for each version of MSER in terms of p,r,f as shown in Fig. 3. It shows the variation of the Δ value on dataset ICDAR 2011 Fig. 3 (a) and dataset ICDAR 2013 Fig. 3(b), in terms of p,r,f obtained using different versions of MSERs. It is evident from the Fig. 3 that in each version of MSER for smaller values of Δ, the p is less and r is on the higher side which is due to the fact that for smaller values of Δ false regions are produced and over-segmentation of true regions occurs. Whereas, for the larger values of Δ, the text mixes with background and therefore r decreases.

The optimal value of Δ for ICDAR 2011 and 2013with respect to different version of MSER is shown in Table 1. As obvious from the Table 1 that for different versions

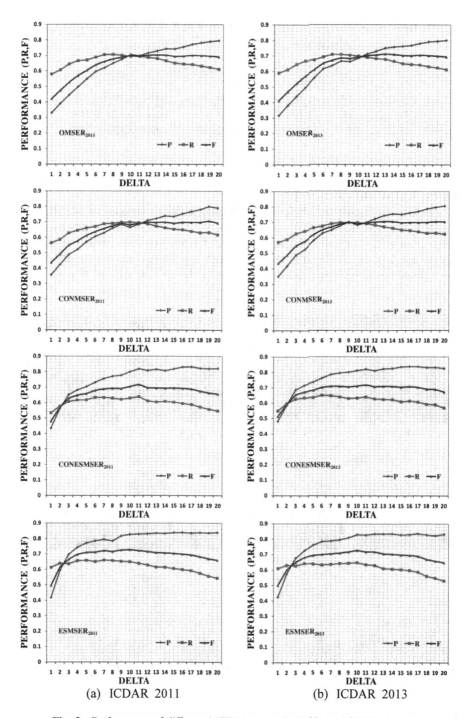

(a) ICDAR 2011   (b) ICDAR 2013

Fig. 3. Performance of different MSER(s) w.r.t Δ (1–20) on ICDAR datasets

Table 1. Performance of versions of MSER w.r.t to Δ on ICDAR Datasets.

Method	ICDAR 2011				ICDAR 2013			
Name	$\Delta_{optimal}$	r	p	f	$\Delta_{optimal}$	r	p	f
PT$_{omser}$	13	0.68	0.73	0.704	13	0.677	0.749	0.711
PT$_{conmser}$	19	0.632	0.80	0.706	19	0.630	0.797	0.703
PT$_{conesmser}$	11	0.639	0.819	0.717	11	0.64	0.820	0.718
PT$_{esmser}$	10	0.649	0.827	0.727	10	0.648	0.83	0.727

of MSERs, the best result in terms of p,r,f is obtained at different values of Δ for both datasets ICDAR 2011 and 2013.

The Fig. 4 demonstrates the effect of Δ using different versions of MSERs on a sample image from ICDAR 2011 dataset [30]. We have shown the results by taking three values of $\Delta_{i, op, f}$ (i = initial, op = optimal, f = final) on each version of MSERs. It is evident from each column of Fig. 4 that texts are detected and localized(shown in blue colored bounding boxes) most appropriate for the optimal value of Δ in each case

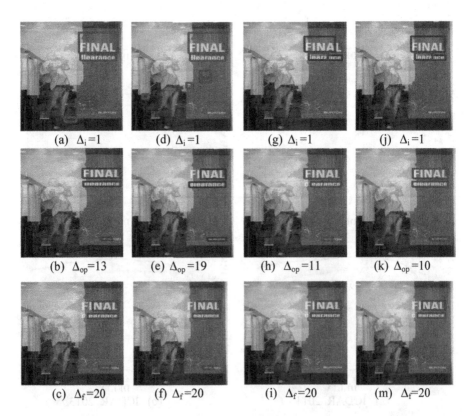

(a) $\Delta_i=1$	(d) $\Delta_i=1$	(g) $\Delta_i=1$	(j) $\Delta_i=1$
(b) $\Delta_{op}=13$	(e) $\Delta_{op}=19$	(h) $\Delta_{op}=11$	(k) $\Delta_{op}=10$
(c) $\Delta_f=20$	(f) $\Delta_f=20$	(i) $\Delta_f=20$	(m) $\Delta_f=20$

Fig. 4. Showing effects of Δ on different version of MSERs. (a, b, c) results by OMSER, (d, e, f) shows results by CONMSER, (g, h, i) shows results by CONESMSER, (j, k, l) shows results by ESMSER.

as compared to initial and final values of Δ. In case of $\Delta = 1$ (small value), the results obtained consists of some false positives and over-segmentation of true regions that reduces precision, whereas in case of of $\Delta = 20$ (large value) the text mixes with the background, therefore, reduces recall. The optimal value of of $\Delta = op$ (having maximum f-measure) is different for each case of MSERs. For Original MSER(OMSER) the optimal Δ is obtained at 13. In cases of Contrast Enhanced MSER (CONMSER), the optimal Δ is obtained at 19 that happen because in pre-processing step the contrast of the image components is enhanced to nullify the effect of blurriness. The contrasts enhance components get stable at higher values of Δ. In case of Edge Smoothing MSER(ESMSER), the optimal value of Δ is obtained at 10 which is the due to smoothing of edges (for reducing blurriness) and removal of extra pixels around the edges of the components that bring downs the optimal value to 10 as compared to previous cases. Lastly, in case of Contrast Enhanced Edge Smoothing MSER (CON-ESMSER), the contrast enhancement is carried out followed by edge smoothing to further nullify the effect of blurriness, the optimal value of Δ increases to 11, due to increase in contrast of the image in pre-processing step.

5.3 Comparison with Other State of Art

In this work, we inspect the Δ parameter for the different versions of MSERs on benchmark datasets ICDAR 2011 and 2013. The outcome obtained by proposed method are examined with other state-of-art in the domain of scene text localization are shown in the Tables 2 and 3 for ICDAR 2011 and 2013 datasets respectively. The results obtained by our CONESMSER using the guided filter and four text specific features $PT_{conesmser}$ at optimal value $\Delta = 11$. Table 2 depicts that proposed method attains p = 0.819, r = 0.639 and f = 0.717 on ICDAR 2011 dataset, whereas Table 3 shows that it obtains precision of p = 0.82, r = 0.64 and f = 0.718 on ICDAR 2013 dataset.

Table 2. ICDAR 2011

Method	r	p	f
$PT_{coneesmser}$	0.639	0.819	0.717
Ghaei [21]	0.72	0.77	0.75
Yu et al. [32]	0.63	0.78	0.70
Li et al. [7]	0.62	0.80	0.70
Neumann [12]	0.65	0.73	0.69
Kim [30]	0.62	0.83	0.71
Merino [14]	0.67	0.51	0.55

Table 3. ICDAR 2013

Method	r	p	f
$PT_{coneesmser}$	0.64	0.82	0.718
Guan [20]	0.67	0.82	0.73
Gomez [19]	0.67	0.78	0.72
Wang et al. [29]	0.73	0.80	0.76
Wang et al. [33]	0.60	0.77	0.68
TextDetect [25]	0.53	0.74	0.62
CASIA [25]	0.68	0.78	0.73

Figure 5 displays the outputs acquired on applying our method to different datasets. The detected text in Fig. 5 is enclosed by rectangles in blue color. This method detects text of distinct colors, fonts, color, orientation & font size. It's gives better results regarding other state-of- the-art work concerning challenges like different lighting conditions, low contrast and blurred images

Fig. 5. Sample images from ICDAR dataset. First and second row shows images from ICDAR 2011, 2013 datasets respectively using $PT_{conesmser}$ $\Delta = 11$ method only.

6   Conclusion and Future Work

We have explored and examined the effect of the Δ parameter of MSER algorithm on the different versions of MSERs concerning the extraction of text regions from natural scene images in current paper. We have varied the value of Δ from 1 to 20 to calculate its optimal value for each version of MSERs. The optimal value of Δ obtained for each MSERs version is different which shows that it affects the performance of the MSERs to generate results in terms of p,r,f. This happens due to the fact that images in the natural scene have varying contrast and illumination. A better version of MSER and tuning of other parameter is needed to recall the lost characters from the noisy images. In future, we intend to investigate this issue to get better results.

References

1. Zhang, H., Zhao, K., Song, Y.Z., Guo, J.: Text extraction from natural scene image: a survey. Neurocomputing **122**, 310–323 (2013)
2. GonzaLez, A., Bergasa, L.M.: A text reading algorithm for natural images. Image Vis. Comput. **31**(3), 255–274 (2013)
3. Ye, Q., Doermann, D.: Text detection and recognition in imagery: a survey. IEEE Trans. Pattern Anal. Mach. Intell. **37**(7), 1480–1500 (2015)
4. Matas, J., Chum, O., Urban, M., Pajdla, T.: Robust wide-baseline stereo from maximally stable extremal regions. Image Vis. Comput. **22**(10), 761–767 (2004)

5. Vedaldi, A., Fulkerson, B.: Vlfeat: an open and portable library of computer vision algorithms. In: Proceedings of the 18th ACM International Conference on Multimedia, pp. 1469–1472. ACM (2010). http://www.vlfeat.org/

6. Li, Y., Lu, H.: Scene text detection via stroke width. In: 2012 21st International Conference on Pattern Recognition (ICPR), pp. 681–684. IEEE (2012)

7. Li, Y., Jia, W., Shen, C., van den Hengel, A.: Characterness: an indicator of text in the wild. IEEE Trans. Image Process. 23(4), 1666–1677 (2014)

8. Boykov, Y., Veksler, O., Zabih, R.: Fast approximate energy minimization via graph cuts. IEEE Trans. Pattern Anal. Mach. Intell. 23(11), 1222–1239 (2001)

9. Pan, W., Bui, T., Suen, C.: Text detection from natural scene images using topo-graphic maps and sparse representations. In: IEEE Computer Society. IEEE ICIP (2009)

10. Epshtein, B., Ofek, E., Wexler, Y.: Detecting text in natural scenes with stroke width transform. In: 2010 IEEE Conference on Computer Vision and Pattern Recognition (CVPR), pp. 2963–2970. IEEE (2010)

11. Neumann, L., Matas, J.: A method for text localization and recognition in real-world images. In: Kimmel, R., Klette, R., Sugimoto, A. (eds.) ACCV 2010. LNCS, vol. 6494, pp. 770–783. Springer, Heidelberg (2011). https://doi.org/10.1007/978-3-642-19318-7_60

12. Neumann, L., Matas, J.: Real-time scene text localization and recognition. In: 2012 IEEE Conference on Computer Vision and Pattern Recognition (CVPR), pp. 3538–3545. IEEE (2012)

13. Liu, Z., Sarkar, S.: Robust outdoor text detection using text intensity and shape features. In: 19th International Conference on Pattern Recognition ICPR 2008, pp. 1–4. IEEE (2008)

14. Merino-Gracia, C., Lenc, K., Mirmehdi, M.: A head-mounted device for recognizing text in natural scenes. In: Iwamura, M., Shafait, F. (eds.) CBDAR 2011. LNCS, vol. 7139, pp. 29–41. Springer, Heidelberg (2012). https://doi.org/10.1007/978-3-642-29364-1_3

15. Chen, H., Tsai, S.S., Schroth, G., Chen, D.M., Grzeszczuk, R., Girod, B.: Robust text detection in natural images with edge-enhanced maximally stable extremal regions. In: 2011 18th IEEE International Conference on Image Processing (ICIP), pp. 2609–2612. IEEE (2011)

16. Tsai, S., Parameswaran, V., Berclaz, J., Vedantham, R., Grzeszczuk, R., Girod, B.: Design of a text detection system via hypothesis generation and verification. In: Proceedings of Asian Conference on Computer Vision, vol. 12, pp. 13–37 (2012)

17. Tian, S., Lu, S., Su, B., Tan, C.L.: Scene text segmentation with multi-level maximally stable extremal regions. In: 2014 22nd International Conference on Pattern Recognition (ICPR), pp. 2703–2708. IEEE (2014)

18. Zamberletti, A., Noce, L., Gallo, I.: Text localization based on fast feature pyramids and multi-resolution maximally stable extremal regions. In: Jawahar, C.V., Shan, S. (eds.) ACCV 2014. LNCS, vol. 9009, pp. 91–105. Springer, Cham (2015). https://doi.org/10.1007/978-3-319-16631-5_7

19. Gomez, L., Karatzas, D.: A fast hierarchical method for multi-script and arbitrary oriented scene text extraction. Int. J. Doc. Anal. Recogn. (IJDAR) 19(4), 335–349 (2016)

20. Guan, L., Chu, J.: Natural scene text detection based on swt, mser and candidate classification. In: Image, Vision and Computing (ICIVC), pp. 26–30 (2017)

21. Ghanei, S., Faez, K.: A robust approach for scene text localization using rule-based confidence map and grouping. Int. J. Pattern Recogn. Artif. Intell. 31(03), 1753002 (2017)

22. Soni, R., Kumar, B., Chand, S.: Text detection and localization in natural scene images using MSER and fast guided filter. In: Fourth International Conference on Image Information Processing (ICIIP), pp. 1–6 (2017)

23. Huang, W., Qiao, Y., Tang, X.: Robust scene text detection with convolution neural network induced MSER trees. In: Fleet, D., Pajdla, T., Schiele, B., Tuytelaars, T. (eds.) ECCV 2014. LNCS, vol. 8692, pp. 497–511. Springer, Cham (2014). https://doi.org/10.1007/978-3-319-10593-2_33

24. He, K., Sun, J., Tang, X.: Guided image filtering. In: Daniilidis, K., Maragos, P., Paragios, N. (eds.) ECCV 2010. LNCS, vol. 6311, pp. 1–14. Springer, Heidelberg (2010). https://doi.org/10.1007/978-3-642-15549-9_1

25. Karatzas, D., et al.: ICDAR 2013 robust reading competition. In: 2013 12th International Conference on Document Analysis and Recognition (ICDAR), pp. 1484–1493. IEEE (2013)

26. Dalal, N., Triggs, B.: Histograms of oriented gradients for human detection. In: IEEE Computer Society Conference on Computer Vision and Pattern Recognition CVPR 2005, vol. 1, pp. 886–893. IEEE (2005)

27. Majtey, A., Lamberti, P., Prato, D.: Jensen-shannon divergence as a measure of distinguishability between mixed quantum states. Phys. Rev. A **72**(5), 052310 (2005)

28. Gonzalez, A., Bergasa, L.M., Yebes, J.J., Bronte, S.: Text location in complex images. In: 2012 21st International Conference on Pattern Recognition (ICPR), pp. 617–620. IEEE (2012)

29. Wang, Q., Lu, Y., Sun, S.: Text detection in nature scene images using two-stage non text filtering. In: 2015 13th International Conference on Document Analysis and Recognition (ICDAR), pp. 106–110. IEEE (2015)

30. Shahab, A., Shafait, F., Dengel, A.: ICDAR 2011 robust reading competition challenge 2: reading text in scene images. In: 2011 International Conference on Document Analysis and Recognition (ICDAR), pp. 1491–1496. IEEE (2011)

31. Wolf, C., Jolion, J.M.: Object count/area graphs for the evaluation of object detection and segmentation algorithms. Int. J. Doc. Anal. Recogn. (IJDAR) **8**(4), 280–296 (2006)

32. Yu, C., Song, Y., Meng, Q., Zhang, Y., Liu, Y.: Text detection and recognition in natural scene with edge analysis. IET Comput. Vis. **9**(4), 603–613 (2015)

33. Wang, R., Sang, N., Gao, C.: Text detection approach based on confidence map and context information. Neurocomputing **157**, 153–165 (2015)

34. Zhang, J., Kasturi, R.: Text detection using edge gradient and graph spectrum. In: 20th International Conference on Pattern Recognition (ICPR), pp. 3979–3982, August 2010

Coconut Tree Structure Analysis - Background Work for an Unmanned Coconut Harvesting Robot Design

Sakthiprasad Kuttankulangara Manoharan$^{(\boxtimes)}$ (iD)
and Rajesh Kannan Megalingam$^{(\boxtimes)}$

Department of Electronics and Communication Engineering,
Amrita Vishwa Vidyapeetham, Amritapuri, India
sakthiprasad221914@gmail.com, megakannan@gmail.com

Abstract. For the designing of an unmanned robotic coconut climber/harvester, we need to model the coconut tree structure especially the tree trunk. The coconut tree trunk is non-deterministic in nature. The variation mainly results in the tree trunk, height, inclination, and treetop. The variation in size/diameter, height and inclination are not same in all coconut trees. In addition to the diameter variation and inclination treetop notches made for harvesting, attack of different organisms, and stem decay due to aging is included for the accuracy. The empirical method is adopted to get some idea about the variation in the coconut tree, in that precisely view the variation of 50 trees in the Kollam district of Kerala, India to reach some conclusion. In this empirical analysis, we tried to include coconut trees with some sort of in variation their structure to make the analysis more effective.

Keywords: Treetop variation · Coconut tree trunk · Inclination · Robot design

1 Introduction

The world production of coconut is 69836.36 million nuts from 12196.00 ha, in that Indonesia, Philippines, India, & Sri Lanka dominating in the production of coconuts. These four countries producing 55585 million nuts, 79.59% of world production. The India contributing 31.02% of overall production. (Source: Asian and Pacific Coconut Community (APCC) Statistical Year Book 2014). In India, Andhra Pradesh state is producing more coconuts than another state. Kerala producing 7429.39 million nuts from 770.62 ha, which is 33.51% of overall Indian production [13]. Coconut tree (Cocos nucifera) of the palm family (Arecaceae) is one of the important crops in India. The lifespan of the coconut tree is generally 80 to 90 years. Coconut tree grows well up to an altitude of 3000 ft. above the sea and flourish under various soil conditions the slender, leaning, the ringed trunk of the tree rises to a height of up to 25 m (80 feet), featherlike leaves. Throughout the tropics, we can found out coconut tree, it is interwoven into the lives of the local people [14, 15]. It is mostly in the low islands of the Pacific where, in the lack of land-based natural property, it gives almost all the required items of life. Coconut tree usually starts bearing after 5 to 6 years of the plantation. The tree trunk is stout and cylindrical, based on the scars present in the stem we can

© Springer Nature Singapore Pte Ltd. 2019
S. Minz et al. (Eds.): ICICCT 2018, CCIS 835, pp. 207–222, 2019.
https://doi.org/10.1007/978-981-13-5992-7_18

determine the age of the tree. In one-year, make 12 to 14 scars. The leaves crowded together in the crown, in that young leaves appears in the center of the crown. Normally crown includes 15 open leaves, 15 younger leaves [2]. Fruits require a year to ripen; the annual yield per tree may reach 100, but 50 is measured good. Yields continue profitably until trees are about 50 years old. The coconut finds its greatest commercial utilization, besides the edible kernels and the drink obtained from green nuts, fiber the husk yields coir, used in the manufacture of ropes, brushes, mats, baskets, and brooms. The cabinets and huts are constructed using decay-resistant, coconut tree trunk (porcupine wood) is used [4, 5, 10]. Empirical modeling has been used for the modeling of a case, which does not have mathematical support. The empirical modeling purely depends on the collected data, so it is helpful for specific types that do not have parametric support. Using the empirical modeling, with the help of different theories and approaches we can establish a relationship between variables. In empirical modeling, from the collected data the analyst gets some initial idea about the tendencies of the variables under consideration [3].

2 Motivation

Harvesting of coconuts becomes a hectic issue for coconut farmers. The educated youth is not interested in this harvesting job due to its risks and health issues. The acute shortage of human coconut tree climbers results in the deterioration of the coconut farming [16]. User-friendly coconut harvesting robot is the solution for this problem. To design a coconut harvester robot we need to identify the variation in the coconut trees. Each coconut trees are unique, so modeling the variations is the solution to make the design more functional.

3 Related Works

Inorsky [4, 8] has given the idea about coconut tree foliage. The coconut trees have alternate foliage, leaves are attached to the stem in either clockwise (Left-handed or L) or anti-clockwise (right-handed or R). SousaI et al. [6] have given the direct and indirect methods are there to find the total leaf area of the plant finding the total leaf area of the plant, obtained by either direct or indirect method. This two-stage study includes. First, an empirical model for leaf area of individual leaves of green dwarf coconut tree was developed and evaluated. A sample of 57 leaves was collected in an intermediate position on the canopy, at an irrigated orchard located at Campos dos Goytacazes, RJ, Brazil (21°48′2″ S, 41°10′51″ W).

The measured length of the rachis (LR) of each leaf and the sum of all leaflet areas (LA) was determined through leaf area meter (LI-3100 area meter, LI-COR Inc., Lincoln, Nebraska, USA). The length of the rachis in the collected leaves ranged from 0.48 m to 3.3 m; the age of plants varied from one to four years. The developed models using linear regression on anamorphosis scheme, using leaf rachis length as independent variable. The six-year coconut tree and three-year coconut trees are two different types, six coconut year tree produces fruit in about six years other in three There are two varieties of coconuts based on color, green type, and red/orange type is explained in [9]. The coconut takes 12 months to fully ripe; coconuts in the same bunch ripen at about same time. A single tree produces multiple bunches at various time in a single year. Coconut husk is an indicator of ripeness, the tender coconut green color changes to brown when it matures [11].

Chattopadhyay et al. [17] have given a method of modeling with the help of image data and empirical data. They collected different variety photos in different viewpoint and create a database. The extraction of the skeleton from the depth image of an apple tree. The tree parts, away from the sensor showing more errors while empirical correction. Fan et al. [18] used three analytical model to optimize the wine quality from the physical and chemical properties of the wine and grape. Fitting analysis, Analysis of variance (ANOVA), fitting analysis, Q cluster analysis are used analytical models for the optimization. A large amount of raw data was required for the effective modeling. Song et al. [19] obtained a relation of chemical and physical components between grapes and wines. Wine quality depends on the properties of grapes, so by obtaining the mathematical relationship between these parameters they graded the wine quality. Elfiky et al. [20] used SbG (Skeleton-b201ased Geometric) features for the reconstruction of the front and back. Circle based layer– layer –aware algorithm is used to find pruning points of the tree branch with an accuracy of 96%. Detection segmentation and modeling were the three steps they used in this work. Xie et al. [21] suggested a 3D model-based method for creating the realistic model of a tree with the help of a collection of example tree models. Using the database of the 3D model generating tree models with complex structure. Similar modeling schemes used in some other fields also Reddy et al. [22] developed cost-effective communication network for fisherman using the intranet. The fisherman's mobile phone gives the details with the help of WiFi facility in the boat through the directional antenna. The values obtained through this communication was theoretically modeled with the help of actual values collected from various places of India. In this experimental modeling, the main parameter under consideration was signal strength fluctuations. Modeling is also used in the computing and software areas. Unnikrishnan et al. [23] gave an idea about the modeling methods adopted in IT and cloud computing areas. Microsoft secure development life-cycle (SDL), STRIDE, Microsofts DREAD model, Trike etc. are the popular threat modelings. With the help of database classify the risks as low, medium and high. Common vulnerability scoring system was used for the susceptibility representation. The burglar sidesteps the authentication is the major issue in the cloud computing. Keyser et al. [24] evaluated the relationship between different parameters of ponderosa pine, like tree size, crown, and stem damage. Tree mortality and morphology were the key features under consideration. Five-year data (2001 to 2005) of 963 trees included a database. Tasissa et al. [25] given a model of the thinning effects on the stem profile of loblolly pine. This modeling was done with the help of data collected and maintained by the loblolly pine growth and yield research cooperative at Virginia polytechnic institute and state university. As per the model, significantly increased from exponent that was evaluated by Akaike's information criterion (AIC) and likelihood ratio test.

4 Coconut Tree Structure Analysis

The coconut tree trunk diameter is varying from the top to bottom, In general, the base diameter is high and top diameter is less compared to the middle. In addition to that, due to different reasons, the diameter is abnormally varying at different heights.

(a)   (b)

Fig. 1. Normal tree trunk variation

In Fig. 1(a) and (b) showing the normal variation of the coconut tree trunk. The abnormal variation may occur at any height from the ground due to various factors like climatic conditions, pest attack, and different diseases. Sudden variation in the tree trunk makes the tree trunk more complex to predict. In this abnormal variation, the tree trunk circumference may less than or greater than the average tree circumference. The abnormal variation of the coconut trunk is shown in the Fig. 1. In that (a), circumference variation close to the treetop, but in (b) the variation is in the middle of the tree trunk.

(a)   (b)   (c)

Fig. 2. Abnormal tree trunk variation

(a)   (b)   (c)

Fig. 3. Coconut tree diameter variation in the base

The circumference variation is close to the tree base in the Fig. 2(c). the base diameter of the coconut tree is comparatively higher than the average value. This abnormal variation is shown Fig. 3. In that (a), (b), & (c) the base circumference value is very large, exceeds 130 cm. This variation does not exceed 50 cm, after that the circumference gradually reduces up to treetop. In the case of the old coconut trees base is damaged, the presence of cracks and roots, shown in Fig. 4. The main reasons for this are lack of proper maintenance and aging. In Fig. 4(a), the 30-year-old coconut tree base is shown, in that cracks are less but in the (b) & (c) are the 40 plus old trees in those trees cracks are also present. In addition to age, improper caring is the reason for this. The surface of the coconut trunk is not smooth small trough and crest formed as part of falling of leaves (Fig. 5a and b). Normally the size of the crest is varying between 2 mm to 5 mm. In some places, for the easiness of the manual harvester, they are making notches or step-like structure in the coconut tree trunk. The harvesting notches, sometimes may deeper (Fig. 6(b)) extend up to 5 cm that affect the health of the tree. Shallow wedges are made normally for harvesting. These notches become affected by different types of insects and funguses and affect the health of the tree (Fig. 6(c)).

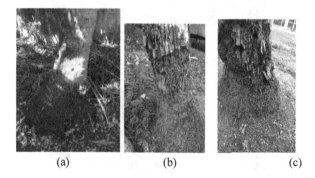

(a)   (b)   (c)

Fig. 4. The base of an old coconut palm

Fig. 5. Tree surface variation

Insects, fungi and some organisms attack the coconut stem; insects usually attack the growing parts. Insects (rhinoceros beetle, palm weevil), mycoplasma-like organisms, and fungi attack coconut palms. Fungi usually attack the portions, where its vitality reduced due to insects, physical damage, and human impact. Most probably, the fungi enter into the stem through the harvesting steps, which is using to facilitate harvesting of the coconut in some countries like the Philippines and some areas of India. Rainwater and dirt collect in the notches cut in the coconut trunk for the harvesting, so the insects and fungi can attack easily through that notch [1]. Figure 7(a)–(c) Showing some of the defected tree trunks. Majority of the coconut trees are inclined with respect to ground, the main reason for this is sunlight availability. Normally the inclination not exceeds 50° (Fig. 8b) but in some cases, it is more than that, especially in the seashore area (Fig. 8a).

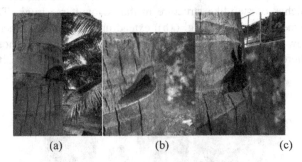

Fig. 6. Harvesting steps in coconut stem

Fig. 7. Defects in the coconut stem

Coconut foliage is also varying in a different tree. Leaf distribution, coconut bunch alignment, dried portion. The coconut foliage depends on the proper harvesting, 45 days is the normal harvesting period if the farmer not maintains proper harvesting period that's leads to misalignment of leaves and lot of dried portions.

(a)   (b)

Fig. 8. Inclined coconut trees

Dried coconut flower parts and spathe have to remove by the harvester during harvesting. Treetop is not cleaned properly then these dried portions accumulated there, results in improper foliage.

(a)   (b)   (c)

Fig. 9. Treetop variation

Figure 9(a) showing the treetop of a well-maintained coconut tree and (b) is a treetop due to improper maintenance and timely harvesting. Treetop may vary due to the pest action, an example for that is shown in Fig. 9(c). Different types pests attack different parts of a coconut tree, like a rhinoceros beetle, black headed caterpillar, the red palm weevil, core bug, and cockchafer beetle. The adult beetle bore into the unopened leaf and the sheathing bract enclosing the coconut flower, the attacked leaves when fully opened show characteristic geometric shapes shown in the Fig. 10.

Fig. 10. Rhinoceros beetle attack

Figure 11 shows the inter-cultivation is the method adopted by the farmers to control the weeds; by this, the aeration of the soil would increase. Husk burial tried to increase moisture content, for that burying fresh or dried coconut husks around the palm. The green and cover crops would help to increase the organic content and prevent soil erosion; therefore, this method is recommended for cultivation in coconut garden.

Fig. 11. Green manure and cover crops

Red palm weevil (Fig. 12) can be identified by the presence of holes on the stem and oozing brown fluid through the hole. In the advanced stage, crown falls down or dry up later when the tree is dead.

Fig. 12. Red palm weevil

Stem bleeding is shown in the Fig. 13. Reddish brown viscous fluid ooze through the developed cracks, this is due to the decaying of tissues in that area. The developed small cracks become big holes in the tree trunk.

Fig. 13. Stem bleeding

Fig. 14. Leaf rot

Leaf rot leads to the gradual weakening of the tree. Blackening of the ends of the leaflets and younger leaves which later break off in its bits is shown in the Fig. 14.

Due root (wilt) disease (Fig. 15) yield of the coconut tree reduces drastically. Abnormal bending, a general yellowing of the leaflets are the main symptoms of this disease [12].

Fig. 15. Root (wilt) disease

Table 1. Varying parameters of the coconut tree

Coconut Tree no.	Base circumference (cm)	Circumference, 150 cm from the base/ground (cm)	Inclination with respect to ground (Degree)	Height (m)
1	64	65	10	4.7
2	78	68	1	5.2
3	82	75	66	7.3
4	72	61	15	8.1
5	84	91	50	12.9
6	102	76	10	13.2
7	112	82	18	2.8
8	90	79	12	10
9	81	79	13	6.8
10	106	81	30	5.4
11	83	74	36	4.5
12	88	75	26	8.6
13	80	60	10	5.7
14	71	61	2	3.1
15	67	40	10	2.6
16	97	78	10	8.3
17	77	68	22	6.3
18	84	69	4	6.1
19	98	88	14	7.7
20	90	72	3	6.5
21	92	79	53	9.6
22	81	70	44	10.5
23	91	64	24	6.6
24	91	82	25	10.1
25	122	86	16	13.2
26	107	79	7	10.4
27	102	69	6	5.4
28	93	74	26	11.8
29	94	73	23	6.1
30	106	58	25	11.1
31	63	66	6	11.4
32	115	74	8	12.4
33	86	50	9	2.9
34	72	43	10	3
35	72	49	2	2.9
36	125	76	4	4.1
37	112	57	4	3.9
38	97	57	11	8.5
39	110	70	26	7.2

(continued)

Table 1. (*continued*)

Coconut Tree no.	Base circumference (cm)	Circumference, 150 cm from the base/ground (cm)	Inclination with respect to ground (Degree)	Height (m)
40	101	72	9	7.8
41	108	68	2	8.2
42	116	74	11	9.9
43	93	67	3	5
44	121	78	22	7.5
45	98	82	6	9.3
46	100	85	9	7.9
47	132	98	16	8.3
48	198	96	3	3.9
49	94	78	45	12.6
50	89	80	20	15.2

Inference

From the graph (Fig. 16) the majority of the coconut trees are inclined 1 to 15° with respect to ground. So we have to design a climber that can climb through the inclined structure. Some of the trees are bending more than 50°. The inclination mainly depends on the climatic conditions, especially availability of sunlight (Table 1).

Table 2. The range of variation of parameters

Value	Base circumference (cm)	Circumference, 150 cm from the base/ground (cm)	Inclination with respect to ground (Degree)	Height (m)
Maximum	198	98	66	15.2
Minimum	63	40	1	2.6
Average	95.74	71.80769	16.74	7.698077

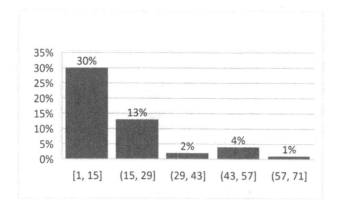

Fig. 16. coconut tree inclination

From the graph (Fig. 16) the majority of the coconut trees are inclined 1 to 15° with respect to ground. So we have to design a climber that can climb through the inclined structure. Some of the trees are bending more than 50°. The inclination mainly depends on the climatic conditions, especially availability of sunlight.

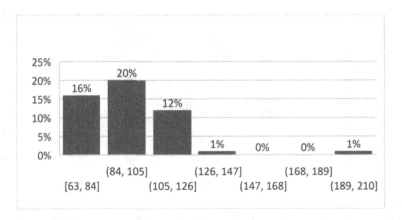

Fig. 17. Base circumference

The base circumference of the coconut tree is comparatively larger than the average circumference. Except for some defected trees, all other tresses have larger base size than middle and top. Therefore, this is the maximum circumference that accommodates by the coconut harvester. From the Fig. 17. Majority of the coconut trees have a base size between 80–100 cm. From the graph (Fig. 18) it is clear that height is the other variable in the case of a coconut tree. The height of the coconut tree depends on the climatic conditions mainly availability of sunlight, type of soil, soil fertility and amount of rain in that area. The variation in height is mainly in a range of 5 to 12 cm. The harvester design has to support to reach this much height.

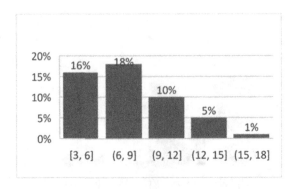

Fig. 18. The height of coconut tree.

The aim of collecting circumference of coconut tree trunk is to get an idea about the tree diameter variation. The mechanism, which is used in the robotic harvester, should accommodate these variations for the smooth upward movement. From the graph (Fig. 19) we got the information that majority of the coconut trees with circumference 65–90 cm (Table 2).

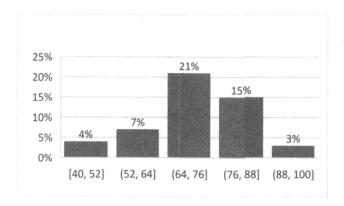

Fig. 19. The circumference of the coconut tree, 150 cm from the base

5 Robotic Designs for Coconut Tree Harvester

The diameter/circumference of the coconut tree trunk varying in different ways in different trees in addition to that some abnormal variation due to pests and other physical agents, to accommodate all these variations the holding mechanism of this robotic unmanned harvester must be a spring mechanism. Due to the presence of the green manure and nitrogen-fixing plants, abnormal tree base and extra roots present in the old trees, we cannot attach the robot directly to the base, In this case, we have to fit one meter above from the ground. So we have to connect one meter above the ground. Weight is the main constraint for this robot, carrying the bot to the desired coconut tree and manual assembly becomes easy when its weight is less. If the weight is high the torque requirement for the motors also increases, which results in addon weight and cost. 2 sets of motors, in each set, contain three or four motors to carry the robot upward and downward. Robot body motors might be dc motors to reduce the cost and weight. Low weight wheels with the tires are preferable. The tree top is unique in each and every tree. In the majority cases the coconut bunch inside the leaves, so we have to cut and remove leaves to reach the coconut stem. To reach the destination for cutting we need a robotic arm with inverse kinematics and for automatic cutting. To reach all the positions using inverse kinematics, 6 DOF arm is required. The end effector of the arm will be a cutter rpm greater than 10000 and torque enough to cut the dried portions of the coconut stem and leaf.

The power supply source must be AC if we use batteries recharging is required in between the harvesting. We can divide the entire robotic system into two sections, mobile unit and ground station. We are required when we use manual control, in that case, two controllers are required one in the ground station and one in the mobile unit. In that case, all the communications between the two stations must be wireless. The camera is essential for an autonomous harvester, using image processing and learning algorithms identify the mature coconut bunch for the cutting. The camera will be placed in the starting of the sixth DOF and work only if the cutter is not enabled. If we are using manual mode camera video is helpful to understand the coconut treetop to the user on the ground. The emergency circuit is also required, to avoid problems related to the connectivity losses, power failure, and hardware issues. We need a dc battery, which is completely dedicated to the emergency circuit.

6 Future Work

We got the range of variation of different parameters under consideration, so include analyzed factors in the design of coconut harvesting robot and make that design functional.

7 Conclusion

The coconut tree structure is non-deterministic; each one of them is unique in different ways. Tree trunk circumference is varying from the base to top in addition to that fungal actions, different diseases; harvesting notches are also made the structure more complex. The majority of the trees are inclined to surface and their heights are different. Treetop is also a varying factor, different diseases, improper harvesting are factors in addition to general factors like availability of sunlight, amount of rain etc. By this analysis, we got an idea about the range of variations in different parameters like tree height, trunk circumference, treetop, inclination, special cases like harvesting notches, and variations due to different fungal and insect actions. Green Manure and Cover Crops restrict to connect/entry of the harvesting robot through the base. This information needs to include in the design of robotic coconut harvester to make the design more effective.

Acknowledgments. We are grateful to Humanitarian Technology Labs (HuT Labs) of Electronics and Communication department of Amrita School of Engineering, Amrita Vishwa Vidyapeetham University, Amritapuri campus, Kollam, India for providing us all the necessary lab facilities and support towards the successful completion of this work.

References

1. Coconut palm stem processing: technical handbook, Produced by Forestry Department: Coconut palm stem processing: a technical handbook. http://www.fao.org/docrep/009/ag335e/AG335E02.htm
2. http://www.agritech.tnau.ac.in/expert_system/coconut/coconut/coconut_varieties.html

3. Empirical Modeling and Its Applications, Edited by Mamun Habib, InTech, Chapters published July 20, 2016 under CC BY 3.0 license. https://doi.org/10.5772/61406, https://www.intechopen.com/books/empirical-modeling-and-its-applications

4. Peter, V., Inorsky, M.: Latitudinal differences in coconut foliar spiral direction: a re-evaluation and hypothesis. Ann. Bot. **82**, 133–140 (1998). Department of Biological Sciences, Union College, Schenectady, NY 12308-2311 USA

5. Written by: The Editors of Encyclopædia Britannica https://www.britannica.com/plant/coconut-palm

6. de SousaI, E.F., et al.: Scientia Agricola: Estimating the total leaf area of the green dwarf coconut tree (Cocos nucifera L.). Print version ISSN 0103-9016On-line version ISSN 1678-992X, Sci. Agric. (Piracicaba, Braz.) vol. 62 no. 6 Piracicaba Nov./Dec. (2005)

7. Pahlm, O., Sornmo, L.: Software QRS detection in ambulatory monitoring-A review. Med. Biol. Eng. Comput. **22**, 289–297 (1984)

8. Inorsky, P.V.M.: Foliar spiral direction: a re-evaluation and hypothesis. Ann. Bot. **82**, 133–140 (1998). Department of Biological Sciences, Union College, Schenectady, NY 12308-2311 USA

9. http://www.cookycoconuts.com/typesofcoconuttrees.html

10. http://www.cookycoconuts.com/coconuthistory.html

11. http://homeguides.sfgate.com/tell-coconuts-ripe-tree-60198.html

12. http://vikaspedia.in/agriculture/crop-production/package-of-practices/plantation-Crops/coconut/coconut-cultivation-practices

13. http://coconutboard.nic.in/stat.htm

14. Megalingam, R.K., Pathmakumar, T., Venugopal, T., Maruthiyodan, G., Philip, A.: DTMF based robotic arm design and control for robotic coconut tree climber. In: IEEE International Conference on Computer, Communication, and Control (IC4-2015)

15. Pramunendar, R.A., Supriyanto, C., Novianto, D.H., Yuwono, I.N., Shidik, G.F., Andono, P.N.: A classification method of coconut wood quality based on gray level co-occurrence matrices. In: International Conference on Robotics, Biomimetics, Intelligent Computational Systems (ROBIONETICS) Yogyakarta, Indonesia, 25–27 November 2013

16. Megalingam, R.K., Sakthiprasad, K.M., Sreekanth, M.M., Vivek, G.V.: A survey on robotic coconut tree climbers – existing methods and techniques. In: International Conference on Advanced Material Technologies (ICAMT)-2017, Dadi Institute of Engineering and Technology, Visakhapatnam, Andhra Pradesh, India, 27–28 December 2016

17. Chattopadhyay, S., Akbar, S.A., Elfiky, N.M., Medeiros, H., Kak, A.: Measuring and modeling apple trees using time-of-flight data for automation of dormant pruning applications. In: 2016 IEEE Winter Conference on Applications of Computer Vision (WACV) (2016)

18. Fan, F., Li, J., Gao, G.: Mathematical model application based on statistics in the evaluation analysis of grape wine quality. In: 12th International Computer Conference on Wavelet Active Media Technology and Information Processing (ICCWAMTIP) (2015)

19. Song, Z., Liu, T., Bai, S.: Modeling based on the effects of grapes for wine. In: 2014 IEEE Workshop on, Electronics, Computer and Applications (2014)

20. Elfiky, N.M., Akbar, S.A., Sun, J.: Automation of dormant pruning in specialty crop production: an adaptive framework for automatic reconstruction and modeling of apple trees. In: 2015 IEEE Conference on Computer Vision and Pattern Recognition Workshops (CVPRW) (2015)

21. Xie, K., Yan, F., Sharf, A.: Tree modeling with real tree-parts examples. IEEE Trans. Vis. Comput. Graphics **22**(12), 2608–2618 (2016)

22. Reddy, D., Parthasarathy, V., Rao, S.: Modeling and Analysis of the Effects of Oceanic Wave-Induced Movements of a Boat on the Wireless Link Quality, pp. 1–2 (2017). https://doi.org/10.1145/3084041.3084073

23. Unnikrishnan, B., Kandasamy, K.: Profiling threat modeling approaches and methodologies for IT and cloud computing. Cent. Cybersecurity Syst. Networks Int. J. Pure Appl. Math. **115**(8), 121–126 (2017)

24. Keyser, T.L., Smith, F.W., Lentile, L.B., Shepperd, W.D.: Modeling postfire mortality of ponderosa pine following a mixedseverity wildfire in the black hills: the role of tree morphology and direct fire effects. Forest Sci. **52**(5), 530–539 (2006)

25. Tasissa, G., Burkhart, H.E.: An application of mixed effects analysis to modeling thinning effects on stem profile of loblolly pine. Forest Ecol. Manage. **103**, 87–101 (1998)

Author Index

Printed in the United States
By Bookmasters